blue
rider
press

THE
INVESTIGATOR

THE
INVESTIGATOR

FIFTY YEARS OF UNCOVERING THE TRUTH

TERRY LENZNER

BLUE RIDER PRESS

A member of Penguin Group (USA)

New York

blue
rider
press

Published by the Penguin Group
Penguin Group (USA) LLC
375 Hudson Street
New York, NY 10014

USA · Canada · UK · Ireland · Australia
New Zealand · India · South Africa · China

penguin.com
A Penguin Random House Company

ISBN 978-0-399-16055-4

Printed in the United States of America
1   3   5   7   9   10   8   6   4   2

Book design by Gretchen Achilles

To the men and women of IGI who helped to create
and continue to sustain our enterprise

AUTHOR'S NOTE

As a lawyer and investigator, my top priority is always my client. My law practice and IGI employees adhere to strict standards of confidentiality, upholding the law and the highest ethical standards. There is nothing disclosed in this book that violates these standards. Some of the stories I've chosen to tell about my experiences involve events that have been cemented in our history, some have been widely reported in the media, and some refer to cases that illustrate universal truths about investigative practice and human nature that I've learned along the way.

CONTENTS

PREFACE

Sometimes I'm asked what makes a good investigator. How do some people develop those skills—curiosity, doggedness, attention to the overlooked details—that are requisites for a successful investigative career?

As a boy, I was active, enthusiastic, and curious. On family trips, I kept a journal, took snapshots, and pored over maps, noting distances. I used that data to educate myself, to hone my skills as an observer. I looked for patterns and associations among things that had no obvious relationship. A good investigator does the same thing: he takes observations and turns them into useful information.

Growing up in mid-century Manhattan, I was the youngest of three boys, all of us born two years apart with summer birthdays. We lived in a seventh-floor corner apartment at 75th Street and Lexington Avenue, the rental that my parents moved into after they were married in 1934 and didn't leave until they died. I shared a bedroom with Allan, my older brother; Bobby, the oldest, had his own room on the other side of the bathroom we shared.

I was born in 1939, and my earliest memories were formed during World War II. Earlier than I can remember, my father left to join the navy as a dentist on an aircraft carrier in the Pacific, the USS *Long Island*. I went with my mother across the country by train at least twice to see him in San Diego when he was on leave.

Neither of my parents was self-confident, and I suspect they had difficulty believing that any product of their union, including their sons, could amount to much. My mother was not particularly maternal, which is understandable considering how little mothering she'd had. Her mother had died, after a long illness and medical treatments in Boston, when my mother was eleven. When the U.S. entered World War I, her father went to Washington with his son, the middle child, to work for a wartime agency. My mother was left behind in New York with her cold, widowed grandmother and youngest sibling, a sister whom she resented. The lack of nurturing in her upbringing greatly influenced her own maternal style.

My father's parents had come to America from Lithuania. They settled in Trenton, where my grandfather owned a hardware store. My father, the youngest of eight children, was eager to move beyond the confines of his Orthodox Jewish home and fully embrace what he thought were real American values. He discovered football in high school and saw that as his ticket out of the immigrant class. He wanted to go to Harvard because of its famous football team, though eventually he was persuaded by an older brother to go as an undergraduate to the University of Pennsylvania dental school, where at least he could play varsity football in the Ivy League.

Once the war was over, my parents wanted to be as conventional as possible in our straitlaced, mostly WASP, East Side neighborhood. After work, my father spent a lot of time at the elite, Jewish Harmonie Club, playing bridge and drinking too much. He was the first Eastern European Jew to become a member, thanks to his well-established father-in-law. My father's standards and his desire to shed his Orthodox, ethnic roots dictated how we were raised: clothes from Brooks Brothers (he adopted "Brooks," formally, as his middle name), high-class private schools, and football. My oldest brother was more intellectual than athletic and Allan, though athletic, was small. So satisfying Dad's desire for a football-playing son became my job.

If I knew then that we were Jewish, I don't remember it. My father always advised us to put "non-denominational" on any form that asked for religious affiliation. My earliest religious experience was at the Catholic church near our apartment, where Henny, my mother's housekeeper, occasionally took me with her to afternoon Mass. When I was at Trinity School on the Upper West Side, I sang in the *Messiah*. My report cards, which I got much later from my mother, indicated I was a satisfactory student and sang with gusto.

In our household I learned early on to be sensitive to temperaments and behaviors. My father was a very conflicted man. His moods were unpredictable and he was often angry. The room I shared with Allan was adjacent to the entrance hallway. When our father came in and we heard him place his hat calmly on the table, all was well. If it bounced off the wall, we knew to try to stay clear of him.

When I was in seventh grade, I played a lousy game of football one day. My father had watched the game with disappointment and increasing anger. I showed Dad my inexplicably swollen ankles, which had slowed me down. He kicked my legs, furious at the excuse. It turned out I had rheumatic fever and was soon hospitalized. I felt abandoned in the hospital for several weeks, including over Christmas, and was allowed visitors only rarely. For weeks afterward, I was usually alone in my room at home. Bobby was away at boarding school and Allan had moved into Bobby's room.

Those long, boring days confined to bed in a small bedroom provided less than cheerful insights into human nature, but they would become essential to my career as an investigator. My parents bought me a television so I could watch *The Howdy Doody Show* and *Kukla,*

Fran and Ollie. When your best friends are television puppets, you must be lonely. Even though it was cold outside, the overheated apartment's windows were open, so I occupied much of my time listening to what was happening outside. My ears were my eyes on the street. I visualized fire trucks, ambulances, and police cars as they went by. I learned the differences in the sounds of people's footsteps, in the ways they greeted one another on the sidewalk. I imagined the daily life outside that was going on without me.

Stuck in bed, I was also attuned to what was happening inside. My parents often fought, and the sounds of their angry conflicts made me want to find a different world. Knowing how to identify fear in someone's voice is a useful tool. So is listening for subtle changes in tone to detect a lie. I became sensitive to the slightest changes in demeanor or mood.

My illness was one of those defining moments that influence some people's lives. I had been told that I might never be able to play football or run again. As I struggled to regain my strength, I vowed to achieve something I could be proud of. I rejected any thought that I was an invalid and pursued goals tenaciously. I felt there was a clock ticking, telling me I had to move forward before time ran out. I guess I still haven't slowed down. I operate best with a sense of urgency, and I still haven't stopped trying to find that elusive sense of contentment that comes with accomplishment.

My father told me that there were two important things to do in life: go to the best schools and play football. I was able to follow that advice in both respects. I attended Phillips Exeter Academy, Harvard College, and Harvard Law School. I played football and was captain of the team at Exeter and Harvard, where I was the first Jewish captain. I was elected despite an effort by a rival who made anti-Semitic remarks against me, ironic considering my complete lack of religious identification.

Football turned out to be an enormous benefit and valuable for my later career. The sport taught me speed and agility, how to analyze what an opponent intends before he does it, and how to gain leverage over someone who is bigger or more powerful. It taught me about teamwork, and connected me to one of my early mentors, Bill Clark, who was the Exeter coach. I soon discovered how useful my familiarity with football was as a conversation starter, especially when I worked as a Department of Justice lawyer in the Deep South.

But after my last Harvard-Yale football game, I couldn't imagine a future. I remember lying on the floor, looking up at the ceiling, and wondering what I was going to do with the rest of my life. I was relieved to be accepted at law school that spring, but had no idea what kind of lawyer I would become.

It was the advice of a senior partner at a prominent New York firm, Lloyd K. Garrison, that set a course for me. He suggested that I apply for a job in the Civil Rights Division of the Department of Justice. That recommendation led to not only an extraordinary first-job experience, but also shaped my future.

I cannot overestimate how much I benefited from strong mentors throughout my early life. I realize that this is a two-way street—that I was very fortunate to have outstanding role models and fortunate also to be able to recognize and respect them. The teachers at my excellent schools taught me how to think critically and to write clearly. I am especially indebted to Henry Bragdon, my American history teacher at Exeter, who instilled in his students his love for history and admiration for public service. I learned about commitment, persistence, and the overriding importance of facts, the "romance in the records," from John Doar and other lawyers at the Civil Rights Division. Under Bob Morgenthau, the U.S. Attorney in New York, I learned to prosecute cases carefully and independently and with only the highest standards of integrity. With Sam Dash and senators on the Watergate Committee like Sam Ervin, I developed sure-footed investigative skills and an appreciation of the importance of bipartisan leadership for a sound government.

I realize that another significant factor shaped my career: the fortuity of being in the right place at the right time. I take no credit for that good fortune, but I recognize it as a critical ingredient in the uniquely varied and somewhat unconventional series of experiences I've had. When I accepted the Civil Rights Division position in 1964, I had no idea that I would be investigating a horrific murder in Mississippi or enabling the famous Selma to Montgomery march. After I was fired by Donald Rumsfeld, I was available to join the team defending Phil Berrigan and the other radical Catholic antiwar activists. And I was available to become an assistant counsel to the Watergate Committee because I hadn't yet committed to a law firm. I was retained by Dr. Sid Gottlieb to represent him before the Church Committee investigating the CIA because I happened to know the agency's special counsel and had no other clients whose cases would interfere. I was hired to investigate the cost overruns on the Alaska pipeline construction because I was in Alaska on another case. Each of these was an experience that most lawyers never have.

It was while I was at Harvard that I learned important early lessons about investigative work. I majored in government and had decided to write my senior thesis on Congressman John McCormack, a popular Boston politician who was then majority leader (and soon to be Speaker) of the U.S. House of Representatives.

Invited to the majority leader's office at the Capitol, I met a man named Marty Sweig, McCormack's chief of staff. Marty was my main point of contact and, for whatever reason, he took a liking to me. Back then, the gulf between Boston's Irish and the historically WASP Harvard was wide. McCormack was honored that a Harvard student was writing about him, and I received significant access to the Speaker and his various meetings.

Late at night I'd hang around the office and hear a man's voice imitating McCormack's Boston accent on the phone coming from McCormack's office. The voice belonged to Marty. That struck me as odd. I was with Marty one day when he opened an envelope from a union leader and a $100 bill fell out. Marty used the money to take me to one of the most expensive restaurants in town, where he seemed to be a regular.

Marty Sweig talked a lot, and I listened carefully. "If anything ever happens to McCormack," he once told me, "I've got to get out of town." He confided that he had a bank account in Switzerland for that purpose. It never occurred to me that this was something he shouldn't have been bragging about.

When I finished my thesis, the *Boston Globe* ran it as a series of articles. In a sense, it was my first investigative reporting, though I didn't really think of it that way. McCormack didn't care much for what I'd written about him, and he called me into his office to berate me in front of his staff. He was especially offended by the parts that quoted him accurately but apparently embarrassed him, as well as parts where I noted some of his habits, such as tossing cigar butts behind the curtain at committee hearings.

Years later I was working in the U.S. Attorney's Office for the Southern District of New York under the legendary Robert Morgenthau. One day when I was in his office to discuss the indictment of Salvatore Bonanno, I heard him mention the prosecution of a highly sensitive political target. The target was Marty Sweig, who was still working for McCormack, then Speaker of the House. Sweig was being indicted for bribery, and had to resign. Marty was like a son to the childless Speaker—which is probably why he got away with so much for so long—and accepting his aide's resignation was said to be heartbreaking for McCormack.

The bigger realization for me was that, at age twenty-one and working on my college thesis, I had come across corruption in the highest level of Washington power. I could have exposed it then, but I just wasn't clued in. Marty Sweig came across as a nice guy to me. I was too naïve to recognize him as corrupt.

The tragedy of Marty's life was that he really didn't need the extra cash. He was at the height of power, working closely for one of the most important men in the nation. Yet he allowed himself to be brought down through his exercise of that power. It wasn't that he needed the illicit money, but that he enjoyed the thrill of what it meant to be able to get it so easily.

In the years since, I have seen a lot of Marty Sweigs. Sometimes they are billionaires. Sometimes they are respected CEOs. Sometimes they are union leaders. Sometimes they are role models. Sometimes they are presidents of the United States. Along the way I have learned a lot about human nature, as well as how much our country, and our sense of truth, has changed.

CHAPTER 1

MURDER OF THE INNOCENTS

O n June 21, 1964, three young men drove cautiously through dusty Neshoba County, Mississippi, in a blue station wagon. The backwater county was known for its violence against blacks and any outsiders intending to help them. Things were so bad that Neshoba had lost most of its black population in the previous few decades. Those who stayed behind were oppressed into timidity. "This is a terrible town. The worst I've seen," Dr. Martin Luther King Jr. once said after a visit to Philadelphia, the county seat.

In 1964, nearly half of Mississippi's population was black, but less than 5 percent were registered to vote. In rural counties where blacks were the overwhelming majority, the percentage of those registered was even smaller. Leaders of the civil rights movement were concentrating on activities to secure voting rights for the disenfranchised black citizens of the Deep South—to challenge the very foundations of racial injustice by giving political power to the powerless.

Hundreds of young people, mostly white college students from the North, flooded into the state to help. The local authorities considered these idealistic outsiders "agitators" and "troublemakers." They took every opportunity to harass, intimidate, and sometimes assault them.

James Chaney, Andrew Goodman, and Michael Schwerner were among those taking part in the "Freedom Summer" of 1964—a program organized by the Council of Federated Organizations (COFO) to encourage and promote black voter registration. Black residents engaged with the Freedom project at their own peril, and James Chaney, a brave twenty-one-year-old black man from Meridian, took on the challenge. He worked with Mickey Schwerner to make preparations for the summer. Schwerner was a twenty-four-year-old leader in the Congress of Racial Equality (CORE) who had moved with his wife, Rita, to Meridian, Mississippi, early in 1964. Working together to make Freedom Summer preparations, the young men had attracted the attention of segregationists. The Imperial Wizard of the White Knights of the Ku Klux Klan had issued an order for Schwerner's death.

In early June, Schwerner and Chaney visited Mount Zion, a small church in the rural outskirts of Philadelphia, whose all-black congregation had agreed to host a Freedom School to prepare black residents for registering. A few weeks later, while Schwerner and Chaney were in Ohio for training with Freedom Summer volunteers, members of the Klan attacked Mount Zion church. They searched the congregation for "Goatee" or "Jew-Boy" (Schwerner's KKK-assigned nicknames), beat the congregants, and then burned the church.

Returning to Meridian on June 20 with the first group of volunteers, Schwerner and Chaney learned of the church burning. The next day, joined by twenty-year-old Andrew Goodman, a Freedom Summer volunteer from New York, they went to Neshoba County, apparently to meet with local activists at the burned-out church and offer encouragement and support. On their way back to Meridian, after dark, they were stopped by Deputy Sheriff Cecil Price, ostensibly for speeding.

Though only one of them had driven the vehicle, all three were taken to the local jail, where they were held for hours without being allowed to make phone calls. Because of the dangers inherent in their work, participants in Freedom Summer had been trained to contact the headquarters at regular intervals. Back at the Freedom Summer headquarters in Meridian, the staff worried that the men had not been heard from. A search began in earnest, and officials from the Department of Justice learned that the three had indeed been held in jail but had been released that evening. They were not heard from again.

On June 23, the FBI found the blue station wagon on the outskirts of the Choctaw Indian reservation, only fourteen miles northeast of Philadelphia. The vehicle had been set on fire, but no bodies were recovered. The clock on the charred dashboard had stopped at 12:45, two hours after the men had been released. During the weeks-long search for the car's occupants, Mississippi authorities dismissed the trio's disappearance as a stunt. Senator James Eastland, a staunch segregationist and powerful Democrat, mocked the idea that Schwerner and the others were in any danger and derided the mystery as a scheme to defame the people of his state. The disappearance of the three men would occupy the attention of much of the country. And my experience with civil rights profoundly changed the course of my life.

When I left Harvard Law School, I had little confidence in my abilities as a practicing lawyer. I had learned a lot of law and theory but had never applied it in a nonacademic setting. Before I began my law studies, I barely knew the difference between a plaintiff and a defendant. I was a scrappy ex-college football player, a little introverted, maybe a little socially awkward, but headstrong in finding my way in unfamiliar situations.

The summer between my second and third years at law school, I clerked at a prestigious firm in Manhattan, where I occupied a tiny windowless office. A loud pneumatic tube dispensed plastic cylinders next to my desk. The contraption made a *whoosh* as it carried messages to my desk from somewhere else in the building. Whenever a cylinder arrived, I opened it to retrieve the paper inside. This was usually a research assignment from one of the partners, which I attended to as quickly as I could. This primitive, impersonal delivery, the 1960s version of e-mail, defined my days.

I remember attending a deposition with one of the firm's partners on an antitrust case in which we represented the defendant company. The deposition dragged on and on as our senior lawyer asked a series of what seemed to me to be at best tangential questions. The room was hot and airless and there were few breaks. Everyone was sweating.

When the meeting finally ended, I asked the senior attorney what that was all about. Why had he kept us in that stifling room for an almost unbearable length of time? The partner proudly told me it had been by design. He had even kept the windows closed to make the environment as uncomfortable as possible.

"What's the point?" I asked.

"Wearing people down until they settle," he replied. "That's the point." I couldn't imagine taking pride in that kind of work. I wanted to make something more of my legal education than that.

At the end of that summer, Lloyd K. Garrison, a senior attorney and great-grandson of the famous abolitionist William Henry Garrison, sought me out. I don't know if he'd caught wind of my disenchantment or not, though he was a pretty shrewd observer of people. In any event, he suggested that a particular government position might suit me better than private practice, and urged me to apply to work for the Civil Rights Division of the Department of Justice, which had a mandate to hire new lawyers. I don't know why he took the time to advise me, but I'm glad he did. His direction put me on a track for a career and a life I would not have had otherwise.

After I returned to school in the fall, Mr. Garrison wrote to me with an introduction to Burke Marshall, the assistant attorney general in charge of the Civil Rights Division. I met with Marshall and other senior officials and was offered a job. After I graduated and took the bar exam, I moved to Washington, D.C., to learn about the law in a place I had never given much thought to—the Deep South.

I joined the Justice Department's Civil Rights Division in August 1964—along with a number of other newly minted lawyers hired that summer. It was a chaotic time—the three civil rights workers' bodies had just been found on August 4, buried in an earthen dam some distance from where Schwerner's station wagon had been discovered weeks before. The discovery of the bodies confirmed for many Americans the depth of Southern white segregationist fervor and habitual brutality—what the Freedom Summer project was up against.

When Freedom Summer began, many Americans, especially the families of the young volunteers, demanded that the federal government protect the activists who went to Mississippi. Though mindful of the dangers, the Justice Department refused their appeals, asserting that the federal government lacked the authority, as well as the manpower, for national law enforcement. I knew enough from law school to understand that our federal system recognizes state authority and defers to state laws for most crimes. The Feds could not charge anyone with murder (except under special circumstances, such as if the crime was committed on federal property or on an Indian reservation). But a federal statute prohibited a person acting "under color of law" from depriving someone of a civil right, including life. It was by way of that law that the Department of Justice pursued the Neshoba murderers.

By midsummer, in response to a $25,000 reward, a witness had come forward. He offered Joseph Sullivan, the FBI's chief investigator on the case, information about what had happened to the three young men. Their bodies were found in a dam at a place called Old Jolly Farm, six miles southwest of Philadelphia. All three had been shot. The white men, Goodman and Schwerner, had each been shot once through the heart. The black man, Chaney, had been shot three times. A medical expert who examined Chaney's body told reporters, "I have never witnessed bones so severely shattered except in tremendously high-speed accidents such as airplane crashes." That may or may not have been the result of the murderers' abuse, as we later learned that the bulldozer used to bury the bodies might have done some of the damage.

Until their bodies were found, there were all sorts of rumors and theories in Mississippi about the fate of the three civil rights workers— that they were dead, that they were in hiding, that they got lost. "They're just hiding and trying to cause a lot of publicity," said Lawrence Rainey, the thick-chested, tobacco-chewing county sheriff. He and his deputy, twenty-six-year-old Cecil Ray Price, were both alleged to be members of the Ku Klux Klan.

Civil Rights Division lawyers were distressed but not shocked by the discovery of the bodies. From the outset it seemed unlikely that they would be found alive. The prevailing theory was that after their release from the local jail, by pre-arrangement, they had been intercepted by the murderers, likely Klan members, on the lonely road to Meridian. They were taken from their car, killed, and buried where their killers hoped they'd never be found.

When the FBI excavated the dam, Agent Sullivan requested that Deputy Price personally help recover the bodies for delivery to the morgue. The message was not lost on anyone, least of all on Price: We know you did this and we're going to make you clean up your mess. According to the FBI agents on scene, Price "picked up a shovel and dug right in, and gave no indication whatsoever that any of it bothered him."

The reaction to what was now officially a murder investigation was widespread and instantaneous. John Lewis, who became a U.S. congressman from Atlanta in 1986, was then a leader of the Student Nonviolent Coordinating Committee and led the Freedom Summer in

Mississippi. He placed blame for the murders squarely on the shoulders of white Americans who had ignored the struggle under way in the South. The question, Lewis said, "is not who killed Andy, Mickey, and James, but *what* killed them." His answer was "apathy."

Investigators immediately suspected that Rainey and Price were involved in the murders. Price had arrested the trio on the questionable traffic charge just after they left Mount Zion, logged them into prison, and then logged them out shortly before they vanished. But evidence to prove what happened later required the involvement of federal investigators. Not surprisingly, state and local law enforcement showed no interest in pursuing the case.

The search for the bodies uncovered the remains of other murder victims. The bodies of two black men, Charles Moore and Henry Dee, were found in a lake off the Mississippi River. Another young man, wearing a "Congress of Racial Equality" T-shirt, was found in the Big Black River. All three had been lynched. No evidence suggested that the local authorities had ever even looked for them.

Leading the investigation for the Justice Department was John Doar, second-in-command at the Civil Rights Division. Doar was a Republican holdover from the Eisenhower administration. He had been retained as deputy by Burke Marshall, Attorney General Robert Kennedy's appointee.

Doar had come to Washington from Wisconsin to be chief assistant to his friend Harold Tyler, who was then heading the division. Years later, I heard him describe his motivation. As a Republican, he believed that the power of congressional Democrats from the one-party South effectively diminished the political power of states, such as Wisconsin, that had two-party democracies. When the civil rights movement began with sit-ins in 1960, he realized that there had been no real advance in civil rights since President Truman desegregated the military fifteen years before. And he knew that nothing would change if progress depended solely on the white power structure in the South.

As attorney general, Bobby Kennedy encouraged Marshall and Doar to pursue lawsuits against voting rights discrimination aggressively. Realizing that he couldn't depend on agents of the FBI, the Justice Department's investigative arm, to provide adequate support, Doar directed his lawyers to gather and analyze facts as well as to prepare lawsuits. And he instructed us to be always right about the facts. That's how my career as an investigator began.

Doar had earned recognition for his role in enforcing desegregation of the University of Mississippi when James Meredith enrolled there in 1962. After Medgar Evers, the head of the NAACP in Mississippi, was assassinated, Doar managed to calm a mob of outraged blacks in Jackson.

Like most Americans outside of the South, I learned about the degradation of African-American citizens through press accounts of Freedom Rides, sit-ins, protest marches, and violent clashes. I was sympathetic, but not particularly tuned in. For a New Yorker attending schools in New England, civil rights activities seemed worlds away.

When I had first interviewed with Doar, the Civil Rights Division was looking to double the number of attorneys on staff who were needed in the Deep South and particularly in Mississippi to handle Freedom Summer activities. Doar appreciated far better than I did that the situation had its dangers. Many of the new hires were law review achievers, which I was not. But I think Doar liked the idea of sending an ex–football player down to Dixie. Maybe he thought that I knew something about how to defend myself.

I later came to the conclusion that my disinterest was a prime qualification in Doar's eyes. A previous Civil Rights Division lawyer who was committed to the movement had gotten in trouble for assisting Martin Luther King Jr. He had been tasked with monitoring Dr. King's activities to keep the department informed about King's plans. On one occasion, when the civil rights leader needed transportation to a rally, the DOJ attorney allowed King to use his rented car. Doar felt strongly that the Department of Justice represented only the federal government; it had to avoid any appearance of working with the movement.

This minor gesture of goodwill elicited an outcry in Mississippi over federal collusion with civil rights "agitators." The backlash was so strong that the local authorities threatened to arrest any Justice Department attorney in their jurisdiction. Doar had no choice but to fire the lawyer. For a brief time, all the lawyers were pulled out of the state so no warrants could be served on them.

Shortly before I went to Washington, I was offered a Fulbright grant to go to Denmark. I told Doar about this and asked his thoughts.

Doar spoke deliberately and with a notable Wisconsin accent. Lean and tall—he was six feet two—he had an air of unassailable authority and integrity. I could see how he had been able to quiet a mob.

"Denmark will always be there," he said. "If you come to work with us, you'll be part of something historic." This was only the first piece of excellent advice he gave me.

As civil rights activities grew, segregationist intransigence and racial violence increased dramatically. In 1963 alone, the nation had seen the assassination of Mississippi NAACP leader Medgar Evers; the inauguration of George Wallace as governor of Alabama, pledging "segregation now, segregation tomorrow, segregation forever"; and the bombing of an African-American church in Birmingham that killed four young girls. Yet nothing had focused Americans' attention on issues of civil rights in the South like the Philadelphia murders did.

The federal government's strategy in Mississippi was to demonstrate a physical presence in the state to send a signal that the days of unchecked brutality by local law enforcement were over and to encourage cooperation from citizens who were tired of the abuses—especially those residents who might have information about what happened to Chaney, Schwerner, and Goodman. The FBI took over the town of Philadelphia for what they called Operation MIBURN (for "Mississippi Burning"). Most of the agents who came to Philadelphia were members of the bureau's organized crime section. The agents came from cities where mob investigations had been going on for years—New York, Chicago, Cleveland, Boston. They had skills and experience that agents who lived in the South lacked, as well as attitudes less accepting of entrenched segregation.

Using tactics learned from Mafia-related operations up north, the FBI infiltrated the Klan with undercover operatives and deployed a variety of methods to undermine the organizations. For example, agents routinely picked up Klan members in Philadelphia and questioned them for hours, attempting to get them to cough up any useful information. After these sessions, even if they proved unproductive, the agents would drive them around in a government car so everyone could see who had been questioned. When they let them out in the middle of town, the agents made a point of calling out, "Thanks for the help." By implying that one had cooperated, the FBI hoped to spread dissension within the Klan and encourage others to rat to save themselves.

While the FBI continued to pursue the murder investigation aggressively, John Doar's strategy for the division's lawyers was to challenge local law enforcement officials under its own legal authority using two post–Civil War federal statutes. One outlawed conspiracy to "injure, oppress, threaten, or intimidate any person" in the free exercise of a constitutional right. The other statute, making it a crime to deprive people of their civil rights while acting "under color of law," targeted law enforcement officials. No one from the federal government had so challenged local authorities in the Deep South since Reconstruction. Doar also directed his lawyers to investigate previous cases of police brutality in the hope of securing indictments in those cases, as well as to learn more about the Klan's and the sheriff's activities.

The division operated under the conviction that if all citizens were allowed to vote, Southern segregation would finally end. We filed lawsuits, county by county, challenging the systems of disenfranchisement. We had to document in detail the pattern and practice of discrimination particular to each county. Mississippi, Louisiana, and Alabama used complex voter registration applications that allowed county registrars to make subjective judgments on whether applicants passed. In Alabama, applicants had to be vouched for by a registered voter, of whom very few were black. Literacy tests designed to exclude illiterate applicants were unfairly applied.

My first assignment at Justice was to examine and analyze records of voter registration applications that the FBI had copied on microfiche. To show just how ignorant I was of all this at the time, I remember wondering why people who couldn't read or write should vote anyway. It wasn't long, however, before I could see the injustice. Some forms required applicants to indicate their race, others asked for their color. African-Americans were denied if they wrote the wrong thing: "Negro" instead of "black" or "brown," or vice versa. This was a trick question that African-Americans could seldom answer to the satisfaction of the registrars. In addition to testing literacy, some applications required applicants to interpret a section of the state constitution to the satisfaction of the registrar, which was almost always impossible for black applicants, even for those who understood law better than the registrars.

The records I examined showed that illiterate whites, who signed their applications with only a scrawled X, had been registered without incident, while black professors, ministers, and college graduates were rejected, even when they were highly literate. As I became more familiar with how the registration applications were used, I fully appreciated the phrase "equal justice under the law" for the first time.

The Philadelphia murders disrupted that agenda as the department went into crisis mode. It was an all-hands-on-deck moment, and I was eager to be involved. My bosses quickly convened emergency meetings on the investigation, with almost every member of staff, including me. A few short weeks after arriving at the Justice Department I went to Mississippi to be part of the murder investigation. Over the next three months, I was in the state for fifty-seven days.

Because I was so green, Doar teamed me with an experienced lawyer, Bud Sather, who was a close friend of Doar's from the Wisconsin attorney general's office. The Civil Rights Division was primarily a civil litigation operation, and Sather's experience as a seasoned investigator was highly valued. My job was to serve as Sather's driver and note taker—to listen, learn, keep my mouth shut, and stay out of trouble. I managed to do a couple of those things.

The town of Philadelphia, Mississippi, is the historical center of the Choctaw Nation. It is in the rural middle of the state, eighty-one miles northeast of Jackson and forty miles northwest of Meridian. When I arrived in 1964, it looked like a movie set for the Old West. Its wooden downtown buildings were bleached a light gray by the Mississippi sun. Pickup trucks coming into town had gun racks.

Bud Sather and I went first to the state capital of Jackson, where the Justice Department had an office in the federal courthouse. We drove east to our lodgings in Meridian, where federal officials stayed while investigating in the area. The federal presence was substantial, with division lawyers and a hundred agents working the case. Members of the military had been brought in to help search for the bodies.

At the office on my first day, I opened up one of the drawers of a file cabinet. Inside were two black revolvers nestled in holsters. I had never held a handgun before, and I picked one of them up.

"Those belong to Walter Sheridan," someone told me. Sheridan was with the FBI and one of Bobby Kennedy's most acclaimed investigators. He had been up against some pretty tough characters in his work with the attorney general's investigation of organized crime and battles with Jimmy Hoffa and the Teamsters. He was known as being fearless; I couldn't imagine that he was afraid of anything. (A number of years later, I had the privilege of hiring Sheridan to work with me.)

"Why are they here?" I wondered.

"Walter always carries them when he's in Mississippi."

What I remember most vividly is that it was hot—the kind of hot I'd never felt before. The humidity was so thick that beads of sweat collected on your brow as soon as you walked outside. Jackets and ties, our standard uniform, were barely tolerable in that environment. Air-conditioning was rare, and the federal government would not cover the extra cost of it in a rental car. The heat was so enervating that more than once I was in danger of falling asleep at the wheel while driving around Mississippi that summer. This did little to bolster my partner's confidence in me.

Neshoba County's Sheriff Rainey and Deputy Price were popular local figures. Among a largely uneducated white population, Rainey and Price were appreciated for keeping order and protecting the community from outsiders trying to stir up trouble. They did not appreciate the national spotlight now shining on their town.

Most of us assumed that Rainey and Price were up to their necks in the disappearances. These guys were not criminal masterminds. But what people *suspected* and what could be *proven* were two very different matters. Because the local prosecutors were not helpful, even what we could prove needed unimpeachable certainty.

Operating according to Doar's strategy, we were going to "get in the faces" of Rainey, Price, and anyone else who might have participated in the murders. Before we left Washington, Sather had subpoenaed the records of the county jail to obtain the names of blacks who had been arrested for violating the county's curfew. (At the time, blacks in Philadelphia were not allowed to be on the street after 9 p.m. most evenings.) Sather also got hospital records of blacks who had been treated for injuries that might have resulted from police brutality. I accompanied Sather to interview these victims to see if any might be effective witnesses in a grand jury. I was exhilarated to be doing this kind of hands-on work.

Many black residents lived in corrugated steel and wood shacks on dirt roads on the outskirts of town. Some houses were patched with old clothes wedged into holes. Indoor plumbing appeared to be nonexistent.

In our white shirts and ties, Sather and I looked totally out of place. When we knocked on their doors, residents thought we were there to collect the rent or to sell them something. Many couldn't read, so showing them a badge embossed with the letters of the Department of Justice was useless. Even if they could read, they didn't have any concept of what the Justice Department was or how the federal government could impact their lives positively. It was as if we had come from another planet.

But when I said I worked for Bobby Kennedy, their eyes lit up, and they understood that we were there to help. JFK had won widespread and lasting affection among blacks after he defended Martin Luther King Jr. when he was imprisoned during a civil rights protest. In August 1963 the president invited King to the White House. The Kennedy brothers, though abstract and distant heroes, cared more about blacks than any other white person in their lives. Many had framed photos of John F. Kennedy on their walls.

Sather knew how to ask the right questions. The first rule he taught me was to learn as much as possible about a witness before coming to an interview. He made a point of memorizing details. As he scoured the witness documents, he picked out details that a less discerning eye would have missed: the time of day of a hospitalization, the signatures on the witness statements, the victim's address. He committed them to memory and knew exactly when to use one to jog a reluctant recollection or to challenge contradictory assertions.

When a witness said something significant, I learned to get him to repeat it several times—to confirm the statement, and to be sure I understood exactly what the witness said and why he believed it to be true. Sather was rarely satisfied with an account from one person. He searched for corroboration from others who might have seen the same event, or from a supporting document. He always asked those we interviewed if anyone else was involved in these incidents or if there had been an eyewitness to the events. These were practical lessons that theory-focused law schools didn't teach.

Sather also showed me that the best way to start an interview was with benign, innocuous chatter to put the witness at ease. A relaxed interviewee was more likely to produce useful information. In farming areas, for example, nothing was more effective than opening conversations with sharecroppers by asking about the local soybean crop.

Knowing that Mississippi's all-white juries were biased in favor of the police, we needed witnesses who were unassailable on the stand: with clean records, straightforward and articulate testimony, and— most challenging of all—the courage to testify. We knew it would be extremely difficult to find witnesses who met all these criteria.

The notes from interviews that we prepared for our superiors were supposed to include our assessment of the witness's quality and highlight instances where their recollections differed from those of others. The first potential witness we interviewed was a man in his forties— let's call him Robert. He lived in a two-room shack with his wife and children. Once he figured out who we were, he welcomed us into his house. I recall that the heat inside was as oppressive as it was outside. From hospital records and X-rays, we knew Robert had sustained a skull fracture when he was arrested for violating the curfew a few years earlier because he had to go out for an emergency errand. By my estimation, he was a damn good candidate. He was open, forthright, and consistent in his answers.

As I scribbled notes in a green cloth-bound ledger, Robert told us that he had broken the curfew because he had to pick up something at a nearby store. The police stopped him and took him to the jail, where an officer used a blackjack to beat him. Robert described this without emotion, as though this was a common occurrence.

We asked if he knew anyone else who might have been treated similarly, or someone who might have witnessed his assault. He gave us a few names. At the end of the interview, Sather turned to me. "Do you have any questions, Terry?" he asked. I didn't have many but I felt I had to say something. So I asked him to clarify a few things he had said that I didn't understand from my notes.

As the news circulated in the black community about our interviews, more black residents came forward to tell their stories. As their confidence grew, we saw the first fissures in a silence born of intimidation and violence.

I quickly learned that Rainey and Price were sadistic bullies. Rainey's reputation was such that his mere presence was intimidating. He and others would drive by in patrol cars and stop black people on the street, issuing nonsensical orders just to see them cower or run. On one occasion at the county fair, Rainey stood in the midst of a group of African-Americans. Without his saying much of anything, they dispersed. I interviewed people who told me about officers showing up at the black community center, staying there until all the young people left. One officer walked around a group of black kids, holding his pistol. "I should blow your fucking heads off," he said, and dared them to try to go for his gun.

I interviewed two black youths, Billy Harris and his friend Robert Hudson, both eighteen, who told me about being picked up for questioning by Price and another officer, Richard Willis. The officers drove the boys to city hall and took them into a back room. Once inside, according to the boys, Price and Willis closed the door. One of them took a leather strap from the wall. I asked Billy to describe it. He said it was approximately three feet long, leather, and about the width of a hand. The strap was placed on the table in front of them.

"Do you want to whip each other," Willis asked, "or do you want us to do it to you?"

The boys decided that if they had to face something like that, they might as well be in control of it.

"Well, then," Willis allegedly said, "who wants to be first?"

By their count, Robert and Billy whipped each other thirteen times. At one point, one of the officers warned, "Don't be whippin' white!"—urging the boys to be more forceful. A witness corroborated this, telling about blue scars she saw along one of the boys' thighs shortly after the incident. I put all of this information in my report.

I interviewed a forty-six-year-old black man named Kirk Culberson who told of being stopped on suspicion of drunkenness. In a bizarre courtesy, Sheriff Rainey offered to hold Culberson's glasses while another officer slapped his face and hit him over the head with a club. Culberson was released from jail only after a bond—much more than Culberson could ever pay—was paid by a white couple he knew. In another encounter with the sheriff, Culberson said he had been beaten so badly that he'd lost some of his hearing.

Culberson showed me a claim he had filed with his auto insurance company seeking reimbursement for treatment of his injuries, which he had described as the result of "falling out of an automobile." In response he received a letter stating: "According to information made available to us, we understand that on January 26, a sheriff attempted to arrest you but you willfully resisted arrest. Under these circumstances, the sheriff had no recourse but to use force in order to apprehend you and his force resulted in your injuries." I heard over and over again similar stories of abuse, mistreatment, and torture by authorities who faced no consequences in the town named after the birthplace of American democracy.

These accounts shook me in ways I'd never expected. Rather than becoming inured to the common, habitual mistreatment of fellow human beings, I became angry. It was disheartening to realize how long this had been going on and how hopeless the situation seemed to those experiencing it. Racism and exclusive white power were so entrenched in the Deep South that no one expected change to come quickly. Of course, racism and official brutality were not exclusive to Mississippi, but I was still naïve about the ubiquity of racial injustice.

The division lawyers were assembling a strong case against the sheriff's office and the KKK for a pattern and practice of inflicting injury on blacks without justification. These were clear and obvious violations of constitutional rights—punishment without due process. The question was whether we had the evidence and witnesses to persuade an all-white grand jury in Mississippi to indict.

The department needed to be absolutely confident that if anyone was charged with federal crimes, the charges would stick. They needed an airtight case, and I wanted to be the one to give it to them.

When Bud Sather left Philadelphia for other assignments, I was temporarily alone. Even though division lawyers weren't supposed to pursue any investigative work in such a violent and unstable community without a partner, I decided that I could continue working regardless of whether I had a partner or not. Foolishly, I figured I knew enough by then to disregard the department's rule.

On one of the days I was out beating the pavement in blazing heat, a black teenager came up to me.

"Mister, you're with the government, right?" he asked.

I nodded.

"Well, I saw them bury those bodies."

The kid told me he had observed the burial from a discreet distance, from a hill overlooking Old Jolly Farm. He provided corroborating details and even identified a pickup truck that he said was at the scene. He said he saw an excavator digging up dirt. He told me he counted up the number of people involved. As I heard this, one thought popped into my head: *Holy shit.*

Using my new investigative skills, I asked him different questions to test his veracity. He didn't appear to be searching for answers. His story remained constant.

When I asked him to describe to the FBI what he'd seen, he was reluctant at first. Providing information like this could easily get him lynched. Just being seen with me was dangerous.

He said he'd tell what he saw only if we agreed to pay to move his family out of Philadelphia. I couldn't blame him for wanting to get out of this godforsaken place. So I told him that if his story checked out, I'd see what I could do to help him.

I was so exhilarated by the impact this chance encounter might have on the case that I couldn't help but brag about my discovery with the attorney who was rooming with me in Meridian. He was a senior lawyer with far more experience in Mississippi. He wasn't impressed.

"What on earth are you thinking?" he asked. "You can't make a deal with someone like that—even to present him as a possible witness— without getting approval. You don't know what you're doing."

I stumbled over my words.

"What the hell are you thinking?" he asked again.

Though I didn't tell him this, what I was thinking was that although I was only a few months out of law school, I was about to break open a major case single-handedly.

"Pick this kid up tomorrow morning," my roommate said. "We'll take him to Sullivan to check out his story."

A little concerned that the bureau would snag my witness, I escorted the youth to the FBI's makeshift headquarters in a motel just outside of Philadelphia the next day.

Joseph Sullivan, who was in charge of the FBI task force, was a legendary figure at the bureau. A widower in his fifties, he was known for total dedication to his cases. He had a reputation for being tough and thorough. In later years, the author Tom Clancy referred to him as "the greatest lawman America ever produced."

The motel rooms used as offices by the FBI were mini-arsenals—filled with handguns, shotguns, and ammunition. Were this known, it could only have increased local anxiety about the federal government's presence in the state. I heard that some agents had gotten into confrontations with Klansmen where weapons had been drawn.

With my young witness, I sat in one of the motel rooms for a while until Sullivan walked in with a group of underlings. I introduced myself to him. He was cordial but showed little interest in me. He quickly turned to my guest and the interrogation began.

Sullivan started off extremely solicitous of the young man, asking him about his background and about what he saw that night. Then he got notably rougher, casting doubt on the story at every turn. He asked the teen repeatedly if he was telling the truth. He went over the facts again and again. Eventually the kid started to get tripped up until he finally started to cry. He said four words that taught me a valuable lesson for the rest of my career.

"I made it up," he said.

He confessed to Sullivan that he just wanted to get his family out of Philadelphia. I later realized that the young man had seen me—correctly—as an easy mark.

After the interrogation concluded, Sullivan came up to me. He was not happy about having wasted his time.

"Listen," he said, "in the future, leave it to the pros." That stung more than any hit I had received in eight years of football.

I got over that embarrassing experience, but I never forgot it. I'd been seduced by the desire to believe him. In my eagerness to be the one to solve the case, I had forgotten that if something seems too good to be true, it usually isn't true. It taught me a simple but important lesson, not to overreach and allow my ambitions to get ahead of the facts.

After flying solo and crashing spectacularly, I was assigned a new partner. Marty was about my age, but shorter and thinner. Like me, he joined the division in the summer of 1964, after graduating with honors from a Midwestern law school. Mississippi was as foreign to him as it was to me. He was more circumspect than I was, and had more practical skills: he had been a licensed driver for years, while I, raised in Manhattan, barely knew a brake from a clutch. We worked together in Mississippi for five weeks, from mid-September to October 16.

One evening, Marty and I drove back to our hotel in Meridian from Philadelphia, where we had gone to interview Freedom Summer organizers. While there we met with Rita Schwerner, Mickey's widow, who offered us an icy welcome. She blamed the federal government for her husband's death, asserting that the Department of Justice could have protected him. I told her we were doing our best to find and punish those responsible.

I had absolutely no doubt that our visit to the Freedom Summer headquarters was observed by the local authorities—that descriptions of us and our car were noted and conveyed promptly to Rainey and the sheriff's office.

As Marty and I drove along a mostly empty highway, we heard a police siren behind us. It seemed to come out of nowhere.

I stopped our car on the side of the road. Knowing as well as I did the reputation of local whites, Marty was anxious. While the officer sat in his vehicle, Marty scanned the darkness behind us.

The officer took his time getting out of his car; he walked deliberately to my window, which was already rolled down because of the oppressive heat. He was an ordinary-looking guy, not particularly threatening. If this weren't in the middle of backwater, racist Mississippi, where Justice Department lawyers were considered undesirable outsiders, I might have been less wary.

"You violated the law here, son," he said to me.

This was complete nonsense but I knew better than to say so. I hadn't been speeding and I hadn't had anything to drink. "What did I do, Officer?"

"Your left tire was on the white line while you were driving," he said. Then he asked for identification. I handed him my driver's license and my government ID.

As the officer studied the documents, I noticed that Marty appeared increasingly anxious.

When the officer handed the ID cards back to me, he asked, "What are you boys doing down here?"

"We're with the Department of Justice," I said, gesturing to my identification. The last thing I wanted to do was explain exactly why we were in Mississippi.

He looked hard at us for another moment—it probably seemed longer than it actually was.

"All right, then," he finally said. "You boys take care now."

I pulled the car from the side of the road. As I drove carefully back to Meridian, Marty seemed still shaken and again looked behind us.

"Marty, what in the hell is wrong with you?" I finally asked.

His eyes were wide. "Didn't you see that pickup truck?" he asked.

"What truck?"

"On the side road," he said. "Filled with a bunch of thugs. They were watching us."

"What about it?"

"I think they were going to do to us what they did to those other guys."

Like Schwerner and Goodman, we were two young Jewish men sent to the South to protect the rights of black citizens. It dawned on me what might have happened had I not shown the officer my Justice Department identification. Until that moment I had been too naïve to be afraid for my life. From then on I checked the rearview mirror often when I drove at night.

B y the end of 1964, John Doar determined that we had compiled enough evidence to charge Rainey, Price, and several others with violating the civil rights of black citizens, including Harris and Hudson, the two youths, and Kirk Culberson, the man assaulted while Rainey held his glasses. In total, thirteen cases were presented to federal grand juries convened in Jackson for violations of Title 18 of the U.S. Code, which covers violations of civil rights by government officials.

These were the first cases ever filed by a government entity against the Neshoba County authorities. Over several weeks, seventy-four witnesses would be called to testify, including many I'd vetted and interviewed myself. The grand jury indicted Rainey and Price on several counts, though dismissed other cases for lack of evidence. But even a single indictment, and the message it sent, was what mattered. These cases were separate from the murders of Chaney, Schwerner, and Goodman, which were still under investigation. But indictments of the Neshoba sheriff officers in the other cases increased pressure to break that case too.

I was in our field office in Jackson that November when word came that a Klansman the FBI had been pressuring had finally cracked. In exchange for immunity, Horace Doyle Barnette confessed his involvement in the deaths of Chaney, Goodman, and Schwerner and implicated about a dozen other people in the crime. Among those implicated: Deputy Price; Sheriff Rainey; Alton Wayne Roberts, a local Klansman; and Jerry McGrew Sharpe, another local. The news of the confession went around our office like a Kansas cyclone.

A copy of the confession was sent to our field office—because of its sensitive nature, it was highly confidential. I managed to get a look at it and jotted down as much as I could in the notebook I always carried for just such occasions. It was powerful.

They [Chaney, Schwerner, and Goodman] went to the Mt. Zion church on June 16. Arrested by Price about 5:30 within the city limits . . . Released at 10:30 at night. They were followed to the city limits by Price and Willis. Killen [head of the Klan] and Sharpe drove to the drive-in in Meridian. . . . They wanted the Lauderdale [MS] KKK to join in whipping them. "You'd better take your beaters." . . . Miss Highway Patrol intercepted them on Hwy 19. Price stopped the car. He placed the three in back of his own car, drove down the road . . . We went left on gravel road. Wayne Roberts ran past us, opened the left door, pulled Schwerner out, spun him around, said, "Are you that nigger lover?" and Schwerner said, "I know just how you feel." And Roberts shot him. Roberts got Goodman out of the car and shot him. . . . Another man, Jordan, said, "Save one for me." He got out of the car. Chaney backed up, stood on the bank on the other side of the ditch, and Jordan shot him. Jordan said, "You didn't leave me anything but a nigger, but at least I killed me a nigger."

I was struck by the bloodlust. I couldn't fathom how anyone could be so eager to kill someone. The Klansman, Wayne Roberts, could barely control himself.

Ironically, had the murders occurred near where the car was burned and abandoned—on the Choctaw reservation—the federal government would have prosecuted the murder case, since the Indian reservation was under federal jurisdiction. But there was no evidence to prove that. The murders were crimes under the jurisdiction of state authorities, and the Mississippi prosecutors were reluctant to press any charges. Incredibly, they cited a lack of evidence. In any event, we knew enough to believe that an all-white jury in a Mississippi state court would never convict.

The alleged conspirators were charged with the only federal crime available to us: violations of the civil rights of Goodman, Chaney, and Schwerner. It was the equivalent of trying Al Capone for tax evasion, but in Capone's case, that tactic worked.

On December 4, 1964, the FBI arrested nineteen people, including Rainey and Price. At their arraignment six days later, the charges were dismissed by a U.S. magistrate who determined that the confession on which the arrests were based was hearsay and therefore inadmissible. The charges, one reporter noted at the time, "seemed to increase their popularity."

"It took me an hour to get to work this morning," Price said the day after his arraignment. "I have to spend so much time shaking hands."

A famous *Life* magazine photo of the conspirators at a court hearing showed them smiling and laughing, with Rainey sitting up in the front of the crew, sockless in cowboy boots, with a bag of his ever-present chewing tobacco in his hand and a wad in his cheek.

In January, Doar and his team persuaded a new federal grand jury to indict all nineteen conspirators, but a month later Judge Harold Cox dismissed the indictments against all but Rainey and Price. Judge Cox was a friend of Mississippi senator James Eastland. Although he had been appointed to the federal bench by President Kennedy, he was aligned with segregationists and a frequent obstacle for the division.

The indictments were just the first step in a long, agonizing ordeal for Justice Department lawyers. It took almost three years, until October 1967, and a U.S. Supreme Court decision to reinstate the indictments before John Doar personally tried eighteen of the men for conspiracy in the deaths of Chaney, Schwerner, and Goodman.

I was among many offering Doar and other prosecutors whatever assistance I could. At the time, the Civil Rights Division was loosely organized and lacked a strict hierarchy, so that we could be mobile. Seniority was gained only by experience. I became one of Doar's "fast ponies"—attorneys he could send on a moment's notice to respond to problems when they arose. We were willing to take on tough assignments without question, like managing tense demonstrations and confrontations. We interviewed victims and witnesses to brutality, gathered evidence for potential prosecution and, in some cases, went into the courtroom. I enjoyed working with a sense of urgency and I was always available. I had no family commitments. My Washington apartment was little more than a mail drop and my social life revolved around my colleagues at Justice.

We all spent countless days in Mississippi, and John Doar's life was not much different. As the columnist Jimmy Breslin once wrote, his life "has been in those nothing motels on the highways or in the dirty-windowed hotels of small cities. It has been spent with people afraid to help him or with people who think about shooting him, in courtrooms where you can't win and with politicians who will not listen." When one of Doar's children was born, the baby was unnamed for weeks until his father could get home, and name him after his boss.

As I came to know Doar better, I learned more about him, especially about when he quieted that mob after Medgar Evers was killed. With his tie knotted and his white shirtsleeves rolled up, standing between angry black protesters with rocks and white police with guns, his impressive presence and careful, strong words averted a massacre. He had pledged to secure justice and managed to persuade hot, grief-stricken, and angry young blacks to disperse.

It wasn't until after I'd left the division that any convictions were achieved in connection with the Philadelphia murders. The ten-day trial before Judge Harold Cox, John Doar's longtime nemesis, was exhausting. The defense attorneys reminded jurors that Doar had helped James Meredith to "invade" the University of Mississippi, and dozens of witnesses testified as to the defendants' good character. On October 27, 1967, the all-white jury rendered what appeared to be a compromise verdict. Rainey and six others were acquitted, but Cecil Price and five others were convicted.

None of the defendants was ever charged by the state, much less convicted, of murder—until nearly thirty years later. In 2005, Edgar Ray Killen, a white preacher and Klansman, was convicted of manslaughter. But in 1967, any conviction of a white person in Mississippi for deprivation of civil rights was a significant achievement.

The Philadelphia murders continue to be shocking. Not only did the conspirators kill the three young men—all nonviolent and defenseless—in cold blood, they did it with glee and impunity. They even fought with each other for the privilege of gunning them down. This case exposed a world that had persisted for decades, a reality that I and other horrified Americans learned of only through the victims' sacrifice and the determination of federal investigators to solve the crime. It was hard to comprehend the conditions of life for dignified people who were treated so badly—a life Hobbes described as "poor, nasty, brutish, and short." But I concentrated on my work with the hope that eventually the division's lawsuits would succeed enough to chip away at blacks' disenfranchisement. Empowering them with full voting rights was the only way I could see to bring about real change. I never imagined that could happen quickly.

On March 4, 1965, I went to Tallahatchie County, Mississippi, to investigate how blacks there were being kept off the voting rolls. Tallahatchie is a rural county in the northwestern part of the state. It is still today predominantly black and poor, with a population in decline since the 1930s. It had a reputation as one of the most racist counties in the state; considering what I'd just encountered in Neshoba, that was quite a statement. I'd heard that black motorists traveling through Tallahatchie were warned to have a full tank of gas because the few gas stations weren't likely to serve them.

As always, when I traveled in local communities, I was conscious of being an unwanted outsider. A few white residents were friendly, but I was generally wary. When I checked into my motel, I showed my Department of Justice ID to the desk clerk. Nothing the clerk said or asked was threatening, but I felt uncomfortable. He directed me to a room on the far side of the building with a window overlooking the nearby highway. Any pickup truck could drive by and speed off quickly into the night. Afraid of being so exposed, I decided to sleep on the floor that night, and placed my mattress up against the window. I traveled through the dusty counties for the next few days, gathering information and ignorant of the drama unfolding to the east in Alabama.

In early 1965, civil rights movement leaders ramped up voter registration efforts, and federal officials in Washington began to plan for new legislation to secure the vote. Movement leaders targeted Dallas and Perry counties in Alabama for a concerted effort to register black residents in Selma and Marion, the county seats. Over several weeks during February, emboldened blacks in ever-growing numbers nonviolently confronted increasingly resistant white authorities. The activity drew the concern of government officials in Washington and the attention of the press. While I was in Tallahatchie, the conflict came to a head in a particularly ugly event.

Despite the brutality of local law enforcement toward the demonstrators, no one had died—until the end of February. Jimmie Lee Jackson, a young black man, participated in a nighttime rally on February 18 to protest the arrest of a movement worker in Marion. When the streetlights suddenly went out, the group was viciously attacked by the local police and state troopers, while a mob of angry whites attacked reporters and news photographers who were covering the events. One of the troopers shot Jackson while he was trying to protect his mother. He died a week later. Martin Luther King Jr. spoke at Jackson's funeral, which was attended by more than a thousand people. King and other leaders of the Southern Christian Leadership Council (SCLC) decided to plan a march from Selma to the state capital in Montgomery for the local blacks to protest Jackson's death and demand the state to enforce their right to vote.

On Sunday, March 7, in the afternoon, approximately six hundred local black citizens began to march along U.S. 80 from Selma to the capital in Montgomery to petition the state government. Leading the march was a young leader from the Student Nonviolent Coordinating Committee (SNCC) named John Lewis and a clergyman named Hosea Williams of SCLC. Walking slowly on the Edmund Pettus Bridge across the Alabama River at the edge of the city, they confronted a phalanx of police and state troopers and a posse of white men that Sheriff Jim Clark had "deputized" that very morning. When the marchers did not immediately disperse, the patrolmen began shoving them. As the march leaders stoically held their ground, they were attacked. The patrolmen fired tear gas, and Clark's posse—some of them on horseback—beat demonstrators with clubs and knocked them to the ground. Seventeen marchers were hospitalized—victims of what was quickly dubbed "Bloody Sunday." The brutal incident was televised across America, interrupting ABC's broadcast of the 1961 movie *Judgment at Nuremberg*; viewers were shocked to see real-life images from Selma contrasted with the film. The Gestapo-like violence against U.S. citizens seeking only the fundamental right to vote, especially in the wake of the notorious murders in Philadelphia, graphically demonstrated to the rest of the country a situation spiraling out of control.

I remember watching the news broadcast in my motel room in Mississippi. It wasn't long before I too was called to Alabama.

The day after Bloody Sunday, Dr. King came from Atlanta to join movement leaders in Selma. They filed a request in federal court in Montgomery for an injunction to prevent the state from interfering with a massive new protest march from Selma to Montgomery. That afternoon, while John Lewis was still in the hospital recovering from his beating the day before, Judge Frank M. Johnson replied that he would not issue an injunction without a hearing, which he scheduled to begin Thursday.

On Tuesday, March 9, Dr. King led a symbolic march from Brown Chapel in Selma to the Pettus Bridge. The marchers didn't attempt to cross the bridge, but the leaders felt they had to organize a protest to relieve pressure while awaiting the hearing. Protests against the Selma violence were being held in cities across the country as well as in Montgomery, where hundreds of SNCC demonstrators, mostly area black students, clashed with police.

Dr. King had asked ministers to join him on this symbolic march, and many clergymen heeded his call. Three white ministers who had just arrived in Selma were viciously attacked after the march by a group of white men when they left a restaurant after dinner. One of them, a Unitarian minister from Boston named James Reeb, appeared to have sustained brain injuries from the assault, and local doctors refused to treat him. Taken to a hospital in Birmingham some two hours away, Reverend Reeb was put on life support and died two days later.

During the Freedom Summer in Mississippi, the Justice Department's insistence on honoring the constitutional limits on federal authority and not acting to protect the volunteers had bothered many Americans. But Bloody Sunday was so big that it was clear that the federal government could no longer stand by when civil rights were being so brutally violated by state authorities. The Department of Justice was now all in, participating in the SCLC lawsuit on the side of the marchers as a "friend of the court."

The hearing before Judge Johnson began on Thursday, March 11, the day I received a phone call from John Doar in Selma, summoning me immediately to Selma, which was 270 miles away from where I was in Mississippi. I headed there at once. Selma turned out to be a pretty town along the Alabama River with several prominent churches and other signs of civilization. The main hotel, the Albert, was modeled after the Doge's Palace in Venice.

I arrived at the Selma courthouse that night and immediately sought out Doar. I found him towering above other lawyers, issuing instructions. He handed me some photographs that had been taken from an FBI surveillance plane during the Bloody Sunday melee. The pictures showed the sheriff's posse on horseback chasing marchers and beating those already on the ground. In some cases, you could see the officers' faces clearly despite the gas masks many were wearing.

"I need you to find some of these victims," Doar said, handing me blank subpoenas. "Then I want you to get them on a bus to Montgomery to testify tomorrow morning."

I started off without a map of the area, or the slightest clue of how I was going to accomplish this. I'd forgone lunch and dinner as I made the long, tiring drive.

"Yes, sir," I replied.

Though I had never been to Alabama before, I figured it couldn't be that different from Mississippi. I headed to the outskirts of town where the pavement ran out, looking for the black part of town. By the time I found it the hour was late and the sky was dark.

I parked my car and began walking toward the series of small houses in the hope someone would answer my knock on their door and tell me something that might help. From one nearby, I heard music playing and a large group of people talking and laughing.

I walked up to the door and displayed my identification to the first person who answered. Carrying some of the FBI surveillance photos under my arm, I said, "I'm Terry Lenzner. I work for Bobby Kennedy." I told them I was investigating what had happened at the Pettus Bridge and showed the photographs to them.

My instincts paid off and I found the members of the tight-knit community eager to help. Almost immediately, someone at the party pointed to a person being beaten in one of the photos and said, "Oh, I know him." Others came over and identified this person and then another.

"Do you want me to get this guy and bring him over?" someone offered, pointing to a figure in one of the photos.

"Yes," I replied. "That would be very helpful." Buoyed by so much willing assistance, I began to believe that I might accomplish my assignment in time.

Having been dispatched to the field so quickly, I was not familiar with most of the details of the incident. So when interviewing a potential witness, I asked whatever questions I could think of: What did you think was going on when the police started moving in on you? Were you hit? How many times? What did the sheriff's posse say to you? Who was near you? Did you see others get hit? I jotted the answers down in my notebook and handed subpoenas to those who seemed the most credible.

I had put together a pretty decent group of witnesses with incredible speed. But my feeling of triumph lasted only a few hours. I got a call the next morning from a Justice Department lawyer in Montgomery, complaining that I hadn't yet sent in a report of my findings. How in the world, I wondered, was I supposed to have gotten that done? It would have been easier and faster if I had been debriefed over the phone. Tension within the department was running high.

The selection of Selma as the site for civil rights demonstrations was not happenstance. Sheriff Clark had a history of brutality and was determined to stop the movement to register blacks in his county. His short fuse ignited quickly, which meant that challenging him was sure to produce drama. He was known to have beaten one prominent African-American woman with a club, ordered mass arrests of protesters, and thrown a black minister down a flight of stairs. Clark, a forty-two-year-old former cattle rancher and World War II veteran, wore a pin containing a single word, NEVER, a signal to blacks that nothing was ever going to change for them. Like Lawrence Rainey, the sadistic Clark was an almost perfect symbol to rally the country against—a man likely to overreach in his tactics and horrify Americans who saw his atrocities on television.

Another reason Selma was a good choice for civil rights activism was that movement leaders knew the division was investigating voting rights violations by the Dallas County registrar there. John Doar told me that before Freedom Summer activities began, he had been visited by Bob Moses, codirector of the Council of Federated Organizations (COFO), the umbrella organization that oversaw the voting registration efforts. Moses knew the division was focusing on particular counties in Mississippi, Louisiana, and Alabama where disenfranchisement was most egregious and federal lawsuits had the best chances for success. He also knew that our resources were limited. There weren't nearly enough lawyers to cover most of the cities and counties in the South where there was racism, violence, or protests. With limited staff we could be in only a few places at one time and had to choose our stands carefully. Doar assumed that Moses, during his visit to Doar's office, had seen the map displayed on the office wall, indicating which counties we were targeting. This was invaluable intelligence for the civil rights organizations.

While we waited for word from the federal court in Montgomery about whether a march could go forward, thousands of people began to arrive in anticipation of participating in the historic event. Every hotel in Selma, Montgomery, and the surrounding areas was packed with lawyers detailed from other divisions at Justice, other federal officials, movement supporters, and members of the press. Much of the Justice Department staff, including me, was relegated to sleeping at Maxwell Air Force Base outside of Montgomery. Demonstrations were held in Selma that I was sent to observe and report on. At one event, I came across a familiar figure peering at a demonstration from behind a tree. He turned out to be John Culver, a renowned Harvard football player and later U.S. senator. John, who was then working for Senator Ted Kennedy, had been sent to Selma to provide a firsthand report.

In some ways I felt as if I was walking through a circus—in one area were National Guardsmen and federal law-enforcement officials, in another were local and state police. Nonviolent protest groups distanced themselves from more aggressive black power leaders. White sympathizers, mostly students from the North, mingled with local black residents. Smaller groups of white residents who deplored the violence confronted mobs of segregationists who insulted almost everyone.

One day when I was hanging around Brown Chapel, the local black church where the demonstrators congregated, I came across a bureau agent I'd met at other demonstrations. We had struck up conversations a few times. He was bored as I was, waiting for a planned demonstration to begin. We chatted about the weather, sports, the usual. When talk turned to the latest demonstration, he said, "This guy King is a real scumbag."

I knew that not all the bureau guys supported the protest activities, especially those who had roots in the Deep South. Some, complaining about the late start to marches, referred to events as operating on "CPT" or "Colored People's Time." Still, I was a little taken aback by his bluntness.

"You mean Dr. Martin Luther King?" I asked. What he was telling me seemed so unbelievable that I wasn't sure he had the name right.

"Yeah."

"Well, how do you know that?"

He leaned in a little closer. "I've heard tapes of him screwing around with women and men."

I guess it was another mark of my naïveté, but it never occurred to me that the FBI—apparently under direct orders from J. Edgar Hoover and presumably with the approval of the attorney general—wiretapped

Dr. King. Why on earth was the FBI spending taxpayers' dollars for something as sordid as that? At the time, Hoover was still considered a hero to most Americans, and this seemed unworthy of him. The disclosure made me skeptical about how much I could trust the bureau to protect civil rights. And it raised questions in my mind about Dr. King as well.

After I heard from a journalist friend that he, too, knew of the tapes, I typed a note to John Doar, telling him what I'd learned about the FBI's wiretaps of King.

I took the note in an envelope, marked CONFIDENTIAL, to Doar's office. A little while later, Doar came down to my office, which was unusual, and asked me to come out into the hallway. He handed me the note.

"Do whatever you want with this," he said. He didn't tell me to destroy it—that wasn't his style—but it was pretty clear that's what he wanted.

I tore it up in front of him. But I didn't throw it away. Instead I kept the bits of torn paper in an envelope and put it in a personal file, where it still resides.

During those days in Selma, I needed to report information back to our headquarters and to DOJ in Washington about what was happening between the protesters and Sheriff Clark and the highway patrol. That wasn't easy. I spent an inordinate amount of time running around looking for an available pay phone and making sure I had the correct change to make calls. One day, I had a bright idea. I had gotten to know some of the residents of a small apartment building near Brown Chapel, in particular a woman I knew as Mrs. Turner. She and I had become friendly—we'd talk about what was happening in Selma and I'd ask her opinions on things and what life was like for her and her neighbors. So, one day, I asked her if I could observe the demonstrations from her apartment and use her phone.

She readily agreed, and we paid her a few dollars per day to use her apartment while she was away at work. Her window offered an excellent view of the demonstrations, and having a phone immediately available was a godsend. Every half hour, I or another lawyer called in to report what was happening.

Mrs. Turner's apartment became a center of activity during the demonstrations once people heard of the arrangement I'd secured. At one point a senior partner from a prestigious Washington law firm, one of several who had come to Selma to monitor the activities, visited the apartment as I was about to leave. Introducing himself, he said, "I was told to talk to you about what I'm supposed to do."

I had no idea what to say. He was probably a capable friend of one of the department's senior attorneys but he looked, truth be told, a little out of his element. Finally, I replied, "You know, Mrs. Turner doesn't like the apartment messed up when she comes home from work. Can you help clean up?"

When I returned about an hour or so later, I found him in the kitchen sweeping, with Mrs. Turner's apron tied around his waist.

By Monday, March 15, we were fairly certain that Judge Johnson was going to allow the march to Montgomery. He was to issue his decree the following day. He asked the movement leaders to draw up and submit to him detailed plans for the march. The logistics themselves were considerable. Since the march would take days to complete, the organizers needed to provide adequate food, water, and safe shelter at night. That afternoon, several hundred students from black colleges in Alabama clashed with police and mounted deputies in Montgomery. When the officers tried to physically break up the peaceful demonstration, some students threw rocks and bottles in response. It was obvious that non-violence would be impossible to maintain much longer.

That evening, President Johnson captured the airwaves to give a momentous address to the nation. He announced that he would introduce legislation to Congress that would end disenfranchisement. I heard the president's speech on the car radio as I was driving to the courthouse in Selma for an evening meeting with Doar. Johnson urged Congress to swiftly enact the Voting Rights Act of 1965 to outlaw the discriminatory practices—such as the arbitrary literacy tests I'd encountered—that had kept blacks in the Deep South from voting for decades. "What happened in Selma is part of a far larger movement which reaches into every section and state of America," Johnson said in his familiar Texas twang. "It is the effort of American Negroes to secure for themselves the full blessings of American life. Their cause must be our cause too. Because it's not just Negroes, but really it's all of us who must overcome the crippling legacy of bigotry and injustice." He concluded by echoing the anthem of the civil rights movement with special emphasis: "We *shall* overcome."

When I first went to work for John Doar, he'd promised me I'd be involved in something historic. The president of the United States was talking about something I was directly involved in and now cared deeply about. As I drove through the dark, empty streets, no one in sight, I believed the president was speaking to me.

The next day, Judge Johnson issued a decree allowing the fifty-four-mile march from Selma to Montgomery to proceed without state interference. I was to be one of Doar's liaisons along the route, assigned to look out for potential problems and witness incidents. We had a considerable presence in Selma at that time, but I felt that I was Doar's personal eyes and ears for the entire walk.

The march was set to begin on Sunday, March 21, and all the different and sometimes warring civil rights organizations in the country were involved in preparations over the next five days. Eighteen hundred members of the Alabama National Guard were mobilized to guard the highway, which was reduced to only the eastbound lane for vehicular traffic. U.S. Army troops, a hundred FBI agents, and U.S.

marshals were to be deployed, and helicopters were to fly overhead to look out for snipers and other dangers.

I walked with the marchers all the way during the five-day march, carrying a walkie-talkie so I could report back to headquarters with almost minute-by-minute accounts. Where the highway was narrow, only three hundred were allowed to march, but the parade swelled to three thousand along wider stretches. Walking out of Selma was by far the worst part. A large group of Klansmen and state troopers gathered by the bridge. They were held back from the vast crowd of jubilant demonstrators by the federalized National Guardsmen, but they yelled vile comments ("Nigger lover!" "Burn in hell!") and jeered. One of them spit at me as I passed. Occasionally I looked at a protester's face—always a portrait of pure hatred and frustration.

As the marchers proceeded along the highway, I scanned the woods for snipers. Instead I saw federal troops stationed there, searching the area or standing guard. As the march progressed, the federal presence was impressive and daunting. U.S. troops marched ahead of us, picking up manhole covers to ensure bombs hadn't been planted. Overhead, a helicopter flew—I spoke to its occupants from time to time, receiving information about what they were observing along the route. At night, the marchers camped in fields belonging to black residents who lived along the route. They held rallies and were entertained by speakers and performers. I explored the campsites to make sure the marchers would be secure, then got a ride to Montgomery to sleep at Maxwell Air Force Base.

Large crowds of blacks came out to watch along the route, lining the highway and celebrating the victory of a successful march. On the last day, as we made our way into the outskirts of Montgomery, things became tense again. There was more shouting from white bystanders, more taunts, more spitting and throwing.

I walked with Doar on those final miles to the statehouse in Montgomery. Though he carried himself with his usual composure, I knew he was relieved, satisfied, and exhausted. The march ended with a concert headlined by Harry Belafonte, Sammy Davis Jr., Tony Bennett, and the folk trio Peter, Paul, and Mary. I stood with Doar and our colleagues almost directly in front of the stage. We all shared a moment of release. This peaceful end to the events that had begun with such violence in Selma only weeks before was all but unimaginable. Everyone was moved, and felt enormous relief and pride for a job well done.

Then, more violence. The day after the march ended, when I was heading back to Washington, a white woman named Viola Liuzzo drove a group of black marchers home to Selma. Mrs. Liuzzo was a mother from Detroit who had come to Alabama to express solidarity. As she drove, a car filled with white men pulled alongside her. One of the occupants aimed a gun at her and fired. She was killed on the highway that we had walked just the day before.

The shocking news was devastating. It shattered the confidence, pride, and hope that the march to Montgomery had encouraged. This murder shook me up even more than when the state trooper had pulled Marty and me over. From then on, I looked to see if cars were following me as I drove around the South. I created my own evasion techniques: slowing down, changing lanes, glancing through the rearview mirror to see if any car was following. For the first time, I was really aware of the dangers. The violence had become random; anyone could be a victim.

I remembered another occasion earlier in the winter in Sunflower County, Mississippi. I'd gone to a black church to interview potential witnesses for a voting rights case. Waiting outside for the service to finish, I listened as Fanny Lou Hamer, a well-known activist, sang "We Shall Overcome." Her beautiful, rich voice and the words were incredibly moving. I felt inspired because in a very real way my efforts were helping these people overcome decades of subjugation. But I also remembered that I was standing in the cold, all by myself, feeling vulnerable. If some segregationists drove by the church looking to make trouble, I was screwed. I was like the character in *The Godfather* who is told to stand outside Vito Corleone's hospital after an attempted mob hit and to make it look like he had a gun in case other assassins happened by.

After the march to Montgomery, along with a few other attorneys I managed the federal grand jury in Selma, seeking indictments for the Bloody Sunday attacks. Doar doubted that we'd get any indictments, but the cases were important to pursue. I worked as hard as I could, helping to prepare cases of police brutality with the best possible evidence. I chose victims who would be the most credible witnesses, such as John Lewis and a woman named Margaret Clay Brooks.

Mrs. Brooks was a slight black woman with two kids who lived just outside of Selma. She had heard about the demonstration planned for March 7 and came to demand her right to vote. She was friendly and polite, and had a beautiful smile. While standing in the line of marchers at the bridge, a trooper grabbed her, hit her with a club, and knocked out all of her front teeth.

After hearing her unequivocal account of police brutality, the all-white grand jurors asked Mrs. Brooks questions such as: "Are you a member of the Communist Party?" "Were you paid to demonstrate?" "Have you ever been arrested?" "How many children do you have?" "Where is your husband?" "Are you on welfare?"

The grand jurors seemed equally unmoved by John Lewis's story. We had a news photograph showing a highway patrolman with a club raised just before bringing it down on Lewis's head, fracturing his skull. Although the patrolman was wearing a gas mask, the FBI was able to enlarge the picture sufficiently to identify him. But the patrolman was not indicted.

Even with sworn testimony from credible victims and witnesses, as well as clear photographic evidence, we did not get a single indictment. This was the ugly truth behind Clark's NEVER pin—that white Southerners were determined to maintain segregation—and why so many black citizens believed the pin's message. I knew Doar was right. We weren't going to persuade all-white grand juries to indict those who were safeguarding the status quo. We needed new grand juries empaneled from voting rolls that included blacks.

That disheartening experience afforded yet another lesson. During the grand jury preparation, I received a memo from John Doar. "You are riding people too hard," he wrote. His note came as a complete surprise. I was a hard worker, impatient, probably brash and maybe too aggressive. I'm sure I wasn't as diplomatic with the other lawyers and investigators as I should have been. My feeling was that we had a lot of work to do and a short amount of time in which to do it. The stakes were high, and the case was important. Doar, a demanding but fair boss, was telling me that I needed to correct my attitude. I took the criticism in stride, but I also tried to learn from it, though not always successfully.

Despite courtroom disappointment, something extraordinary did come of our efforts. The brutal attack in Selma, coupled with the murder of civil rights workers in Mississippi, provided the impetus for Americans across the country to embrace the cause of equal rights in the South. They lobbied Congress and their representatives responded. On August 6, 1965, President Johnson signed into law the Voting Rights Act that he had urged Congress to enact less than five months before. The law prohibited literacy tests everywhere, and mandated federal oversight of registration and voting in counties that had a history of racial discrimination.

When the Supreme Court later validated the Voting Rights Act's prescriptions, it cited the Civil Rights Division's record of painstaking county-by-county lawsuits. John Doar and Burke Marshall deserved credit for that. For the black citizens of Selma, one effect was dramatic and immediate. In 1966, with an electorate that now included a large proportion of black voters, Selma's Sheriff Jim Clark was voted out of office.

The first elections under implementation of the Voting Rights Act were primaries in May 1966. In March, I went to Perry County, contiguous to Selma's Dallas County, to prepare for the election. My DOJ predecessor had been so dogmatic that the local authorities refused to deal with him. Mindful of that, I opted for a different approach. I wanted to deal with the most moderate and potentially cooperative official in the county, and asked the local FBI agent whom he thought I should approach. He quickly named T. O. Harris, the city of Marion's chief of police. He called Chief Harris to introduce me, and the three of us met the next day for breakfast.

The chief was personable, had a good sense of humor, and spoke with apparent sincerity. We met at a small café in Marion, where Harris insisted on ordering my breakfast: cornbread and buttermilk. Then he watched with a sly grin as I choked it down. In the South, the easiest way to find common ground was to talk about one of three things: trucks, guns, or football. I knew nothing about the first two, but I could do football. We got along almost instantly.

"I know you have a complicated situation, and Washington doesn't have all the answers," I told him. "But if we work together, maybe we can figure out some way to avoid ugly incidents here and get the Department of Justice out of your hair."

He nodded in agreement. Harris was an educated man—he was pursuing a doctorate in education—and didn't want violence in his county any more than I did. He introduced me to Mary Auburtin, the Circuit Court clerk who was in charge of voter registration in the county. She had been sued by the DOJ for her office's discriminatory practices. Yet she too was quite friendly. I figured the two were glad to be rid of the lawyer I had replaced. But they had another reason to want to work with me: under the Voting Rights Act, the federal government could in effect take over the entire voting process in a county, bringing in federal regulators and usurping local control altogether.

Over the next two months, the three of us spoke regularly. Mrs.

Auburtin was a thoughtful, gentle lady who actually became a lifelong friend. Both she and Harris wanted the elections to go smoothly. As the primaries drew closer, I sat in the chief's office while he called the local Ku Klux Klan head. "No one is going to cause any problems in my county," I heard him say, "or I will arrest you boys on the spot."

Despite his demeanor, the chief reflected the white community's fears that encouraging blacks to vote would bring greater turmoil. "Listen, Terry," he told me at one point. "We are going to allow everyone who's registered to vote in my county. But I want you to know that we are going to empty the hospitals and bring to the polls every white person we can find. Got a problem with that?"

"Not at all," I responded. "Anyone eligible to vote should do so. That's what this effort is all about." I was so impressed by the cooperation of these officials that I sent a memo to Doar recommending that Perry County be allowed to conduct its own primary without federal interference, though the county's reputation was so bad that my request never had a chance.

The Voting Rights Act quickly altered the political situation in Selma, but change came more slowly in Perry County. Although they outnumbered whites, many blacks eligible to vote were still reluctant to register. When they had tried in the past, their houses had been firebombed and they'd lost their jobs. They remembered Jimmie Lee Jackson, the local church deacon who was killed in Marion after a voting rights demonstration just a year before, and whose death prompted the march that became Bloody Sunday. Even with the full support of the federal government, many were not going to rush to the polls. They wanted to wait and see what happened.

Decades later, John Doar and I made a return visit to Selma for one of the annual commemorations of Bloody Sunday. While I thought I'd understood the impact of what had been accomplished in the 1960s, I didn't fully appreciate it until I went back more than forty years later. This time, all highway patrolmen were African-Americans. I turned to one of them and said, "You look a lot different from the patrolmen I encountered the last time I was here." He laughed appreciatively. I was very moved by this new reality for the people of Selma, and had a much deeper appreciation for the sacrifices made by men like Medgar Evers, James Chaney, Mickey Schwerner, Andrew Goodman, and Dr. King.

My experiences with the Civil Rights Division offered lessons in investigative work that I never received at law school nor could have gotten by working at a law firm—lessons that formed the basis for my later career. I discovered the good that government action can accomplish. I also learned under John Doar's tutelage how important it is to search diligently for and document factual truth. Despite the obvious extremes of the injustices we verified, he never allowed his lawyers to take shortcuts. Every one of the many voting rights cases the division brought under his guidance was carefully prepared with detailed analysis of every registration application in the subject county.

The division also introduced me to my wife, Margaret Rood, a Washington native who was a summer intern there when I arrived. Margaret was the first of a series of young women who came to the division to work in a new position of "research analyst," what today is called a paralegal. We became engaged during the riots in Washington that followed Dr. King's assassination on April 4, 1968. As I was staying with her and her family one weekend, mobs of angry demonstrators took to the streets, smashing store windows and parked cars and setting fires. A curfew was imposed—so we were stuck at home. I had tried to speak with Margaret's father on previous visits, but he was always unavailable. This time he couldn't go anywhere, so I could finally ask for her hand. We were not the only couple that the division produced. In all, ten marriages came out of it around that time.

The minor role I'd played in advancing civil rights—realizing one of President Kennedy's and Johnson's stated goals—had an enormous effect on my outlook and my work since. I had no inkling then of the roles I would play in two more high-profile aspects of Johnson's administration: his "war on poverty" and the escalation of the war in Vietnam.

CHAPTER 2

ZIG WHEN OTHERS ZAG

In early August 1965, between trips to prepare for the Selma grand jury, I was summoned to the attorney general's office on the fifth floor. I had been up there once before. When I was living in the Harvard Varsity Club during my final year of law school, I had noticed an old photograph of Bobby Kennedy's football team gathering dust. Since the photo seemed forgotten, the manager of the club allowed me to take it. Shortly after I began work at the Justice Department in 1964, I asked to see Kennedy and presented him with the picture. He was pleased to receive it, talked a little about the team, and sent me a thank-you note afterward.

Kennedy had resigned his position at the end of September 1964 to run for the Senate from New York. As his replacement, President Johnson eventually appointed Kennedy's deputy, Nicholas Katzenbach, who had been the acting attorney general after Kennedy left. He was a tall, dignified forty-three-year-old with a quiet, understated demeanor. He'd been in office for about nine months when he greeted me.

It was unusual for a young staff lawyer to be called upstairs to a private meeting in the AG's office. I wondered what I had screwed up so badly that required such high-level attention. Though it was a humid August morning, Katzenbach was cool and affable. His quiet manner belied a forceful personality. His office was large, elegant, and imposing, as was Katzenbach. John Doar was there too. After pointing me to a seat, the attorney general did most of the talking.

"Hello, Terry," he said. "John tells me you have done a good job covering demonstrations in the South."

"I appreciate that," I replied.

"We have a protest coming up this weekend here in Washington. It's an antiwar demonstration, and I'd like you to help us cover it."

His tone, while not anxious, suggested concern. The protest was scheduled for the weekend of August 6, 1965, to coincide with the twentieth anniversary of the nuclear bomb the U.S. dropped on Hiroshima at the close of World War II. It was one of the first antiwar demonstrations to take place in the nation's capital. Considering the violence that resulted from civil rights protests in Mississippi and Alabama, I couldn't blame Katzenbach for being concerned.

"Can you explain what you mean by 'cover' the event?" I asked.

"We'd like to know what's going to happen before it happens," the attorney general replied.

"Okay," I said. I understood they didn't want to be surprised by anything, but I was not entirely comfortable. I didn't want to mislead anyone about my role. The Civil Rights Division was charged with protecting citizen's rights, and these marchers were exercising a legitimate right. I thought it would undermine the department's credibility if I went there undercover. "I'd like to go there dressed like I am now, in a suit," I said. "And I plan to show my Department of Justice identification to anyone who asks me why I am there."

"Fine," Katzenbach said with a nod. "That's the only way I'd have it."

He gave me a card with a telephone number that he said would provide me with direct access to him. I was to call him immediately if

I had any useful information. Though our meeting was short and cordial, I left still struck by the mood. I'd worked for the department for
a year, but I'd never been called to do a special project for the attorney
general. It impressed upon me the singular importance of this mission
to the United States government. Perhaps the Justice Department
officials feared violence similar to that in the South. In retrospect,
I wonder if they wanted an observer to document any overreaching
police response. Certainly, the FBI would be on the scene, but maybe
Katzenbach was not confident that the marchers' rights would be sufficiently respected.

I tried to imagine how to "find out what was happening before it
happened." All I could think of was to adapt the tactics I'd learned in
the South: to be alert as a passive observer, notice everyone and everything, and report regularly to my superiors.

On that Friday, about a thousand protesters assembled in front of
the White House. I joined the crowd of protesters, just as I had said
I would, in a suit and tie. Most of the marchers were in T-shirts and
jeans or shorts. I ambled among them, looking for anything interesting. The crowd was made up mostly of young people, none of whom
looked particularly threatening. They carried signs against the draft
and the Vietnam War. There was marijuana smoke in the air. Quite
fortuitously, I spotted an acquaintance I knew from Harvard who had
come all the way from San Francisco to join the protest. Making my
way to him, I told him I was observing the event for the Civil Rights
Division. He provided helpful information, pointing out the leaders
among the crowd: Dr. Staughton Lynd, a Yale professor, and Dave
Dellinger, editor of a pacifist magazine. He then told me their goals,
including petitioning the White House and staging some sort of demonstration at the U.S. Capitol.

Their plan was to demand to present a petition to President Johnson. If the White House refused, they would occupy the driveway
until they were arrested. (This was before high security guarded

federal buildings and Pennsylvania Avenue became closed to traffic in front of the White House.)

This was the first real piece of intelligence about future action that I'd gathered, and I was eager to report it to the attorney general. I went to a telephone that I had found earlier at the Park Police station in Lafayette Park, directly across from the White House. I showed the officer there my identification, and asked if I could use the phone. I then reached into my pocket for the phone number that Katzenbach had given me. When I dialed it, the attorney general answered right away, to my surprise.

"Mr. Attorney General, I've been with the marchers across from the White House," I told him. "I've got a report on what they are about to do."

I relayed what I had learned.

"Okay, wait a second, Terry," Katzenbach replied. "I'm going to hook in the White House." Within a minute or so, he was back on the line. "Okay, Terry, repeat what you just told me." I didn't know who at the White House was on the line listening in, and I never learned who that person was.

I again outlined the plan as I had heard it. Silence followed.

"So that's what's happening," I added, waiting for someone to say something.

Finally I heard Katzenbach ask, "So what should we do?"

Being barely a year out of law school, I was eager to hear how the government would handle this. But the line was silent.

"Terry," Katzenbach said after several seconds, slightly exasperated. "You're there. What should we do?"

What should we do? I wondered. *He's asking me?*

I was only a rookie, and I began to worry about my government asking someone like me to make decisions. I told him the only thing that made sense. "I think someone should accept the petition. You might even send the agent who looks like the president to receive it."

I'd heard the president usually had at least one Secret Service agent who looked somewhat like him. I thought if that guy came out to accept the petition, the marchers would at least be momentarily unnerved.

"Okay," the attorney general replied. That was it, and he was off the phone.

I crossed Lafayette Park to rejoin the crowd in front of the White House. Minutes later, a man who slightly resembled Lyndon Johnson walked out of the West Wing. As the protesters near me watched silently, the man continued down the driveway until he stopped at the black iron gate guarding the White House entrance. Addressing the protest leaders, the agent introduced himself, and said he would accept their petition on the president's behalf.

Members of the group shared surprised looks. The protesters had wanted a confrontation with the White House. Now they didn't know what to do. When the agent left with their petition in his hand, the marchers took a vote. Some voted to leave without incident while others opted to "sit in" on the sidewalk overnight.

The protest continued through the weekend. On Monday, the demonstrators gathered at the Lincoln Memorial, chosen intentionally to honor the site where Dr. King had delivered his "I have a dream" speech two years before. From there the demonstrators would make their way down the Mall to the steps of the Capitol.

D.C. police were out in force, and the Capitol police were also girded for havoc. I learned the House and Senate entrances, floors, and galleries were packed with security people so that none of the demonstrators might find a way to enter and disrupt congressional proceedings. A cordon of police officers carrying guns made a conspicuous display surrounding the Capitol grounds.

When the marchers got to the Capitol steps, red paint splashed on the pavement and spattered on the front line of marchers. I thought the protesters did this to evoke the blood of Americans and Vietnamese killed in the war, but the next day's *New York Times* said the paint was thrown by counter-demonstrators to symbolize the "red" Communism of the peace advocates. As the marchers expected, the police quickly moved forward to arrest them. The marchers went limp on the Capitol steps. Police officers lifted the marchers one by one and literally threw them into nearby police buses. The way this was carried off, treating human beings like sacks of potatoes, struck me as unnecessarily harsh.

I walked to the officer standing by the bus and displayed my identification. "I'm with the Civil Rights Division," I said.

He stared at me.

"What you are doing seems to be imposing punishment on these people without due process of the law."

Unblinking, the officer replied, "Get the fuck out of here." After watching about sixty demonstrators tossed into buses, I followed his advice.

The following week, Katzenbach called me back to his office. Thanking me for the job I did, he gave me a copy of the letter he was going to have put in my personnel file, attesting to the fact I'd participated in the march under the attorney general's orders. If I were ever under suspicion because my face appeared in an FBI surveillance photo of the demonstration, I'd have evidence that I was not there to demonstrate. This was something I hadn't thought of. Katzenbach knew that an FBI photo of me standing next to a protester could kill a government career.

I continued to work at the division for more than a year, through 1966, investigating and pursuing cases of racial injustice. Toward the end of my tenure there, I was thrilled to be part of the implementation of the 1965 Voting Rights Act, which finally guaranteed African-Americans their right to vote. Our lawyers covered many bases to make sure that new registrants were able to vote in time for the 1966 primary and general elections. Those elections were historic in the Deep South. I knew there would be more groundbreaking work at the Civil Rights Division, but I didn't see myself as a career lawyer there.

When I was ready to move on to a new career challenge, I considered various options. Private practice in a law firm held little allure, but legal programs sponsored by President Johnson's new "war on poverty," especially the celebrated California Rural Legal Assistance program, seemed enticing. At the same time, I was bold enough to consider the U.S. Attorney's Office in the Southern District of New York (Manhattan). This "Cadillac" office, headed by the legendary Robert Morgenthau, usually hired only the brightest young lawyers—law review and Supreme Court law clerk types—which I wasn't. But I applied anyway. John Doar told me that if I wanted to argue cases before a judge and jury, Morgenthau's shop was supreme. "That's where you'll get the best experience as a trial lawyer," Doar said.

The U.S. Attorney's Office in New York City was undoubtedly prestigious. Morgenthau, its leader between 1961 and 1969, set the standard for prosecutorial and ethical leadership. I didn't have the superior credentials of most of the assistant U.S. attorneys in Morgenthan's shop, so I was thrilled, honored, and a bit terrified when I was hired. It was most intimidating to see on the walls of the various attorneys' offices their photographs with the Supreme Court justices for whom they had clerked and framed cover pages of the law review articles they had authored. On my first day, as I was sitting in my office, I heard a knock on the door and met an FBI agent asking for a search warrant. I had no clue how to produce one but, trying not to appear completely helpless, I went down the hall in search of guidance.

After years of working on behalf of rural citizens whose rights were denied and abused, often by law enforcement officials, my new job in New York as a federal prosecutor was definitely different. It never occurred to me to question this particular turn in my career, but it did, apparently, seem odd to some people. Shortly after I arrived, one of Morgenthau's deputies came into my office. "I hear you've been working for civil rights for the Negroes," he said. "I hope that won't affect your ability to put one of them in jail if the need arises."

I was taken aback by the comment. Weren't the U.S. Attorney's offices and the Civil Rights Division branches of the same Department of Justice, both trying to enforce the same law?

"No, sir," I replied. "I can't imagine that my work in civil rights would affect my ability to prosecute criminals here."

I was solely responsible for monitoring and prosecuting the federal criminal cases assigned to me as a member of the organized crime unit. The FBI and other federal agencies provided information and investigative resources, but developing each case was up to the lawyers. Without anything but perfunctory approval from my superiors, I could impanel grand juries and subpoena potential witnesses. The authority and scope of our inquiries was so broad I could see how easily our power could be misused or corrupted. Fortunately, Mr. Morgenthau was a man of great integrity. If our office made a mistake or overreached in a prosecution, he insisted that we readily admit it.

The organized crime unit focused on the five families that made up New York's Mafia. I was assigned to monitor the Genovese crime family. Originally founded by gangster Lucky Luciano, the Genoveses were a large, powerful family—once dubbed the "Rolls-Royce" of organized crime. Its known members were under constant federal surveillance. I received FBI reports every day on who was having lunch or dinner in which Italian restaurant that was known to be associated with the family. The FBI sent agents to these restaurants, most of them in the East Village, to note license plate numbers of cars parked nearby to compare to a database. I advised colleagues and friends to avoid those restaurants, no matter how excellent the food.

One of the Genovese family's activities included stealing credit cards right out of the factories where they were made. The cards were distributed to Genovese associates, who used them for thirty days and then discarded them before the frauds could be detected. One person implicated in the scheme was Tino Barzini, the manager for Frank Sinatra Jr. Tino was using stolen cards to fly Mr. Sinatra and his band around the country for free. I'd learned that Frank Jr. was scheduled to appear at a club in the city on a particular night. I asked an intrepid federal marshal to go to the club and serve him with a subpoena. It was not easy to get to Sinatra directly, but the marshal on the case was a creative and unusual guy. He decided to go to a performance and waited for Sinatra's last set. When he sang his father's classic "My Way," Sinatra stretched out his arms and the marshal slapped into his hand a subpoena ordering him to appear before the grand jury the next day.

The next morning, Sinatra's lawyer came to my office. "I have Frank outside," he said. "He hasn't done anything wrong, but he's worried about the photographers. Where are you keeping them?"

I said I didn't know what he meant.

"Wherever Frank goes, there are always photographers," he said. "We don't want anyone taking a picture of him going into the grand jury."

I looked down the corridor and saw that it was empty. "Where is Mr. Sinatra now?" I asked.

"He's hiding in the elevator well."

When I finally persuaded Sinatra's lawyer that the U.S. Attorney's Office was not in the business of tipping off photographers, he brought us the singer, who seemed suspicious and wary. I greeted Mr. Sinatra and led him into the grand jury room.

Once we were in the chamber, the foreman asked the witness to raise his hand to be sworn in. Then he asked him to state his name. "Frank Sinatra Jr.," he said in a whisper.

He was asked his place of residence.

"Hollywood, California," came a soft reply. Some of the jurors leaned forward as they struggled to hear him.

"Mr. Sinatra, why are you whispering?" I asked.

"I have to sing tonight," he said quietly. "I don't want to strain my voice." Considering my later experiences with the Hollywood crowd, this surreal response should have proved instructive. No evidence ever surfaced linking Sinatra to the crimes, but his manager was indicted and ultimately went to jail.

When I worked in the Civil Rights Division, I was confident that the federal government was reliably on the right side of justice. My experience in the U.S. Attorney's Office gave me a different perspective. For example, our attorneys and federal investigators uncovered massive corruption within the Internal Revenue Service. A shocking number of IRS agents were taking bribes in exchange for fixing tax returns. At one point we planted a recording device in a baby carriage to pick up conversations with an IRS agent who was meeting someone for a payoff in a city park. Among my first cases was an indictment of a gambling institution involved with organized crime. Just the day before trial, I was disconcerted to learn that a key witness, an undercover agent, was having an affair with one of the targets of our investigation. Later, when I prosecuted Salvatore Bonanno, of the Bonanno crime family, on charges of using stolen credit cards, I had concerns about the FBI's wiretap of a conversation with Bonanno. The agent assured me everything was on the up-and-up, but something about it made me uneasy.

I knew that my work as a prosecutor was worthwhile and significant, and I appreciated being one of an elite group of lawyers. But I was afraid to get sucked into the rhythm of a prosecutorial mindset, of seeing everyone as a perp, every suspect as a liar. Toward the end of my second year, I began to wonder where it would lead. I couldn't see myself as a career prosecutor, nor as a criminal defense lawyer in New York. Fortunately, once again, my path was diverted by my old mentor John Doar.

Doar left the Department of Justice at the end of 1967 after securing convictions in the federal prosecution of the Philadelphia, Mississippi, murder case. He moved with his family to New York, to direct a project founded by Robert Kennedy to rejuvenate a desperately poor section of Brooklyn. Shortly after settling in New York, Doar was asked by Mayor John Lindsay to head up the New York City Board of Education. Though this was a nonpaying job for Doar, as school board president he was allowed to hire staff—one person with an annual salary of $15,000. When he asked me to be his assistant in early 1969, I agreed and left the U.S. Attorney's Office.

At that time, the New York City school system was in turmoil. In response to attitudes emboldened by antipoverty initiatives, Mayor Lindsay had decentralized the city's school system, authorizing some local boards to control public schools with "community standards." When unionized teachers were fired by local boards, the teachers went on strike citywide. John Doar tried to reestablish order while maintaining community authority. We had a lot of dramatic encounters with passionate teachers and community advocates. In the end, the state legislature in Albany dismantled the city's school board, and oversight of the city schools reverted to the state.

So in the late spring of 1969, I was out of a job. I had been married for almost a year. My wife, Margaret, a Washingtonian who had gone to college in New York, was reluctant to embrace the big city as a permanent family home. By this time, Lyndon Johnson had left the White House, his departure hastened by the divisive war in Vietnam. A very different president, Republican Richard Nixon, had been elected in 1968 on a "law and order" platform.

Doar told me that he knew someone in the new Nixon administration whom he thought I'd get along well with: Donald Rumsfeld. Like Doar, Rumsfeld was a Princeton graduate, though somewhat younger. "He's become head of the Office of Economic Opportunity," he said. "I think you should go talk to him."

I looked carefully at Doar. "You want me to work for the Nixon administration?" I asked. The new president was anathema to almost everyone I knew. I wasn't much of a fan myself.

"Terry, do what I do," he said. "Zig when others zag."

I knew that Doar still considered himself a Republican. There was no one I respected more than John Doar, and his advice sparked something in me. I agreed to go to Washington to meet with Don Rumsfeld.

The Office of Economic Opportunity (OEO), created and first directed by R. Sargent Shriver in 1964, was the central agency of President Lyndon Johnson's war on poverty. OEO's operations depended on federal funding of community-based organizations to try to level the playing field for poor Americans through research, advocacy, community action, education, and legal and health services. Opposition to the war on poverty had been part of the GOP campaign platform, so the new president's agenda for this new agency was not clear. Rumsfeld was a Republican wunderkind, a very young congressman from Chicago's North Shore suburbs who gave up his seat to take on OEO at his president's request. No one knew what would happen to OEO under Nixon, but many of its advocates were suspicious.

When I first met with Rumsfeld, I found him enormously likable. He was dynamic and personable, and had a great sense of humor. He'd been a high school football star and college wrestler, and, nearing forty years old, had lost none of that energy. He seemed very hardworking, and had a boundless sense of curiosity. Rumsfeld did not strike me as an ideologue with an agenda, but rather as a practical man who wanted to make things work. I had an instant rapport with him.

In June 1969, I joined the impressive young staff he'd collected, several from Princeton—including Bill Bradley, the basketball player on break from the Knicks who was later a senator from New Jersey and ran for the Democratic presidential nomination in 2000, and Jim Leach, on his way to becoming a congressman from Iowa. Initially, I was Rumsfeld's special assistant. I worked in his office, and watched him deal with an incredibly complicated and frequently dysfunctional organization.

The antipoverty program brought together well-intentioned people, many experts in diverse fields such as early childhood education, agriculture, nutrition, healthcare delivery, community organizing, civil rights, and jurisprudence. Head Start, VISTA, and Job Corps were all created as part of OEO. Its primary division was the Community Action Program (CAP) that funded local organizations of poor people to benefit their communities. While antagonists viewed OEO as just another wasteful federal bureaucracy, a lot of creative energy and federal money went into funding meaningful programs that could operate effectively at local levels. But managing it all was extremely difficult. Many departments didn't have adequate filing systems. Funding requests from local programs lingered for months. Guidelines for selecting and shaping programs were vague and often contradictory. At one meeting with some of the research and development staff who developed experimental programs, I asked them, in total seriousness, "Do you R&D guys throw darts at the wall to decide what projects to fund?"

By midsummer, Rumsfeld offered me a choice of three positions at the agency—to remain as his special assistant, to head the Legal Services Program, or to become OEO's deputy general counsel.

"Deputy?" I asked. "Why not general counsel?"

Rumsfeld roared with laughter. He'd already enlisted a prominent lawyer from a major Chicago law firm to take that job.

I decided I was old enough at twenty-nine to not want to be anyone's special assistant, so I chose to take on Legal Services. I wanted to remain within the legal arena, and it seemed like an interesting challenge. From my days in the segregated South, I knew how African-Americans were denied access to government programs and services. And I soon learned how many other poor people in America—in urban ghettos, in Appalachia, on Indian reservations, in migrant worker camps—were being similarly deprived.

My decision to take on Legal Services left vacant the position of the director's special assistant. The job was quickly filled by a serious young man from Wyoming named Dick Cheney, who came over from a congressional office. That set the stage for a Rumsfeld-Cheney partnership that continued over the next four decades.

The Legal Services Program (LSP) operated according to guidelines established by an advisory committee composed mostly of members of the organized bar. The guidelines required that representatives of poor people be on the local programs' governing boards, and that the programs provide services in all noncriminal areas of the law. That included not only direct legal representation of poor clients, but also class-action lawsuits on behalf of groups of clients, and advocacy for reform of federal and state laws, regulations, and practices. The program had 2,200 lawyers, 850 offices, and a $58 million dollar budget. It was called the largest law firm in the world.

It was easy to embrace the Legal Service Program's mission and to champion the dedicated lawyers who represented poor clients. So I made a decision early on that I was going to try to make Legal Services do exactly what was envisioned. This was also Don Rumsfeld's intention when he offered me the job. When he arrived at the OEO, Legal Services was under CAP, and Rumsfeld elevated it to be on par with CAP as a separate division. He saw Legal Services as the premier program within OEO because, as he told me, it allowed people to settle problems through lawyers in courtrooms instead of with mob violence. In announcing my appointment, Don committed publicly to providing poor clients "with representation and advocacy before all institutions and at all levels of government."

In August, shortly after I assumed my new position, one hundred lawyers from Legal Services programs across the country came together in Vail, Colorado, for their first national conference. I went to Vail to introduce myself. The lawyers knew little about me, and many assumed that any Nixon appointee would be trouble.

I arrived in my usual suit and tie, and looked out of place among the casually dressed lawyers, many with long hair and wearing jeans and tie-dyed shirts. Undoubtedly, my appearance fit their image of a conservative bureaucrat. They were primed for revolt—issuing a list of demands to ensure that the Legal Services headquarters in Washington would continue to support their activities. The atmosphere in Vail did not exactly improve when I commented on their choice of locale. A reporter picked up my comment "Your clients aren't out here," which made an irresistible front-page headline. I was profiled in the *New York Times*, which reported on my appointment and meeting with the lawyers in Vail.

After things calmed down, I told the lawyers that I was confident that once they understood my views, they would be satisfied with my leadership. "We are not going to disband the program," I said, "or allow politicians to interfere with the goal of representing poor clients as competently as highly paid lawyers represent rich clients." I let them know that we would continue to support class-action lawsuits and law reform. By the time I left Vail, we had reached a level of trust that grew the more they got to know me.

Back in Washington, I educated myself about the depth and breadth of my responsibilities and assembled a senior staff of some pretty remarkable people. I hired as my deputy Frank Jones, a native Mississippian who had worked with the Chicago Legal Aid Bureau. Dan Bradley and Mickey Kantor, who later became President Clinton's U.S. Trade Representative, had been associated with the South

Florida migrant program. The two women on my senior staff were Kimba Wood Lovejoy, later a federal court judge, and Mathea Falco, who has since devoted her career to drug abuse policy after serving in President Carter's White House. I sought advice from my friend Charles Nesson, who had just become a professor at Harvard Law School, and from Monroe Price, another law professor who continues to be a creative and out-of-the-box thinker. In my office, I was very ably assisted by Dottie Smith and by Barbara Campbell whose sharp intelligence and ready humor often made my day.

I learned gradually that the close relationship I had developed with Rumsfeld during the six weeks I was his special assistant didn't hold much water against the authority of longtime OEO staffers and those newcomers who had been close to Rumsfeld for years before he got to OEO. Frank Carlucci, whom Don had arranged to be transferred from the State Department to head up CAP, had been Don's roommate at Princeton. Another close Rumsfeld friend was Don Lowitz, a Chicago lawyer, who became OEO's general counsel.

Time became my enemy too as I rushed to deal with political crises erupting across the country over Legal Services programs and lawsuits. I had to fly to Vermont to pacify the governor, who was upset that the LSP office had not closed in honor of the July 20 landing on the moon. Arizona senator Barry Goldwater was upset that Legal Services lawyers representing a group of Navajos had sued the Tribal Council. The Missouri governor vetoed the Legal Services Program in St. Louis based on press reports of inappropriate lawsuits. After the bar association deemed the charges to be unfounded, Rumsfeld overrode the governor's veto. But the governor then vetoed the Kansas City, Missouri, program, citing "apprehension" over what he said were my statements urging increasing aggressiveness by Missouri Legal Services lawyers whom we had evaluated as too timid in the past. After the Camden, New Jersey, program was revitalized, the new director became involved in a lawsuit against the city for failing to relocate poor residents who were forced to move to make way for a new highway. After Legal Services lawyers there filed a defamation suit against the Camden police chief for calling black community leaders "hoodlums," the county bar association withdrew its support for the program. In Louisiana, the state bar association called for an investigation of all LSP attorneys in the state when a program in Baton Rouge sued the police department after four black teens were shot by the police. We had a problem in Berkeley, California, when the program's board voted to support the Black Panther Party in conflict with local authorities, using heated rhetoric that horrified the local bar.

One of our early challenges involved the mayor of Chicago, the legendary and all but indomitable Richard M. Daley. Mayor Daley chaired the Community Action Agency under which the Legal Services Program in Chicago operated, and he had barred Legal Services lawyers from suing the city or from representing groups. And the office spaces that were allocated to the Legal Services Program were totally inadequate. One adjoined a gymnasium, where our clients lined up on the bleachers while waiting to talk with lawyers. That office was virtually shut down whenever there was a game, band practice, or other event. At another office next to an elevated train line, all conversation between the lawyers and their clients was interrupted every few minutes when a train went by. Clients were often referred to an "urban life advisor" instead of meeting with a lawyer in confidence. It was impossible to attract good lawyers to the program under those conditions. I decided that it was important for my office to directly fund the Chicago program to take it out from under Mayor Daley in order for the program lawyers to be effective.

When I made efforts to change that by filing a lawsuit against the city, I was called to the office of Chicago-area congressman Roman Pucinski, who was a Daley acolyte. "The mayor isn't going to agree to what you're trying to do," the congressman said. He looked at the red phone on his desk. "I'm going to call the mayor now and tell him you are insisting on pushing this through." After he finished his phone call, the congressman told me, "If you continue to pursue this course, the fire department will close down your office tomorrow and the utilities will be turned off." He said that the city would basically harass us to death. I looked at Pucinski—who struck me as a thug and lackey masquerading as a member of Congress—and was convinced even more that we should sue the city.

I told Rumsfeld about these threats and asked what we should do. Don was from Chicago and the congressional district he had represented included a small part of the city. He knew the power of the Daley machine. To his credit, he told me to move ahead with my plans. I thought it was a gutsy call. Our lawsuit succeeded.

One of the most fractious issues was in California, where Ronald Reagan had become governor in 1967. One of LSP's flagship programs, California Rural Legal Assistance (CRLA), was a thorn in the side for California's growers because of lawsuits on behalf of migrant workers. Growers in Colorado and Florida also complained about lawsuits that LSP programs brought to improve housing and work conditions for migrants. CRLA also challenged Reagan's welfare and Medicaid policies in successful lawsuits. I had to fly to Sacramento to defend the program after CRLA's lawsuit against the state hospital system resulted in a judgment that restored $220 million for Medicaid beneficiaries that the governor had cut. Governor Reagan was determined to bring an end to the annoying lawsuits brought by federally funded lawyers against him. He and other Republican governors were vociferous with complaints to the Nixon White House about Legal Services programs.

Since LSP's legal victories were validated by most appellate courts, the solution for the program's opponents had to be political. In the fall of 1969, my efforts to support individual programs were interrupted by a major legislative challenge in Congress, where the administration's bill to reauthorize OEO was challenged by amendments in both houses. With Governor Reagan's urging, Senator George Murphy of California pushed through the Senate an amendment that would give governors legal power over any aspect of the Legal Services programs operating in their states. If the Murphy Amendment was enacted, the entire Legal Services Program would be eviscerated. In the House of Representatives, an amendment was offered to give the states control over most antipoverty programs, including Legal Services.

The Murphy Amendment elicited tremendous support for Legal Services from bar associations and private lawyers, who organized emergency efforts to lobby Congress. Since I didn't trust OEO's Office of Government Relations to adequately fight against the amendment, I tasked Mickey Kantor with organizing our assault on the House. And Rumsfeld became vitally engaged. Using his legislative experience and contacts as a congressman, Don joined me as we went from office to office in the House to stop the amendment.

We worked closely with Wisconsin congressman Bill Steiger, a close friend of Rumsfeld's. At one point Steiger called me to the Capitol and told me were going to lose the vote unless I could come up with language for the legislation that would satisfy members of Congress from farm states who were worried about lawsuits on behalf of migrant workers. Steiger told me we needed to demonstrate that OEO intended to rein in our lawyers. So, as tourists walked by, I sat down on the floor outside the House chamber and began writing. I scribbled some lines on a piece of paper stating that no lawyer could take any action except in accordance with the American Bar Association's canon of ethics. "This is great!" Steiger said after reading it. "It sounds really tough." Of course, what I'd written was essentially meaningless. Everything Legal Services lawyers did already satisfied the ABA's canon.

My amendment was accepted and the House of Representatives voted down that part of the bill that would have given governors control over legal services. The final legislation reported out by the conference committee kept intact the integrity of LSP. Our success further infuriated many governors. They vented their frustrations to the White House, where I had already become known as a troublemaker who, in Nixonian terms, "didn't play ball."

My problems were not brought on only by Republicans. I encountered plenty from LSP advocates too. As America's involvement in Vietnam dragged on with no end in sight, antiwar demonstrations increased, as did the rift between liberal and conservative America. At the same time, the rise of the black power movement led to racial unrest. After Dr. Martin Luther King's assassination in April 1968, riots broke out in many cities. The antipoverty program was designed to address inequalities, and OEO was ground zero for much of this activity.

The security measures we're accustomed to today, especially since 9/11, didn't exist then; government buildings were open to the public. (When I first got to the Justice Department, for example, neighborhood kids used to roller-skate in the building's hallways.) Now the public's intrusion into government buildings began to hold more risk.

I once was in a meeting with Rumsfeld when a group of protesters burst into our building, came up to his office suite, and tried to break down the door to force their way into the director's inner office. Thinking quickly, Don and I shoved his desk against the door. When the protesters managed to nudge it open, we'd shove the desk back until security people came to our rescue. This sort of thing happened more than once.

During a particularly heated Vietnam War protest in May of 1970, Don and I watched from the rooftop of our building on Nineteenth Street as a mob of antiwar protesters stormed the city. As thousands of people, some wearing football helmets for protection, poured through the streets, I felt as if I were watching a revolution. To guard the White House from the teeming mobs that day, buses were parked along the iron gates that surrounded the grounds. Younger members of the administration were called to the White House to confer about engaging the protesters in discussions about the war. At the White House Mess, I overheard someone from Vice President Spiro Agnew's staff carrying on. "If these hippies try to break through the buses," the guy said, "we have machine guns."

Some months later I was in a meeting of the OEO Legal Services board when a group of Howard University law school students showed up and occupied the room. These minority students wanted a $1 million grant for the law school and believed the agency was discriminating against them. Don realized there was no way to reason with them—they were there to make demands, not negotiate. To pacify them, he asked me to take them to a conference room on a different floor. I did so and talked with them for a while, getting exactly nowhere. I knew I'd have to try to leave so that they could not later claim that I'd been free to do so. Unsurprisingly, as I tried to leave the room, the group physically obstructed my departure.

Hearing that I was basically being held hostage by this group—which included some pretty sizable guys and a young law student named Jerry Rivers, aka Geraldo Rivera—Rumsfeld rushed over. He forced his way in, grabbed me by the arm, and tried to pull me out of the room. The occupiers let Rumsfeld through but closed in around me as I tried to exit. I wasn't going anywhere.

So I did what made the most sense. I waited them out. After a while, the crowd became hungry and bored. Their stunt was running out of oxygen. Finally, they said I could go up to Rumsfeld's office with a message. They demanded that the grant be awarded that day or they were going to stay and refuse to let me leave.

I looked at them skeptically. They wanted me to leave the room, make their demands, and then come back?

When I went upstairs, I gave Don their message: "They want a million-dollar grant or they're staying put."

He laughed. "Tell them if they're not out in ten minutes, I'm going to have them arrested." I went back downstairs and delivered the ultimatum from outside the doorway. True to his word, Rumsfeld had them in custody within the hour.

Being at OEO exposed me to occasional White House perks. OEO senior staff spent one weekend meeting at Camp David, and another evening with their spouses on *The Sequoia,* the presidential yacht. As one of the very few members of his senior staff not to be a Nixon fan, I was subject to Rumsfeld's occasional efforts to broaden my perspective. My wife, Margaret, and I became friends with Don and his spirited wife, Joyce. One day, they invited us to join them at a White House Sunday prayer breakfast that President Nixon hosted. This was one of the few times I met Nixon in person. Seen on television, Nixon was a tough-talking, powerful presence. But as I listened to his awkward comments in person, I found him more odd than impressive.

The first time I met Nixon was in the Oval Office at a small gathering of OEO officials. He gave a rambling speech about the greatness of America. There were lots of things a leader could cite to support that claim, but what Nixon chose to highlight was the fact that America's suicide rate was lower than that of Scandinavian countries. So when we went to the White House for the prayer breakfast, I didn't know what to expect.

I knew that Rumsfeld's friendly relationship with the president was growing. As director of OEO, Rumsfeld was a member of Nixon's cabinet—he had insisted on that when he accepted the OEO job—and by early 1970 he was spending more and more time at the White House. My name was known to some there because of complaints they'd received about Legal Services lawsuits.

After the Sunday worship service concluded, Margaret and I stood in a receiving line to shake hands with the president. When we approached him, Nixon shook hands with Don and smiled. Don gestured to me. "This is Terry Lenzner, Mr. President." Knowing how

Nixon respected athletes, he added, "He was captain of the Harvard football team."

Nixon shook my hand, smiled, and moved to greet the next guest— my wife. He was shaking Margaret's hand when he figured out what he wanted to say to me. "So you're the one causing all the problems," he said. Margaret didn't know how to respond, at least to the president. As we left the White House, she told me, "Your days are numbered."

As Don became more involved at the White House, the pressure on him to rein in Legal Services became more intense. I've no doubt that he heard plenty of complaints at cabinet meetings from colleagues discussing LSP suits against federal agencies, and charges that they were politically motivated. It didn't matter that most of those suits were filed before 1968 against Johnson administration officials, or that it was the courts, not LSP, that decided the cases. Eventually, Don agreed to bring over from the White House a guy named John "Fat Jack" Buckley. Buckley moved into an office at OEO as director of the inspection division, supposedly there to evaluate different OEO programs. But I noticed he took a particular interest in my activities. He spent a lot of time around the Legal Services offices when he had no apparent reason to be there. I once delivered a speech to a small gathering in New Orleans. When I looked out at the group, there was Buckley, taking notes. (I learned later that Buckley also monitored the presidential campaign activities of Democratic senator Ed Muskie, one of Nixon's most formidable rivals for the 1972 presidential election.)

In late February, I was called to a "training session" for OEO inspectors to describe the Legal Services Program and answer questions about specific issues. I pointed out the absurdity of trying to redress legal problems of the poor on only a piecemeal basis through representation of clients individually. For example, the five lawyers in a California program took in 6,800 cases in the previous fiscal year, a caseload that couldn't possibly be handled effectively. I said it was like trying to bail out the ocean, that such an approach could not produce substantial change. Most of the cases were similar, and handling them individually would lead only to a never-ending cycle. I described how much more effective Legal Services representation is when the programs identify priorities for lawsuits to tackle the most pressing problems affecting groups of clients. I authorized Clients Councils to work with the programs' boards of directors on defining priorities, and the programs drew on training and technical assistance provided by six law schools in specific areas of legal rights, including education, consumer fraud, welfare, economic development, housing, and medical law.

In May, I funded a new program designed to serve poor people in Appalachian Kentucky and West Virginia. This regional program was unique—encompassing parts of two states and addressing a wide range of legal issues peculiar to the region. I recruited my Civil Rights Division colleague John Rosenberg to inaugurate the Appalachian Research and Defense Fund (AppalReD) program in Kentucky. John moved to Prestonsburg, Kentucky, in 1970 with his wife and infant son and stayed for thirty years. AppalReD's initial target was the coal industry, recognizing the direct relationship that existed between the coal economy and the profound poverty of the local people. As for every lawyer who worked under John Doar, John Rosenberg's eight years working on civil rights cases in Mississippi had taught him the vital importance of careful preparation of lawsuits. The first-class law firm that he established for AppalReD proved successful in investigations and legal action against coal companies as well as federal and state entities to address problems in such areas as mine safety, stripmining, environment, health, and housing, as well as in providing poor residents with lawyers to handle individual cases.

I thought we were on a roll, but by the early summer of 1970 the poverty program's opponents were again hatching plans to restrain OEO legislatively. In anticipation of the American Bar Association's annual convention in August, its president, Bernard Segal, issued a warning about "ominous danger signals flashing around the OEO

Legal Services Program." He urged ABA members to be "vigilant to maintain the professional independence and integrity" of the program and its lawyers, citing the "storms of protest" evoked by LSP "successes in cases of public and social concern, the so-called law reform cases."

I suppose that my dismissal from OEO on November 20, 1970, was inevitable. Legal Services activities were creating headlines the Nixon folks couldn't tolerate, as I was doing my best to defend controversial programs and personnel. Rumsfeld was taking too much heat from the White House, and our relationship became strained. In New Orleans, the program was being sued for representing criminal clients (which we were not allowed to do). When I learned the program had been cleared of those charges, I let them know without consulting with Rumsfeld. In October, he had ordered me not to travel from Washington without central office approval. I knew what kind of fight I was in, so I traveled to New York anyway to meet with the *New York Times* editorial board. The paper had championed the Legal Services Program, and I wanted them to know about the effort that was under way to gut it. For Rumsfeld, that defiance was the last straw.

When I returned from New York late in the day, my secretary said, "Everyone is waiting for you in Rumsfeld's office." I knew what was coming. In fact, I brought a cigar with me to the meeting and lit it up in reaction to what was about to happen. Don told me that he wanted my resignation because he believed I was no longer willing to comply with his instructions. I told him I'd resign only if he'd appoint my deputy, Frank Jones, in my place. Frank was an African-American lawyer from Chicago who had grown up in Mississippi. He was also as hardcore about the mission of OEO as I was, if not more so. That idea was a nonstarter with Rumsfeld, so he fired me.

Because the situation at OEO was so politicized, the response to my dismissal was significant, reported for example with a photograph on the front page of the *New York Times* above the fold. Editorials and letters in that paper and many others lambasted Rumsfeld and the

White House. Sargent Shriver, brother-in-law to the Kennedys and OEO's first director, and other Washington politicos rallied to defend Legal Services. One of my assistants, Mickey Kantor, who was preternaturally astute at politics, founded Action for Legal Rights to promote the cause with a fund-raiser at Shriver's suburban Washington estate. My so-called heroism led to my election to the Harvard University Board of Overseers the following May. I was the first candidate ever elected by petition.

My deputy, Frank Jones, was also fired. He had lost an eye, and often wore a patch instead of his glass prosthetic. (I was told that Frank left his glass eye in the top drawer of his desk for his successor to discover.) Frank amplified matters by accusing the administration of racism, which was not an opinion I endorsed.

At a press conference after our dismissals, I said the decision was "political . . . caving in to the political interests, like Reagan." I accused the Nixon administration, with a dramatic flourish, of supporting only "bargain-basement justice" for the poor.

The Legal Services Program was fundamentally changed after I left. In 1971, the idea for an independent corporation to manage legal services for the poor began to gain momentum as a way to insulate the program from political influence by removing it from the president's administration. President Nixon advocated this, asserting that such a corporation would make legal services "immune to political pressure . . . and a permanent part of our system of justice." The Legal Services Corporation was created in 1975. Two decades later during welfare reform, federal funding of legal services was drastically cut and poverty lawyers' activities were restricted, including a prohibition on class-action lawsuits. Since then, a number of legal service providers have given up federal funds entirely and many existing programs rely only on private funding.

I look back on the old Legal Services Program with pride in its mission and accomplishments, as well as with disappointment over what it did not achieve. There were twenty million poor Americans then; today there are fifty million living below the poverty line. My experience at OEO was enlightening—and sobering. It taught me a lot about politics, that what motivates even the most high-minded politicians isn't necessarily justice. It also taught me that politics and money often trump facts, especially where the poor are concerned.

But that's all in hindsight. The days after my firing were pretty rocky, especially since I was about to become a father for the first time. Emily was born on November 29. (It was rumored at OEO that Joyce Rumsfeld had said to her husband, "Don, you can't fire him now. Margaret's about to have a baby!") Arriving at a career crossroads yet again, I needed to find new work to do, and suddenly the options looked limited. I had spent my career working for the government. Crossing the president of the United States in such a public way had made me radioactive.

After my firing, though I had become a cause célèbre to many people who didn't know me, I felt alone. I hated being at loose ends and didn't appreciate being the martyr that my liberal friends envisioned. Government jobs were now closed to me and the private legal establishment had little interest in me. Then a man I didn't know at all went out of his way to help me. Edward Bennett Williams was one of the most prominent figures in Washington, D.C. He was the founding partner of a premier law firm, Williams & Connolly, and had represented many big-name clients.

Williams brought me into various cases at the firm. He introduced me to lawyers in different parts of the city. He took me to lunch at the famed Palm restaurant, where he knew that all the other well-heeled diners would see him sitting with me. He became a mentor and a friend.

I don't know why Williams decided to do this for me. He had liked the Legal Services Program a lot, and was concerned about what would become of it. But I think he also wanted to send a message to people in the nation's capital: that when somebody does the right thing, at least in his view, and gets totally destroyed by it, Edward Bennett Williams will stand beside them and help them get back up. Williams's assistance would play a major role in the years ahead.

On November 27, 1970, J. Edgar Hoover testified in a closed-door Senate hearing. The legendary FBI director was almost seventy-six years old, frail, and nearing the end of his life. He requested $14.1 million to hire 1,000 additional field agents and 702 clerks. As justification for the additional funds, Hoover announced that the bureau was investigating an "incipient plot" by "a militant group, self-described as being composed of Catholic priests and nuns, teachers, students, and former students" to undermine the American government and force an end to U.S. involvement in Vietnam. He identified the ring-leaders as Philip and Daniel Berrigan, two brothers, both of whom were Catholic priests and had become known for dramatic demonstrations against the war and the military draft. Both men were featured on the FBI's "Ten Most Wanted" list for destroying draft records.

Initially tied to the civil rights, black power, and antipoverty movements, the antiwar movement began to take off on its own in the late 1960s. The draft was random, enlisting young men over the age of eighteen by lottery. Those enrolled in college or graduate school could be deferred. As the need for troops expanded, and U.S. operations in Vietnam began to seem more dubious, the draft became ever more contentious. Young men scrambled to avoid it. Some became conscientious objectors, rejecting war in all forms; others fled to Canada to avoid being called up. Increasingly the draft appeared to be skewed toward the poor and minorities who were unable to use deferments.

Beginning in 1967, radical Catholics inspired by the Berrigan brothers carried out at least twenty-two nonviolent, dramatic raids against draft boards and corporations they saw as abetting the American war in Vietnam, destroying draft records in Selective Service offices where they were stored, often by pouring blood on them for dramatic effect. Others joined the Berrigans in digging symbolic graves outside the homes of various officials whom they believed had some responsibility for the conduct of the war. J. Edgar Hoover, the archenemy of Communism, felt these actions threatened the United States. He was determined to prevent further disorder.

An aide to Hoover leaked the FBI director's sensational charges to the *Washington Post*. In response to a flurry of media attention, Nixon's attorney general, John Mitchell, felt he had no choice but to pursue the case, as he put it later, "to get Hoover off the hook."

On January 12, 1971, the Justice Department announced indictments of Phil Berrigan and six others on charges of conspiring to destroy Selective Service records, kidnap Nixon's National Security aide, Henry Kissinger, and blow up the heating systems carried through tunnels under federal buildings in Washington, D.C.*

Dan Berrigan—a Jesuit priest, noted poet and playwright, and Phil's older brother—was named as a conspirator but not charged as a defendant. The government chose to prosecute the case in Harrisburg, Pennsylvania, near Lewisburg prison, where Phil Berrigan was serving a term for destroying draft files with homemade napalm. The locale led the group of defendants to be known nationally as "the Harrisburg Seven."†

As the Berrigan brothers had received enormous notoriety over the years, the trial quickly garnered national attention. Well-known lawyers were called in for the legal defense. Led by former attorney general Ramsey Clark, the team included civil rights attorney Leonard

---

*The grand jury continued to meet, resulting in two superseding indictments. In the end, the initial charges were reduced, and seven defendants were charged.
†In addition to Phil Berrigan, the other defendants were Sister Elizabeth McAlister, Father Neil McLaughlin, Father Joseph Wenderoth, Pakistani journalist Dr. Eqbal Ahmad, Anthony Scoblick, and Mary Kay Scoblick. The government also cited as conspirators, but did not charge, Father Daniel Berrigan, Sister Beverly Bell, Marjorie Shuman, Paul Mayer (a married priest), Sister Jogues Egan, Thomas Davidson, and William Davidson.

Boudin—whose daughter, Kathy, was then sought by police for her role in violent antiwar actions; Paul O'Dwyer, a New York lawyer who later was president of the City Council; Father William Cunningham, a lawyer and a Catholic priest; and local counsel Tom Menaker.

Having become a mini-celebrity among Nixon opponents, I was brought into the case by my friend Charlie Nesson. Nesson was then a young professor at Harvard Law School whom I'd known when he was Doar's special assistant at the Civil Rights Division for several months and knew my work there. I'd enlisted his help with some Legal Services projects. Knowing my experience as a litigator with a background in investigations, he recommended me to Ramsey Clark. Though prominent litigators, none of the other attorneys had much background in basic fact gathering.

I had questions about our involvement in Vietnam, but I'd never actively opposed the war. In fact, the assistant attorneys in New York routinely arraigned draft dodgers who refused to comply with draft board summonses. But I believed that every defendant deserved legal representation. The Harrisburg case sounded interesting, and offered reasonable remuneration through contributions to the Harrisburg defense fund, so I signed on.

Trying the case in Harrisburg made sense for the government. There were two military armories in the area, and the conservative community offered a jury pool that was expected to be unsympathetic to the antiwar protesters. It seemed to me that the government had everything in its favor. The prosecution claimed to have letters written by the defendants that proved their criminal collusion—and testimony from an informant, a man named Boyd Douglas, who had befriended Phil Berrigan in Lewisburg Penitentiary, where they were both inmates. And they had a judge, a Nixon appointee, who was not at all sympathetic to peace activists. This was one of those can't-lose cases coveted by prosecutors.

I met with Phil Berrigan for the first time at Danbury Federal Correctional Institute in Connecticut, where he had been transferred prior to the trial. In the prison visitors room, Phil was surrounded by nuns and other priests. This group was warm and welcoming: their greetings usually took the form of hugs—which I was not used to. As they gathered together, they recited prayers and produced small containers of wine that they had smuggled in. At first I didn't know what to think, but as my visits continued, I found their ritual communion, performed by Father Berrigan, incredibly moving. Facing the full weight of the federal government against them, they focused on prayer, meditation, and reflection on Jesus. Many of the times I met with Phil, he delivered a homily before we began our legal discussions. Phil took time to discuss the Gospels with me and told Bible stories and parables that held new relevance for me.

To the federal government, Father Berrigan was Public Enemy Number One. But I found a warm, open man who quickly shared the story of his life—a background that explained clearly why he came to be sitting behind those iron bars.

Phil had been an army man who came out of the Depression-ravaged middle of America to serve his country in World War II. During one of his first battles in France, his unit was involved in a friendly fire incident. When a tank company panicked in the fog of battle, Phil witnessed the spectacle of Americans unwittingly killing other Americans. He told me of other times when he had seen "perhaps a dozen" trucks of dead soldiers being driven back from the front, an image of "frozen corpses with rigid arms and legs bumping on tailgates as the trucks bounced over the cobblestone." At the end of the conflict, Berrigan visited a bombed-out city where bodies of dead children and elderly lay unburied and rotting in the sun. These were images he never forgot.

Returning from the war, he joined the Josephite order, founded in 1871 to serve newly freed slaves, and became active in the civil rights movement. He was the first Catholic priest to participate in the Freedom Rides protesting racial discrimination in the South, and studied the nonviolent practices of Gandhi and King. By the midsixties, he turned his attention to protest against a war he felt was morally unjustifiable.

Phil freely admitted he was guilty of antiwar resistance activities. He was proud that his and his brother's focus on the draft turned many in the U.S. against the war. Phil described how they had destroyed Selective Service records by throwing blood on draft records and burning them with napalm. He described how they had cased offices so they could attack them when the buildings were vacant and no innocent could get hurt. They would sit outside the offices in station wagons for hours, charting the comings and goings of the staff. By 1971 their activities were well known—Phil and Dan had become symbols of the antiwar movement.

While the federal government seriously pursued the charges against the Harrisburg Seven, many questioned the case as a Hoover obsession. Henry Kissinger was quoted as joking that the plot was the brainchild of "sex-starved nuns." Though many considered the priests heroes, not everyone in the antiwar movement was a fan of the Berrigans. As the movement developed, the more professional organizers considered them naïve and dangerous to the movement's success. But because they were unquestionably sincere and men of the cloth, the government was threatened by them. The Nixon administration spent more than $2 million on the Harrisburg Seven prosecution.

Central to the prosecution's case were letters exchanged between Phil Berrigan and Sister Liz McAlister, a nun and peace activist with whom Phil was romantically involved and soon married secretly. Boyd Douglas, Phil's fellow inmate at Lewisburg, was often the go-between for them. In one intimate letter, Liz described a plan "to kidnap—in our terminology, make a citizen's arrest of—someone like Henry Kissinger." Before giving the letter to Douglas for him to pass on to Phil, McAlister wrote an attachment: "Boyd—the enclosed is dynamite and I mean it."

Berrigan replied that Liz's plot was "brilliant but grandiose . . . Nonetheless I like the plan and am just trying to weave elements of modesty into it." That Berrigan would put musings like that in writing and have them delivered by a fellow prisoner that he didn't know very well only underscored the defendant's naïveté and trust.

I had no doubt that Phil and his colleagues believed that, if left alone with Kissinger, they could convince him that American involvement with the war in Vietnam was wrong. To them, the morality of their view was so obvious that no one of good conscience could disagree. But I was satisfied that the abduction and heating tunnel plans never got beyond casual musing. In fact, there was no indication of any overt action to bring the plan to fruition. It was clear to me the conspiracy the government alleged was never implemented, and nothing more than a colorful fantasy of idealistic people who believed their devotion could change the world.

We knew the best defense would hinge on undermining the credibility of the prosecution's star witness, Boyd Douglas, and placing a question in the jury's mind about his motivations. Douglas was not only a convicted felon, he was also instrumental in encouraging the defendants. He had been allowed to leave Lewisburg prison regularly to take classes and work in the library at Bucknell University nearby. This was how he became Berrigan's courier. He took letters from the prison and mailed them when he got to the campus. A professor he befriended was the receiving point for communications to Berrigan from the outside. I scoured the statements Boyd Douglas made to the feds, as well as his grand jury testimony, other statements he made, and articles in the college newspaper, the *Bucknellian*, that he wrote to promote the resistance movement and enhance his campus standing as a revolutionary.

Among my first tasks was to put together a chronology of Douglas's history, including a timeline of his recent meetings and phone calls interspersed with activities of the Catholic resistance. I identified his acquaintances, Bucknell girlfriends, and fellow inmates to interview. The chronology totaled sixteen typed pages, listing everything from Douglas's 1959 enlistment in the army to every phone call or meeting he had with defendants in the present case. Just thirty years old, Douglas had been in prison on a number of occasions—for impersonating a federal officer, forging checks, disorderly conduct, and desertion from the U.S. military. He was a known drug user, and records showed he had twice attempted suicide. In 1968, he had received $15,000 from the federal government in settlement of his claim that he'd gotten cancer through a medical experiment when he was imprisoned. The more I learned about Douglas, the more obvious it was that he was far from an ideal witness for the prosecution.

As the trial approached, I was unusually anxious. I'd never before had trouble sleeping, but I found myself often waking at night. Any error on my part might lead to lengthy prison sentences for people I had come to care about. A lawyer is supposed to remain emotionally detached from his clients, and I usually did that. But I found it hard in this case, because I liked Phil and the others and their commitment to peace so much.

During the months preparing for the trial, I worked out of Ramsey Clark's office in Washington. Once the trial began, I drove with Clark every Sunday afternoon to Harrisburg, where the defense team headquartered in a rented house. It was like a college dorm, with a party every night. It wasn't long before I booked a hotel room where I could work in relative peace.

Each member of the defense team represented several defendants, so there were overlaps among us. I worked with other lawyers on the defense of Phil Berrigan, but my clients were Phil Berrigan, Father Neil McLaughlin, and Dr. Eqbal Ahmad.

The Harrisburg case pioneered the use of consultants to guide lawyers in jury selection. They helped us to ascertain how likely a prospective juror was to convict, based on personal history, profession, and other characteristics. The first four weeks of the trial were spent questioning prospective jurors. We struck more than one candidate whose opinion about the defendants was a variation of "they should be hung."

I knew from prior prosecutorial experience that jurors whose jobs required them to tangle with the federal government were often inclined to question the government's case. One of the potential jurors we considered was an accountant. Picturing accountants as simply hard-nosed number crunchers, some of the defense lawyers wanted to excuse him. But I argued that his experience challenging government regulations on behalf of his clients meant that he might be good for the defense. "These guys spend every day of their working lives fighting against the government," I insisted. "He'll be sympathetic." That turned out to be true, and it may have helped us enormously that the accountant was chosen as the jury's foreman. Not every choice was a win, however. We kept a woman whose sons had been conscientious objectors, believing she'd be sympathetic to our side, only to learn later that she was actually against our case from the beginning.

The trial finally began on January 24, 1972, more than a year after the defendants had first been indicted. Phil came to court daily in handcuffs and chains. The courthouse became an ever-growing spectacle. Nearly every leftist luminary came to Harrisburg— Howard Zinn, Joan Baez, William Kunstler, Tom Hayden, and Noam Chomsky—along with reporters from dozens of newspapers and television networks. Bob Hope joked about the plot to kidnap Kissinger: "They suspect three priests because the ransom note was written in Latin." Many other Americans—what President Nixon famously called his "silent majority"—viewed the Berrigans and peace activists as anything but a laughing matter: Communists and traitors who were undermining their country and aiding the enemy in a time of war.

Before the trial, I met with Phil in his cell. He handed me eighteen typed pages. This, he said, was the opening statement he wanted to read to the jury and, by extension, to the nation. "We have never conspired to bomb or kidnap anyone," the statement said. "While the government *has* conspired to bomb and kidnap . . . kidnapping millions of Indochinese by single expedients of bombing them out to forcibly relocate the survivors to refugee camps." He labeled the Selective Service Act's conscription of young men as "certainly immoral and possibly illegal" and charged that the government had "virtually kidnapped millions of young Americans" through the draft. The statement went on to rail against American policy with respect to the Soviet Union and sharply criticize the military—in a region of the country that depended heavily on the defense industry. Berrigan's manifesto praised Boyd Douglas "as a friend." Phil wanted the jury to know that "none of us bear him any resentment or rancor."

That Phil sincerely believed all of this and thought that he could convince the jury of his views spoke volumes about the distance between his vision of the world and mine as a lawyer. Boyd Douglas had pretended to befriend Phil so as to betray him, and had given Phil's private and intimate correspondence to the FBI in exchange for a few bucks. Yet Phil wanted to tell the jury what a swell guy Boyd was. Douglas was preparing to damn Phil Berrigan and his friends with incriminating personal letters he had obtained through supposed friendship. Boyd Douglas was no swell guy. He was immoral and malevolent. What Douglas did not know, however, was that I had obtained some letters of my own.

Through interviewing students at Bucknell, I quickly learned that Douglas had seduced female students by claiming to have close ties to the radical Catholics, and had involved several friends in his betrayal. By the time the trial was under way, they had read about Douglas's collaboration with the prosecution. They were distressed about having been used, and were happy to talk to us. I asked them about their interactions with Douglas. Had he ever given them gifts? Had he ever written to them? "Oh, yes," some of the women said. "He sent me this card," or "He wrote me a letter." I asked if I could read them. They all said yes. The government had already interviewed most of the women but had never asked about any correspondence. I hoped the letters would come as a complete surprise—not only to the government but to Douglas as well. "Listen," I added when I left each woman, "if the government comes around asking you any questions, I'd appreciate it if you didn't tell them about the letters."

Under the prosecution's guiding interrogation, during the trial, Douglas portrayed himself as a flawed but patriotic ally of the United States government who had turned against dangerous criminals. For several days on the stand in cross-examination, Douglas listened respectfully to questions asked by my colleagues on the defense team. None of the questions seemed to make much of an impression on the jury.

Most of the lawyers cross-examining him focused on his being a plant for the FBI at the prison. From what I could tell, that approach wasn't working. Jurors knew Douglas was flawed, but they thought he was reforming. I wanted to illustrate that he was not trustworthy.

I was the third or fourth defense lawyer to have a shot at Boyd Douglas. When it was my turn to cross-examine him, I stood and asked, "Did you ever tell anybody you were a 'nonviolent revolutionary'?"

Immediately the prosecutor rose to object, stating that the witness had answered the question previously. To my surprise, the judge also came to Douglas's defense by offering testimony on the witness's behalf. "I think he said before that he didn't," the judge said.

After squabbling with both the judge and the prosecution, I went on. "Did you ever tell people on or off the campus that you were committed to and believed in strategic sabotage?" I asked Douglas.

"No," he replied.

"You never said that?" I asked. "You never advised anybody of that?"

"I don't recall that," Boyd replied. "No."

Then I showed him one of the letters I'd obtained from my interviews, a letter he had sent to a woman at Bucknell, and asked him to identify the handwriting as his own. He did.

I then read the letter aloud: "This is where I am at politically: A made, totally committed nonviolent revolutionary who believes in strategic sabotage . . ." He'd also written: "There may be an interesting project that would interest you after the turn of this year . . ."

I kept reading until I reached his sign-off at the end: "Take Care. Right On. Peace. Boyd." I paused for just a moment before reading the letter's final line: "P.S. Please destroy this letter."

I turned back to the witness, whose face seemed a bit paler. "Mr. Douglas, there is a reference to 'an interesting project' after the turn of the year. What was that in reference to?"

"It was in reference to the tunnel system," Douglas replied.

"In reference to what?" the judge asked. He seemed as surprised as the jury.

"In reference to the tunnel system, Your Honor," I replied.

At this point, I heard another objection—not from the prosecutor, or the judge, but from the defense table. Leonard Boudin, the famed civil rights lawyer who rarely shied from the spotlight, jumped into the action by offering a statement that made little sense to anyone. It was so strange that the prosecutor rose to add, "I object to Mr. Boudin interrupting Mr. Lenzner."

"I have other clients here," Mr. Boudin replied, "and I don't believe this interruption is unwise."

After Boudin rose on another occasion, really just to insert himself in the procedure, even the prosecutor whispered to me: "Can't you keep your own guys in hand?"

Boudin had interrupted because he was irked that I was making headway with letters he knew nothing about until that very moment. I had told none of the defense lawyers except for Ramsey Clark. I was afraid the correspondence would be leaked to the press and the value of surprise would be lost. Clark had agreed with me. As leader of the defense team, he usually wanted everyone on the team to feel included, but he was also a brilliant strategist. As for me, I didn't care as much about that collegiality as I did about winning the case.

As soon as Boyd lied the first time, I knew I had him. In a good cross-examination, you get to a point where the witness doesn't know what's coming next and starts to visibly struggle to keep his story straight. This happened to Boyd Douglas, who suddenly came off as totally flat-footed.

Douglas admitted it was he, not Berrigan, who first brought up the plot to bomb heating tunnels. He admitted to having alias identifications and making a series of misstatements to the FBI. When I presented another of his letters, he admitted to asking for $50,000 from the FBI as a reward for the information he was providing. As for a list of instructions that Berrigan allegedly had dictated to Boyd for the plot to kidnap Kissinger, Douglas admitted that he had not given the memo to federal authorities until after J. Edgar Hoover discussed the "insidious" plot to abduct a high-ranking official to the U.S. Senate.

My cross-examination was the subject of numerous press reports, with some reporters referring to me as "rumpled" and carrying a "battered briefcase bulging with work." At least I fared better than Boyd Douglas, who, under intense questioning, was described this way by the press: "He slumps, pouts, his pudgy mouth sullen."

Of the many blows to Douglas's credibility, I thought the most damaging was the evidence—by his own hand, no less—that he was a cad. In one letter I presented to the jury, Douglas had proposed marriage to a woman, telling her he had terminal cancer. He wrote an intimate letter to another woman during the same time he was romancing her roommate. To another woman Douglas wrote, "I have given my life to the struggle," and then added, "I get warm vibrations from you . . . I want our relationship to be real for both of us." He lied to one woman, claiming that scars on his leg were from machine gun wounds he sustained in Vietnam. There were nine females on the jury. For most of the trial the jurors had sat emotionless, giving little indication as to their leanings. But that changed with Boyd Douglas. One reporter noted that, as they heard Douglas's testimony, the women on the jury "swallowed smiles and stirred in their chairs."

During a break in the cross-examination, Phil Berrigan pulled me aside. "Terry, don't you think you are being too hard on Boyd?" he asked.

I looked at him, slightly incredulous.

"We have to respect humanity," the priest said.

"Phil, this is the only way to win this case," I told him. Though what he was saying was unrealistic, there was something touching about it too. Despite our different approaches, I had come to respect and like Phil and many of the other defendants. But I knew that I couldn't let his attitude soften mine; otherwise, he would likely end up in jail with a substantial sentence.

On March 21, 1972, one of the most important government witnesses, the FBI agent who handled Boyd Douglas, took the stand. The agent—code-named "Molly"—tried to defend Douglas's credibility. But, crucially, he testified that he had referred to Douglas as an "accomplished confidence man" in a memo to J. Edgar Hoover. Just in case the jury missed the point, we called Boyd Douglas an outright liar every chance we got.

Having worked with bureau agents in Justice Department jobs, I had seen varying levels of integrity and quality, and was more cynical and questioning of the government than I might have been otherwise. During the trial, for example, an FBI agent testified he had questioned some of the priests after a local police officer had stopped them for speeding. I doubted that story. "If the defendants were stopped for speeding," I asked the agent, "then how did you just happen to be in the same location to question them?" He then admitted that he had called the local police ahead of time to set up a reason to stop the car.

By the close of the prosecution's case, the defense team faced a critical decision. Should we put our clients on the stand and risk their antiwar sermonizing? Or should we rest our case without their testimony, gambling that the jury would find the government's evidence was insufficient to prove its case? I had mixed feelings about this. We had witnesses ready to further discredit Boyd Douglas. Some of the information would be very damaging to the government's case. But I also knew the decision not to call witnesses would be a major surprise—and surprise has its advantages.

It was a gutsy call, and Ramsey Clark made it. When it was the defense's turn to present its case, Clark rose from his chair and told the stunned courtroom that, since the government hadn't proved its case, we would therefore call no witnesses. Moving to summations, Clark was far more eloquent than I could have been.

"What distresses me most is the government's effort to paint people with an enormous passion for peace as violent," the former attorney general said. He compared the antiwar views of the defendants with those of the martyred John F. Kennedy. Quoting Kennedy as saying, "'I look forward to a day of peace and freedom,'" Clark added, "That's why he was killed—violently, with a gun. These defendants also say, 'We look forward to a world of peace and freedom.'" When he was finished, one of the jurors brought a handkerchief to her eyes.

But closing arguments weren't over. Each lawyer made his own statements. My closing summation tended more toward the facts. On a blackboard, I listed the names of other Berrigan associates who had been named during the trial. "If this is a major conspiracy requiring the full attention of the federal government," I asked, "then why aren't these other people named in the indictment?" It didn't concern me that I was making a controversial point by focusing the spotlight on the defendant's friends and others who had escaped being charged. The case, I maintained, was a selective prosecution to punish well-known antiwar activists.

Boyd Douglas, I added, "was the one with the bit in his teeth about illegal projects . . . a streetwise confidence man. He had larceny in his heart from the very beginning."

"The defendants will always seek peace," Clark said. "The defense continues to proclaim their innocence—and the defense rests."

The jury was to decide guilt or innocence on ten counts: three for conspiracy to kidnap Kissinger, destroy federal property, and interfere with the draft; and seven counts for sending letters into and out of federal prison without the warden's consent. On the first day of their deliberations, after meeting for seven hours, jurors asked the judge for a blackboard and a rereading of the judge's instructions on the law. This told me there was at least some disagreement in the jury room. After thirty-three hours, the jury reported to the judge that it was deadlocked. The judge told them to go back, but the result did not change. The jury failed to reach a verdict on the conspiracy charges. It did, however, find Father Phil Berrigan and Sister Liz McAlister guilty of smuggling the seven letters. Despite the guilty verdict on these minor offenses, I considered the case a victory.

Shortly after the verdict, Liz McAlister sent me a card. On the cover was a picture of Washington crossing the Delaware, and inside was the inscription "You've revolutionized my life." She apologized to me and the other lawyers for the "pain" the case caused us. In truth, we had received enormous criticism for coming to the defense of the Berrigans. But it was nothing like the criticism they received every day. "The process wasn't as neat and easy as it could have been," she wrote, "but it was real and it was human and that may be more important."

I knew how she felt. The Berrigan case was an eye-opener for me in a number of ways. It was my first glimpse of the federal government from the other side of the courtroom. I listened to wiretaps of the men and women I was defending. Wiretaps had meant something different to me when I was a prosecutor and government lawyer than they did when they were targeted on defendants whom I liked, respected, and called friends. It was unsettling to hear people I knew holding conversations without any idea the government was listening.

The Berrigans demonstrated how people who don't have a lot of power can have a huge impact on public policy through public opinion. The Harrisburg defendants were confident about their beliefs—and ready to go to jail for them. The consequences of their actions didn't scare them. As someone who'd tried to keep emotional distance by avoiding that kind of extreme commitment and active witness, my participation in this case had a profound impact on me. It was the first time that I had felt someone's fate in my hands, something I found more challenging than I had imagined it would be. I received an education in how to handle sensitive documents like Douglas's letters, and it taught me to trust my instincts: a juror I had fought hard for played a vital role. It changed me in ways that I still probably don't fully understand.

A less profound result of my work on the Berrigan case is that I suddenly found myself a darling of the political left. Which was jarring, since I never saw myself as an ideologue of any kind. That would soon become clear enough to my new supporters.

In the spring of 1973, about the same time the Watergate probe was heating up, testimony was heard in the trial of *U.S. v. Ellsberg.* Daniel Ellsberg was a former military analyst who had served in the Defense Department under Secretary of Defense Robert McNamara. At the RAND Corporation where he worked subsequently, Ellsberg obtained a series of classified documents about the Vietnam War going back to the days of the Kennedy and Johnson administrations. Excerpts of those papers were leaked to the *New York Times,* which published them in a series that started on June 13, 1971, under the relatively innocuous article title of "Vietnam Archive: Pentagon Study Traces Three Decades of Growing U.S. Involvement."

The "Pentagon Papers," as they soon became known, revealed high-level assessments of the situation in Southeast Asia that were far more pessimistic than the U.S. government had been telling the American people. The casualty estimates for the war, for example, were far higher than was publicly disclosed. The documents, as an editor of the *Times* later put it, "demonstrated, among other things, that the Johnson Administration had systematically lied, not only to the public but also to Congress, about a subject of transcendent national interest and significance."

The Nixon administration couldn't have cared less about the Johnson White House, but they were furious about the unauthorized disclosures of classified material and the potential damage done to their own efforts in Vietnam. They decided to prosecute Ellsberg on charges of espionage, theft, and conspiracy. Demonstrations against the war were escalating, and the trial promised to be even more highly publicized than the case against the Berrigans.

Ellsberg portrayed himself to the media—very effectively—as a noble man of action and a potential martyr, a patriot who put the country's interests ahead of his own. "I felt that as an American citizen, as a responsible citizen, I could no longer cooperate in concealing this information from the American public," he told the press. "I did this clearly at my own jeopardy, and I am prepared to answer to all the consequences of this decision." To this day, he remains a folk hero to many of the left. To many on the right, he is considered a "rat" and "traitor." Many Ellsberg defenders assumed I agreed with him too. I didn't know, frankly, what he was. I appreciated the government's compelling need to maintain the secrecy of confidential information. At the same time, the information Ellsberg leaked had shed significant light on the controversial war effort and how the government had deliberately hidden its prospects for success from the American people.

As preparations for the trial were under way, I was invited by Charlie Nesson, who was involved in Ellsberg's defense, to fly out to

California to meet with Ellsberg. I found a well-spoken man of about forty years of age, thin, with dark hair and piercing blue eyes. He was a graduate of Harvard (where he received a Ph.D.) and Cambridge universities, and had served in the Marines. Ellsberg did not look like a man fearing a criminal prosecution. If anything, he seemed to be enjoying his celebrity. Some wealthy person on the coast put him up at a swanky estate overlooking the Hollywood Hills.

I met Ellsberg behind the house by the pool. He was wearing a swimsuit and a pullover and chatting amiably with his friend Tony Russo, an associate at the RAND Corporation and a codefendant in the case. Russo had been given immunity in the trial in exchange for his testimony against Ellsberg.

When I introduced myself to the two men, they barely said hello and kept up their discussion. At one point I overheard Ellsberg openly discussing with Russo the people to whom he had given documents for safekeeping and where they had been stored. He mentioned various women by name. I wasn't sure they understood the law, because what Ellsberg was doing was alarming. Not only was he giving information to Russo, a witness for the prosecution, that could be used against him at trial, but Ellsberg was also putting targets on the backs of all the friends who had assisted him.

"Dan, I have to stop you right there," I said. "Tony here is under subpoena to testify against you. You can't give him this kind of information."

Ellsberg looked at me as if I were speaking gibberish. "You don't know what you're talking about," he said. "We're friends." He told me, basically, to scram.

After that exchange, I visited a few of the people Ellsberg had named as associates—people who had aided and abetted him to copy and disseminate the Pentagon Papers. One of them was an attractive blond woman who lived in a house on the beach in Malibu. When she told me that she was visiting the United States from Sweden on a temporary visa, I became alarmed, knowing that her status made her vulnerable to pressure from the federal government. I couldn't imagine why Ellsberg would have stored these sensitive papers with someone like that. Did he think her foreign nationality would somehow protect her? Or did he want to impress beautiful young women with how he was outmaneuvering the federal government? What was worse, he seemed to care not at all that his friends who possessed the papers were vulnerable to prosecution. If any of them received immunity and still refused to testify before a grand jury, the federal government could put them in jail for the life of that grand jury—up to eighteen months. I had just come out of a four-month trial for people I had some respect for—the Berrigans. I didn't need to spend three or four months with someone's out-of-control ego. I knew it was going to be a huge, high-profile case, but I told Ellsberg's defense team I wasn't interested. I didn't see myself working for a guy like that.

During Ellsberg's trial, it was revealed that senior Nixon officials had ordered a break-in of the office of Ellsberg's psychiatrist to gain information to discredit Ellsberg. That revelation added to the shock waves emanating from the wobbling White House just when the Senate Watergate Committee was beginning its investigation in April of 1973.

CHAPTER 3

DIRTY TRICKS

In March of 1969, less than two months after Richard M. Nixon took office as president of the United States, one of his most trusted aides, John Ehrlichman, made a low-profile trip to the VIP lounge of the American Airlines terminal at LaGuardia Airport. Ehrlichman was a serious man with a frequently grim expression and dark hair in a comb-over. He was an unquestionable power in the White House. In a nod to his German heritage, critics later accused Ehrlichman of forming, along with Chief of Staff Bob Haldeman, a "Berlin Wall" around the president and the Oval Office that supposedly kept others out of the information loop. But Ehrlichman and his high-level associates needed trusted outside operatives, the kind of people who would follow instructions without asking questions. One of these was the man Ehrlichman had traveled to the airport lounge to meet.

Anthony Ulasewicz was fifty-one years old. The son of Polish immigrants, he served in the U.S. Army during World War II and then joined the NYPD's Special Service and Investigation Division. Before

he retired, his duties included protection work for dignitaries and celebrities traveling in the city, a list that included Dwight D. Eisenhower, John F. Kennedy, and Soviet premier Nikita Khrushchev.

Ulasewicz was said to be an excellent investigator, a loyalist with
good instincts, smart and discreet. This was exactly the kind of person
John Ehrlichman was looking for. Ulasewicz would be paid $22,000 a
year (about $140,000 in today's dollars) and use an American Express
credit card under the pseudonym Edward T. Stanley, proof of a clear
intention to deceive.

Ehrlichman had a list of special assignments that he made clear
were of interest to President Nixon personally. Some of them touched
on the bizarre. For example, Nixon had lived in an apartment in New
York City that he sold in 1945, and Ulasewicz was asked to find the
names and addresses of everyone who had lived there over the ensuing
twenty-four years. The reason for the request was not disclosed. This
type of investigative and surveillance work continued to grow and included a phone call Ulasewicz received on July 19, 1969, from another
shadowy Nixon associate, Jack Caulfield. "Get out to Martha's Vineyard as fast as you can, Tony," Caulfield said. "Kennedy's car ran off [the
Chappaquiddick] bridge last night. There was a girl in it. She's dead."

Ulasewicz and Caulfield were among the first members of a clandestine group established by senior Nixon officials to monitor perceived
enemies of the president. Contrary to conventional wisdom, what became known as the Watergate scandal did not begin with a break-in of
a hotel and office complex on the eve of the 1972 election. It actually
began in March of 1969, in that first meeting in the VIP lounge of
LaGuardia Airport.

Ask anyone today about the Watergate scandal, and the names
you most likely will hear—other than Richard M. Nixon—are
Bob Woodward and Carl Bernstein. The *Washington Post* reporters,

aided by their editor, Ben Bradlee, played a crucial role in uncovering an abuse of power that ultimately reached the Oval Office and led to the first presidential resignation in American history. That version focuses on the June 17, 1972, break-in of Democratic Party offices and subsequent cover-up. But the Watergate break-in was only one part of a much more elaborate scheme. What most people remember today about Watergate was shaped by a media narrative established early. It was built around crimes stemming from a single incident that Nixon defenders, somewhat successfully, diminished as "a third-rate burglary" or, as Nixon himself tried to put it, an error in judgment. His biggest fault, as he once put it, was not dealing "decisively or more forthrightly" with the break-in.

That is not why Watergate should be remembered. It certainly doesn't tell the full story. As in many investigations, much that the public learned was limited to the headlines of the moment. As a result, some of the most important elements of the scandal, including why the break-in occurred, were overlooked, minimized, or omitted.

Four decades later, lingering questions remain unanswered. When Charles Colson, special counsel to Nixon from 1969 to 1973, died in 2012, the *New York Times* wrote in his obituary, "To this day, no one knows whether Nixon authorized the break-in or precisely what the burglars wanted." This was incorrect. Many of the answers were discovered in the Senate Watergate Committee investigation. The public just never got to hear the full story.

I was involved in this investigation from the beginning. Working with other investigators, we uncovered issues and problems that continue to haunt our politics today. The direct assault on democracy through use of undisclosed funds and beneath-the-radar attempts to damage opposition party campaigns were critical aspects of the larger Watergate scandal.

I was at home in Washington when I saw a news story in the June 19, 1972, edition of the *Washington Post*: "GOP Security Aide Among

Five Arrested in Bugging Affair." Investigators are inclined to see many things as suspicious, and this story about a break-in of the Democratic Party headquarters at the Watergate was immediately suspicious to me. The circumstances were unusual. For one, some of the perpetrators named were Cuban exiles who came out of the anti-Castro movement. For another, the burglars were so inept that they were discovered by a security guard making his routine rounds. Oddly, they also carried address books documenting their ties to the White House. I assumed that these guys were acting on higher orders. I didn't surmise whose they might be, but I never thought this would lead to the president or his senior officials.

During that summer, national attention focused on the presidential contest, and especially the contentious Democratic Party Convention in July that nominated George McGovern. Watergate was discussed, if at all, only on the fringes, primarily among those who saw the ghost of Richard Nixon in every dark shadow. The break-in received little attention, even in Washington; it was a subject of curiosity at cocktail parties, but not much more.

Thanks to dogged reporting by the press (notably Woodward and Bernstein), and Judge Sirica's suspicion that a cover-up was occurring in his courtroom where the burglars were being tried, the Watergate story continued to grow with revelations of improper activities by the Committee to Re-Elect the President and administration officials. It did not get buried, like the Democratic ticket, in Nixon's 1972 reelection landslide. Even as Nixon took his oath of office for a second term, pledging to "bring down walls of hostility" and "build bridges of understanding" to address the ongoing domestic conflict over Vietnam War policy, the questions about the Watergate break-in and his administration's involvement began to win the attention of the United States Congress.

On February 7, 1973, the United States Senate, with a Democratic majority, voted 77–0 to establish a select committee to "conduct an investigation and study of the extent, if any, to which illegal, improper, or unethical activities were engaged in by any persons, acting individually or in combination with others, in the presidential election of 1972, or any campaign, canvass, or other activity related to it." Senator Sam Ervin, a seventy-six-year-old Democrat from North Carolina—a dignified, white-haired, thick-jowled, self-described "country lawyer"—was appointed chairman. The seasoned Tennessee senator Howard Baker, a serious-looking man with dark hair and horn-rimmed glasses, and a reputation for bipartisanship, was named the Republican vice-chairman. Senator Ervin had insisted that no senators with presidential aspirations be allowed on the committee—a decision that narrowed the pool of candidates and minimized partisan bickering.

The Senate Resolution opened up a broad area of inquiry into the break-in, the cover-up, and any other improper activities related to the 1972 presidential election. One of the principal requirements of an investigation is that the participants make no judgment or assumption as to where the investigation may lead or its ultimate results. I don't believe any senator or staff member believed that this would end up implicating the president or his senior officials. At most, it might lead to legislation to prohibit unfair campaign practices.

After several months as director of the Center on Corporate Responsibility, an advocacy group trying to encourage corporations to adopt policies more sensitive to domestic and global issues, I was frustrated; the Center was not action-oriented. They either didn't know how or didn't care to fight. I did try, however. For example, I hired a *New York Times* investigative reporter as well as the famed Walter Sheridan, whom I'd met in Mississippi. I asked both to help me look into one of the key issues of concern to the center—the funding of various political campaigns for the 1972 elections. Before long, this very issue would preoccupy me in quite a different fashion.

When the Watergate Committee was being formed, Edward Bennett Williams, knowing my frustration, performed another beyond-the-call-of-duty favor for me and recommended me to the committee's new chief counsel, Sam Dash. A recommendation from someone like Williams, of course, carried weight. After a quick meeting where he proclaimed my credentials "great," Dash asked me to join his staff as one of three assistant chief counsels.

I was excited to work as a lawyer and investigator again. It's hard to imagine today that a job on the Watergate Committee staff wasn't considered a plum appointment, but at that time there probably weren't many capable lawyers contending to join an ad hoc congressional committee. Luckily for me, I was available. My colleagues as assistant co-counsels were James Hamilton, a Washington lawyer from South Carolina, and David Dorsen, whom I'd known when we were both prosecutors in the U.S. Attorney's Office in New York. When we were hired in March, no one knew which aspects of the investigation we'd be assigned to focus on; there were plenty of initial facts and issues to get our arms around.

It wasn't long before my past came back to haunt me. Early in April, I learned from Dash that the White House was objecting to my appointment, and that Ervin had been pressured to fire me. Ervin told Dash that my presence on the staff would be embarrassing to the committee because I'd been fired from OEO by Nixon's order and because I'd represented defendants in the Berrigan trial. Ervin cited unnamed people "who are part of the Democratic establishment" who claimed I was a disgruntled ex-administration official with an ax to grind and a "radical leftist background."

Dash countered that my defense of the Legal Services programs that led to my ousting was a positive for the team, and that I had had the support of the American Bar Association. He pointed out that my association with the Berrigans had been in a strictly legal capacity, and claimed that I was the kind of tough prosecutor they needed. Ervin demurred that my background would lead people to "think that we have a Nixon hater on our staff who cannot be objective."

Senator Ervin didn't know me at all. There was little reason for him to put his reputation and that of the committee on the line to keep me on board. But Dash recognized that my abrupt departure could also taint the integrity of the committee and of his leadership. When he was appointed chief counsel, I learned he had insisted on a letter of agreement with Ervin acknowledging that he could select his own staff, conduct the investigation independently, and follow the trail of facts wherever it led. Before giving up, Dash persuaded Ervin to meet with me, at least to announce his decision to me personally.

When Dash described the situation to me, I was stricken. As we walked to Senator Ervin's office, I felt like a kid being marched to the principal's office. The senator looked at me with a kindly face that concealed shrewd eyes. As he talked or emphasized a point, his eyebrows flickered up or down.

"Now, Terry," he said in his Southern drawl, "some folks are real upset about your being hired."

"So I understand," I said.

"I can't have the committee starting under that kind of controversy," he said. "I'll probably have to let you go."

I scrambled to defend myself. I asserted that the activities some were condemning me for, however controversial, were undertaken in my profession as a lawyer. I told him about my work in the Civil Rights Division and as a prosecutor in New York, both for the Department of Justice. I even pointed out that being a member of the Harvard University Board of Overseers should indicate that I was hardly a left-wing radical. I had one final thought, to appeal to a Republican authority.

"Mr. Chairman, I understand that Senator Baker is a fair man," I said. "Would it be all right if I talked with him first?" I figured I had nothing to lose in appealing to the Republican vice-chairman.

Ervin shrugged but was noncommittal. "Let me think about it," he said.

It was a Friday, so everyone agreed to wait until Monday. But by the time our conversation ended, I was devastated. I had been so eager to become involved in this unfolding investigation, and knew I could be an asset. I left Capitol Hill early in the afternoon with the feeling that it was all over.

Later that afternoon, Dash called our house. "Ervin's changed his mind," he said. "See you on Monday." Dash didn't explain the reasons for the chairman's reversal, assuming he even knew. I never knew what changed Ervin's attitude, either. But I do know that Dash went to bat for me. In hindsight, I appreciate too the significant risk that both he and Ervin took in keeping me on board.

I quickly developed an appreciation for Sam Ervin. He was interesting to watch. His face had distinctive features and was very expressive. He had a great sense of humor and quoted Scripture constantly. The latter quality was very effective—it played to his homey Southern roots, and also allowed for the Nixon administration's actions to be viewed through the moral judgments of the Bible.

Positioning himself as an "old country lawyer" not only allowed Ervin's constituents to relate to him but also, not incidentally, led his opponents to underestimate him. In fact, Ervin was a legal scholar steeped in constitutional law. I remember sitting behind him during the first day of the hearings, watching him read a Supreme Court case. My heart sank; he seemed completely divorced from the testimony under way. When it was his turn to question the witness, however, his incisive inquiries demonstrated he'd somehow managed to follow every word of the proceedings.

Ervin had a rare knack for appealing to politicians across the spectrum. "Sam is the only man we could have selected on either side who would have the respect of the Senate as a whole," Senator Mike Mansfield, the Democratic majority leader, once said. He was right. By and large, most of the senators were leery of an investigation that might taint the president. The Republicans certainly didn't want to go there, and neither did many of the Democrats. Ervin, to his eternal credit, allowed us to pursue the facts wherever they led. It is beyond doubt that he was truly indispensable to the committee's success.

Howard Baker was Ervin's equal. They worked together well, which was invaluable for minimizing partisan attacks. Baker shared Ervin's moderate demeanor and tone, and was just as sharp. Though Baker was as committed to his party as Ervin was to the Democrats, he too was reasonable, pragmatic, and willing to follow the facts as they developed. Though loyal to President Nixon, Baker was not determined to exonerate him at all costs.

Of the five other senators on the committee, the two who struck me as the most engaged were Republican Lowell Weicker of Connecticut and Daniel Inouye of Hawaii, a Japanese-American and a Democrat who'd lost his right arm during World War II. They asked good, intelligent questions. Inouye was a victim of Chairman Ervin's habit to call a vote by asking the senators to raise their right hands, then hastily adding, "Except you, Danny." Inouye laughed good-naturedly every time.

Senator Weicker was what might be called a "renegade." He was one who did not hesitate to disagree with his party's leaders. Despite Ervin's admonitions, Weicker had thinly concealed presidential aspirations and was prone to leaking information to the press. At first, I found this a serious problem, though I'd later see Weicker's leaking in a more positive light.

The senators on the committee whom I found to be less impressive during hearings were Republican Edward Gurney of Florida and two Democrats, Herman Talmadge of Georgia and Joseph Montoya of New Mexico. Talmadge was said to be very close to the Nixons—I didn't expect much from him, and I wasn't proven wrong. Senator Montoya seemed often disengaged; perhaps the testimony was over his head. When it came time for him to question a witness, he'd begin by saying, "State and spell your name," even though that witness had been testifying for hours.

During one executive session when I was making a presentation on issuing subpoenas to President Nixon's brothers and his longtime secretary, Rose Mary Woods, Montoya was unusually active at his seat behind the semicircular rostrum. He seemed to be carefully scribbling notes the entire time I talked. His attentiveness was so out of character that I wanted to see what he thought had been so significant in my presentation so I could adapt the technique in the future. As soon as I had a chance to look at the piece of paper, I saw he'd written "Senator Joseph Montoya" over and over. It looked to me like he had been practicing his signature.

Considering the Watergate Committee's ultimate success, one might imagine it operated well from the beginning. In fact, so much new information was reported daily that we were scrambling to adjust to the constantly changing landscape. When I came on board, the committee was still hiring lawyers, researchers, and investigators on an ad hoc basis. Some were hired for their credentials, others because they were friends of friends, still others because they were connected to senators or prominent politicians. As a result, our staff varied greatly in quality.

Sam Dash was a very smart professor of law who often asked good questions. But I never knew how extensive his investigatory experience had been. Dash complained that Fred Thompson, the lead counsel for the Republican minority, constantly leaked information to the White House. That didn't surprise me. I told Dash that if the circumstances were reversed, he'd similarly feed information to a Democratic White House.

However much Thompson may have aided Nixon's staff, they clearly didn't trust him. "Oh, shit," Nixon once said about Fred. "He's dumb as hell." Fred wasn't dumb. And he wasn't about to be pushed around, not by the Democrats or the Republican White House. No-body owned Fred Thompson, which is probably what really upset the Nixon team.

I liked Thompson a lot, though undoubtedly he was more laid-back than I was. He had a Southern way about him—measured, delib-erate, droll—that proved useful in getting Republican and Democratic staffers to work well together. At least one member of his staff accom-panied us on nearly every interview.

Like his mentor, Howard Baker, Fred had a pragmatic approach to the investigation. He also demonstrated a strong ethical backbone. When I developed information that one of his investigators had a pat-tern of leaking information about our activities to the press, Fred heard me out, assessed the evidence, and concluded I was right. The guy was fired.

Fred was so genuine and comfortable in his skin that it seems hard to believe that he could become someone else, as he did when he be-came an actor. I suppose it helped that many of his roles were varia-tions of his own personality—tough, Southern, folksy, principled.

Two of the best investigators I ever worked with were on the Water-gate Committee. Marc Lackritz was a brilliant young lawyer I hired just out of Harvard Law School. He introduced me to Mary deOreo, who became an accomplished investigator. The other was Carmine Bellino, a former FBI agent who had assisted Robert F. Kennedy's Senate inves-tigation of the Teamsters. Bellino was a forensic accountant with exemp-lary skills. Forensic accountants are adept at piecing together complicated financial information and following money trails.

Before the Watergate hearings began in May, I spent weeks flying around the country meeting with various witnesses. Bellino some-times came with me. Early on, we flew to California to talk to Presi-dent Nixon's personal lawyer, Herb Kalmbach. We asked to see bank records and other information relating to money we had learned was provided to the Watergate burglars. Kalmbach calmly replied that those documents had been destroyed. My heart sank. Not Carmine's. "That's not a problem, Mr. Kalmbach," he said. "I'm going to sit right here with you and reconstruct all those files."

He did exactly that, for hours at a time, over a couple of weeks. Focused and dogged, Carmine left no stone undisturbed. He subpoenaed many vendors and companies in Key Biscayne, Florida, where Nixon and his close friend, Bebe Rebozo, each had homes. He asked for Kalmbach's index cards, containing his daily schedule and notes.

Carmine discovered that Kalmbach controlled money paid to campaign operatives including the Watergate burglars. He managed to pull together tax records to build an elaborate chart tracing various campaign funds to all sorts of noncampaign purposes, such as Nixon's purchase of a Harry Winston necklace for his wife's birthday. Unlike a lot of other people, Bellino did his work without bragging about what he accomplished. I recognized how valuable his skills were, and later I would use him as the model for seeking out forensic accountants on future cases and for my investigative company.

Other committee staffers were less impressive. Some were favorites of the senators and came from their home states. They liked to line up in the hallways after committee sessions and chat up reporters. Others just seemed to like saying they worked on the Watergate Committee; no matter what was happening, they came in at nine and left at five. Of utmost importance to many was the opportunity to sit behind one of the senators during the hearings in order to be captured by TV and press cameras for all their family and friends back home to see.

Rufus Edmisten, a North Carolinian who had headed a small subcommittee for Ervin, was named deputy chief counsel. In fact, Dash received his own appointment only after making a deal with Edmisten. In typical Washington fashion, the deal was that Rufus would push Dash very hard for the job if Dash agreed to Rufus as his deputy.

Rufus was totally loyal to Ervin, his patron. He also was a real creature of the Washington culture. Shortly after he came to the committee, he asked the Senate administrative people to create a special chair for him to use behind the rostrum. The chair had no arms and was on wheels. Whenever a senator asked a question during the hearings, Edmisten in his armless chair wheeled over so that he was wedged right beside the questioner. With that technique, Rufus Edmisten became one of the most photographed staff members of the Watergate Committee.

One member of the staff who stood out was Scott Armstrong. Armstrong was a very good and resourceful investigator, but he created a variety of problems. There were elements of his background that I thought could be troublesome. Most problematic was that his good friend from Yale was Bob Woodward, who continued to investigate the break-in, and had remained close to him since. I was concerned that Armstrong's friendship with Woodward might supersede his allegiance to the committee. Dash asked me to interview Armstrong before hiring him, though ultimately he hired Armstrong before listening to my concerns.

Armstrong did help Woodward break a number of stories on the investigation. In one instance, the leak was so severe that Armstrong was suspended from the committee. He was the primary source for a *Rolling Stone* article that criticized the committee staff and senators. He eventually returned, but it took a long time for him to regain my trust.

As mentioned, not everyone was dying to join the committee staff. At the United States Attorney's Office, I had worked with a terrific senior criminal investigator for the IRS named Marvin Sontag. I thought he'd be an excellent addition to our staff, so I called him up.

"I'm an assistant chief counsel on the Watergate Committee," I told him. "I'm heading up of the investigation, and we need someone like you."

He paused for a second. "Let me see now," he said. "You're asking me to leave New York and my job of twenty-five years to go to

Washington to investigate the president of the United States? And you think I will be able to go back to it after I do that? Are you crazy?" Like so many others, he thought the president and his administration would walk away from the investigation unscathed. He assumed there was no future for anyone involved in it.

For some time, the committee staff didn't even have a workspace. Through a friend, Jim Flug, who worked for Senator Ted Kennedy, I managed to find a place to work temporarily in Kennedy's office. Good thing the White House didn't know about that.

Eventually tiny makeshift offices were found for us in the Senate auditorium of the Russell Senate Office Building, an ornate edifice with dark corridors and marble floors. My office was located directly behind the stage and was one of the few with a door that could be closed for privacy. The Watergate hearing room was directly upstairs. My only access to the outside world was a narrow window giving me a view of the rest of the staff. With piles of papers and reports stacked on my desk and spilling onto the floor, it was obvious to visitors that the appearance of my office was not my top concern.

There were a few issues that confronted us early on which, if decided differently, would almost certainly have helped the Nixon administration survive the hearings. The first came from Archibald Cox, the special prosecutor that attorney general–designate Elliot Richardson appointed in May to investigate the Watergate break-in. After hearings had begun in mid-May, Cox came to Chairman Ervin in June and urged him to scrap plans to televise our hearings. The special prosecutor felt that public hearings would complicate his efforts to assemble an independent and impartial grand jury. He also did not want his witnesses exposed to the televised testimony of potential co-conspirators, which might help them craft their own stories. Some senators and even one of my co-counsels were inclined to agree. But Dash and I argued that it was imperative that the Senate committee not cave to the Department of Justice. For one thing there was no guarantee that Cox or Earl Silbert, the U.S. Attorney presenting to the grand jury, would withstand pressure from the attorney general and the White House. Ervin thought about it and decided to go forward. The chairman believed strongly that the American people had a right to hear as much as possible about the case. I would find, however, there were exceptions to this rule.

Another issue involved soap operas like *General Hospital*. The senators, who were politicians first and foremost, were risk averse almost throughout the entire investigation. They were terrified that long, drawn-out hearings would annoy their constituents, particularly those outraged by the preemption of their favorite daytime dramas. To my continued disbelief, this was an ongoing concern; so great, in fact, that the senators seriously deliberated a proposal put forward by Senator Baker that would have been disastrous. He suggested immediately bringing before the committee senior White House officials who might have information about the break-in and cover-up: former attorney general Mitchell, Haldeman, Ehrlichman, and Colson. That way the hearings wouldn't last too long and the soap operas could return to the airwaves.

I argued to Dash and anyone else who would listen that if we brought all the big names before us early, we wouldn't have any idea what to ask them. We had no trail of evidence, no affidavits from witnesses, no way of challenging what they said.

The most effective way to begin an investigation is to start with the people at the lowest levels and move up the chain. Dash shared this view. Fortunately, Senator Ervin and the others were easily convinced. If they hadn't been persuaded, I have no doubt the Watergate hearings would have had a very different result.

There were no established procedures for congressional investigations, how to amass evidence, or what to do with evidence when it was found. Even today, very few law schools provide that education. The issuance of subpoenas was informal. Probably 99 percent of them, except for those most politically sensitive, were signed by Senator Ervin's auto-pen machine. Among the first things I instructed my investigators to do was create witness trees, listing all the employees of various organizations—the White House, the Republican National Committee, and the Committee to Re-Elect the President (CREEP). I wanted to know what role each person played, and who their assistants and secretaries were. I asked my team to assemble all biographical material and press coverage on the individuals that could be found.

Our first targets were those at the lower rungs of each organization—the support staff in the offices of major figures, those who kept their schedules, took their dictation, typed up their notes, and sometimes listened in on phone calls or sat in on meetings. I assumed that these subordinates, though well informed, generally didn't intend to participate in a cover-up. They might not even know that a cover-up was in progress. They had far less invested in the administration's spin than those at the top, and also were far less likely to be complicit in any wrongdoing that they needed to cover up.

Some of them were disgusted by what was happening in the administration and actually sought us out. Almost from the beginning of the investigation, we received calls from staffers asking to meet with us privately. I worried that some of these might be setups—to get us to divulge information or to say something that would indicate hostility to the president and raise questions about our objectivity. I made a point of instructing committee staff to be careful about shooting their mouths off, either about Nixon or any of his people.

When interviewing witnesses, I used the lessons I'd learned during my days in Mississippi and Alabama. I instructed my investigators to assemble as much information as possible about a witness before an interview so we knew what questions to focus on. I also made sure that every witness was always asked: "Is there anything else you wish to add that we haven't covered?" Eventually we added a second question to be asked at the end of every interview: "Are you aware of a taping system that may have been in use anywhere in the White House?" We'd heard that President Johnson had installed a tape-recording system in the Oval Office, and we wondered if Nixon might have continued this practice. As we all know now, that turned out to be an extremely important question.

A few weeks after I was on the job, I sent Ervin a memo suggesting how the investigation should be broken up as well as which investigator should be assigned to what issue. To this day I don't know what right I had to do any of this. At the time, that wasn't a question I considered. Most of the people on the committee staff did not have much investigative experience and for the most part they seemed to welcome my suggestions. So much was being revealed every day that was hard to process. My recommendation was an attempt to make order of the chaos.

Before sending the memo to Ervin, I sat down with my co-counsels, David Dorsen and Jim Hamilton, to figure out how to divide up the various aspects of the investigation. Not surprisingly, Jim Hamilton wanted to focus on the "big" case—namely the Watergate break-in and cover-up. That was fine by me—I wanted to avoid the limelight and avoid causing the committee any more trouble than my appointment already had. Dorsen was an experienced investigator, and he was interested in following the money. So along with assisting the overall investigation, I sought permission to focus on a lesser aspect: the allegations about the Nixon campaign's "dirty tricks" against Democratic opponents.

Initially, however, my primary focus was on the start of the hearings and the information we were gathering.

One aspect of the White House that amazed most of us was the depth of President Nixon's paranoia. His entire team believed they were victims, constantly under siege. They assumed their "enemies" were as devious as they were. Key figures in the Nixon administration believed that the Democrats, aided by sympathetic media, had information they planned to use to take the president down. To discover what ammunition the opposition had, and to counter with derogatory information about Democrats, Nixon hired private investigators Jack Caulfield and Tony Ulasewicz.

When I interviewed Caulfield in New York, I found him a pretty cooperative witness. He didn't think he'd done anything wrong. In fact he was using his experience working for Nixon to set up his own investigative company with Tony Ulasewicz, catering to Republican clients. The twelve-page memo suggested that an under-the-radar campaign operation pursue "offensive" activities against the Democrats that included: "surveillance of Democratic primaries, convention, meetings, etc."; "'black bag' capability (discuss privately)" including "all covert steps necessary to minimize Democratic voting violations in Illinois, Texas, etc."; "penetration of [Democratic] nominee's entourage and headquarters with undercover personnel"; "derogatory information investigative capability"; and "any other offensive requirement deemed advisable." It was stunning that a proposal of this nature had been put in writing. And ridiculous that these guys all wrote and talked like they thought they were G-men. They might have even believed it.

Tony Ulasewicz was extremely cooperative. He was a New Yorker with a notable Brooklyn accent. He had a somewhat threatening aura when I first met him; he looked and talked like he'd just stepped out of a mob movie. An excellent investigator, he put together an impressive thirty-three-page report on his investigation into Senator Kennedy's involvement in the death of Mary Jo Kopechne on Martha's Vineyard—complete with a chronology, summary of theories and speculation, list of unanswered questions, and statements from Senator Kennedy and several others involved in the case. I could almost imagine President Nixon fingering through it and analyzing every detail. "The January 1970 inquest into the death," Ulasewicz maintained, "raised perhaps as many questions as it answered, and many of the contradictions that appear in the testimony taken were left unresolved."

I talked with Tony Ulasewicz many times. He helped me put together a long list of the various assignments he undertook at the request of the Nixon high command. One list denoted fifty-four separate investigations, including: allegations of a "wild party" attended by Ted Kennedy in Hawaii (which, Ulasewicz noted, turned out to be false); allegations that Donald Nixon Jr., the president's nephew, was involved in "love-making groups" at Three Forks, Sierra Madre; supposed antiwar activities of doctors and nurses at Jefferson Hospital in Philadelphia; "scandals" or "skeletons" in the background of Hubert Humphrey, Nixon's 1968 Democratic opponent; investigating the offices of the pollster Lou Harris in Manhattan; traveling throughout Maine to look for "skeletons in the closet" of Senator Ed Muskie; allegations of a "wild party" in Phoenix attended by senators Kennedy and Tunney (also said to be unfounded); allegations of a "wild party" in Hollywood involving Kennedy, Tunney, and Reagan; "checking out" a comedian named Dixon who was impersonating the president; reports that the Speaker of the House, Carl Albert, was involved in "improper behavior" at a Washington bar called "The Zebra Room"; and on and on. Even Tony didn't know what some of these things were about. The list indicated a paranoid White House, chasing whatever gossip or rumors caught their fancy. Tony received many of these assignments directly from Ehrlichman. Tony said he'd worked with major international celebrities for years but that Ehrlichman was the first one who really seemed to throw his weight around.

Another scheme targeting Nixon's "enemies" was hatched by a particularly gung-ho aide named Tom Charles Huston. The Huston Plan proposed electronic surveillance of "agitators," using the IRS against Nixon opponents, and the authorization of break-ins to find information about political opponents. Some of these ideas, Huston noted, "were clearly illegal."

Implementation of the Huston Plan was thwarted by an unlikely obstacle. Some of these schemes proved too much for FBI director J. Edgar Hoover, who was used to running his own investigations of supposed enemies. Among the documents we obtained from our subpoena of the White House was an August 8, 1970, memo from Huston to H. R. Haldeman, Nixon's chief of staff. Hoover, the memo asserted, "has become totally unreasonable and his conduct is detrimental to our domestic intelligence operations." The memo—stamped TOP SECRET—went on to say: "At some point, Hoover has to be told who is president." Huston's final paragraph exemplified the White House paranoia: "For eighteen months we have watched people in this government ignore the president's orders, take actions to embarrass him, promote themselves at his expense, and generally make his job more difficult. It makes me fighting mad." Almost everyone outside a small circle was considered an enemy or a would-be traitor.

The most significant and reliable information we had was what had been revealed in Judge Sirica's courtroom. On March 23, after sentencing most of the Watergate burglars, Sirica read a letter that James McCord, one of the defendants, had written to him asking for guidance about how to be truthful in testifying to the grand jury and to the Senate committee. McCord's letter included a list of bombshell assertions: that political pressure had been applied to the defendants to plead guilty and remain silent, that perjury had been committed during the trial, and that there were others involved in the Watergate operation who had not been identified.

The suggestion that this scandal might reach well into the White House was followed by another major development. On April 6, John Dean, the White House counsel, contacted Dash and offered to cooperate. In his letter to Judge Sirica, McCord had named Dean as a White House staffer who "was knowledgeable of and involved in the

Watergate operation sequence." Dean was already meeting secretly with the special prosecutor and was to testify before the grand jury. He said he would turn over documents and offer himself to interviews with committee investigators. I wasn't in that first meeting, but when I saw the notes he provided, it was the first clue I had that the bungled burglary might have ties to the White House and the president himself. These developments dramatically increased interest in the hearings and opened up the very real possibility that the president of the United States had been involved in illegal activity.

Dean was a wunderkind who had come to Washington from Ohio. He was always well tailored, appropriate looking, clean cut. In my first encounter with him, Dean seemed more intent on bragging about the number of women he'd attracted than in offering high-minded views of the appropriate use of executive power. Dean was obviously skilled at self-preservation, and I was not confident that anything he would tell us would be true. I told Sam Dash, who was obviously pleased with the first "big fish" we'd caught, that we needed to independently verify the information Dean provided. After all, Nixon's people couldn't trust him. Why should we?

Dean, who had been appointed by Nixon to "probe" the Watergate break-in and involvement of White House aides in the matter, had previously declined to cooperate with the committee staff. Nixon had ordered White House aides not to testify, citing "executive privilege," a presidential prerogative that protects information within the president's immediate office from congressional scrutiny. The traditional use of this concept allowed the president to invoke it for anyone working in the office of the president. Of course, use of this device placed the executive effectually above the law. Ervin called it "executive poppycock."

Ervin was so incensed by the lack of cooperation that he issued what was called a "double-barreled challenge" to the White House. He threatened to send the Senate's sergeant at arms to arrest any White House aide who defied his subpoenas. After weeks of public pressure, Nixon offered to allow select aides to testify in secret, away from television cameras. Ervin immediately rejected the offer, arguing that the public had a right to hear from administration officials directly. The tough old country lawyer repeated his vow to order arrests. Meanwhile, Senator Weicker, whose Republican credentials added credibility to the committee, said that any White House aide refusing to testify publicly should resign.

The pressure on Dean intensified in the press. An article written on April 3 by the widely syndicated columnist Jack Anderson—one of the most read reporters in his day—quoted sources on the Ervin Committee saying they had found instances where Dean had committed perjury in response to questions from the FBI about Watergate. "It is a federal violation to make a false statement to the FBI," Anderson pointed out. Other news stories revealed that McCord had named Dean as one of the people behind the Watergate break-in, along with former attorney general John Mitchell and White House aide Jeb Magruder. The press began referring to Dean as one of Watergate's "chief plotters."

It took time to negotiate Dean's cooperation with the committee. As it happened, Senator Weicker lived near John Dean, and the Republican senator spent a considerable amount of time trying to get his neighbor to cooperate. With his reputation under siege, Dean began to distance himself from his boss. Leaks began to appear, reported even by conservative columnists Rowland Evans and Robert Novak, that Dean was urging Nixon to reconsider his refusal to allow him and other aides to appear before the committee in public session. Perhaps Dean was trying to save his own skin, since he had already begun cooperating with the committee without Nixon's knowledge. And apparently Dean won that battle with the president. On April 18, Nixon announced a stunning reversal. He would allow Dean and others to testify before the committee after all. Nixon also announced that Dean's probe into the Watergate matter had "categorically" proven that no one in the senior reaches of the government had committed any wrongdoing. "I condemn any attempt to cover up in this case," Nixon said in a press conference, "no matter who is involved."

In late April, while the Watergate probe was heating up, testimony was heard in the trial of the *U.S. v. Ellsberg* that exposed further examples of the Nixon administration's subterfuge and the president's habitual paranoia. Ellsberg's trial on federal charges of espionage, theft, and conspiracy had begun in Los Angeles in January 1973 before Judge William Matthew Byrne.

I respected Judge Byrne and know him personally. For this reason, when investigators sought to question him, I recused myself. But Byrne said he would talk only to me. On the phone, Byrne revealed that some time earlier, John Ehrlichman had asked to meet with him. They met on a park bench in Los Angeles, where one of the president's top aides offered Byrne a position as FBI director. It was clear to Byrne that the offer was being made only if the judge suppressed evidence in the Ellsberg trial about the administration's involvement in breaking into Ellsberg's psychiatrist's office. Byrne, being a man of integrity, of course refused the deal. The attempted bribe was a major revelation and the beginning of the end for senior Nixon officials.

On April 30, 1973, fewer than two weeks after Nixon allowed Dean and other aides to testify, the president announced the resignations of his two top aides, Ehrlichman and Bob Haldeman. He also said that John Dean had been fired. In a televised address to the nation, a clearly stressed and emotional Nixon tried to make Watergate a thing of the past—saying he accepted responsibility for mistakes in judgment by underlings and had been misled by advisors about the extent of linkages to the White House. If he thought that mea culpa would suffice to excuse the Watergate break-in and satisfy questions about his administration, he badly miscalculated the mood of the committee and of the public. Dean apparently had tried to get Nixon to grant him immunity from prosecution, but Nixon, realizing Dean was turning against him, refused. Only then did Dean turn to the committee. He was in search of friends.

In our first meeting with him, the trim, bespectacled Dean did not seem the slightest bit remorseful about turning against the president or the men with whom he had worked closely for years. Nor did he seem embarrassed by his own role in the administration's schemes. Instead, he was resentful and bitter toward them. He had not liked being publicly appointed by the president as the internal investigator of the Watergate break-in, a probe that he told us was never seriously undertaken.

There were many unsung heroes in the Watergate saga. John Dean was an oversung one. Many in the news media fell in love with him—an affair that for some lasts to this day—perhaps because he had a tremendous facility for remembering facts, delivered clever and earnest-sounding lines, and was blowing the whistle on a president whom many citizens disdained. The main narrative in the media soon became that Dean was a noble "man of conscience" who turned against his former boss and sacrificed his high position to expose wrongdoing. I never saw him that way. His main motive, understandably, was self-preservation.

Dean confirmed the existence of Nixon's infamous "enemies list." In fact there was actually more than one list. The initial one was expanded to include almost every major politician, business and labor leader, and journalist who had ever said anything bad about Nixon. Dean gave the list to us as part of his preparation for testimony. The enemies list was, of course, another stupid thing for the Nixon people to document. What did it mean? What had they intended to do with it? One strange plot Dean described was to incapacitate Jack Anderson, a columnist on the enemies list, by infecting his steering wheel with a substance that would make him unable to drive. Committee senators and staff listened to such things in disbelief, struggling to comprehend what we were hearing about the leaders of our democracy.

Dean told us another curious thing. During meetings in the Oval Office with the president, Nixon would occasionally walk away from him and mumble words that Dean couldn't hear. Nixon was an odd duck, but this was unusual even for him. Dean surmised that Nixon might have been taping their conversations. That suggestion certainly piqued our interest. Ironically, when Dean began to feel uncomfortable at the White House, he started taping conversations with his co-conspirators for his own purposes—including one with Jeb Magruder that he handed over to us. "John, can we talk here?" Magruder asked nervously at one point. "Yeah," Dean replied deceptively.

On May 17, 1973, Senator Ervin gaveled the hearings into session. All three major networks preempted soap operas, game shows, and other programming to broadcast the hearings live—with committee members, staff, and witnesses bathed in bright klieg lights. The hearings were rebroadcast by PBS in the evening, and rehashed during the networks' evening news. One survey found that 85 percent of all U.S. households tuned in to at least some portion of the hearings.

Ervin had announced that phase one of the hearings would cover the break-in and cover-up related to Watergate, phase two would involve campaign financing, and phase three would be for hearings on the "dirty tricks" operations. Press and public were eager for the show to begin. Unfortunately, none of the blockbuster witnesses were ready to testify. We were still interviewing them and conducting background investigations. We needed more time to prepare, so I fought to put on a guy who was innocuous. I was criticized at the time and later that we didn't start the hearings with a bang, but I think he set the scene by providing valuable background.

Therefore the hearings began much as our investigation did—with lower-level witnesses offering background and context. The first witness, at my behest, was Robert C. Odle Jr., the office manager of the Committee to Re-Elect the President, who provided background on CREEP's operations. Though unexciting, Bob could explain what CREEP was supposed to do, who operated within it, who controlled the organization, and how it related to the White House.

It was not until late June that John Dean appeared to testify. As everyone expected, he made major headlines. Dean implicated Nixon directly in the scandal. He testified that the president was intimately involved in discussions about covering up the Watergate break-in.

Dean's five days of testimony, June 25 through 29, riveted the country. He entered the hearing room accompanied by U.S. marshals who were also guarding his home after a death threat letter surfaced. Some of what he said in his full day's opening statement had been leaked and published in the press before, but seeing him live on TV coolly describing nefarious White House activities and the president's involvement with the cover-up was gripping. It was during the hearings that Dean shared with senators his famous warning to Nixon that "there is a cancer on the presidency." The White House had begun a counterattack the week before, when the hearings had been suspended suddenly while Nixon met with USSR president Leonid Brezhnev. Pro-Nixon columnists vilified the Judas, and even some who distrusted Nixon disparaged Dean. Republican National Committee chairman George H. W. Bush was among those delegated to blast Dean for "dragging the president into this thing." Bush questioned Dean's credibility, saying that his recollections appeared "a little hazy." After Dean's testimony, the Senate adjourned for the July 4 holiday, and the hearings didn't resume until July 10.

On July 12, I was having lunch with Sam Dash when he informed me that the White House was putting forward a surprise witness who was to testify that afternoon. We didn't know exactly what was planned, but we expected the witness would try to rebut the most damaging aspects of Dean's testimony—conversations that Dean claimed had involved the president.

"His name is Richard Moore," Dash said. "Know him?"

"I know him," I replied. Moore was a White House counsel who advised on public relations. He had worked with Dean and sat in on a number of the meetings with Dean and the president. Because I didn't trust Dean, I had gone on my own to interview Moore at his lawyer's office to get his recollections of various events and check his story against Dean's. I had also obtained White House logs to see if Dean's supposed dates and times of meetings matched with the official records.

"Great," Dash said. "He's your witness. He's going on right after lunch."

With less than an hour to prepare, I immediately abandoned my lunch, corralled Marc Lackritz, the investigator who had attended my earlier session with Moore, and ran out of the cafeteria. John Mitchell had just concluded two and a half days of testimony trying to respond to what Dean had revealed about him. We had been so busy with Mitchell that I was unprepared for any surprise witness. I hoped I might run into Moore as I made my way to the hearing room. As I recalled, he was gregarious and friendly. I figured if I saw him, I could find out what he was planning to say. (The White House had violated our standard agreement with its witnesses by refusing to release Moore's prepared opening statement.) Fortuitously, I found him standing in the hallway. He remembered me, and we chatted amiably. I posed a series of questions, the same I planned to ask in the hearing room, which he did not hesitate to answer.

Moore's opening statement was long, detailed, and appeared to have been carefully written. He was clearly there to discredit everything Dean had said. His opening statement read, "Much of my testimony will involve my recollections about conversations with the president and John Dean. The good faith recollections of one party to a conversation often differ from those of the other." As he talked, Lackritz and I scoured through notes from our earlier interview, trying to get a handle on what questions to ask. The hearing was the center of the country's attention and being carried live on television channels across America. I felt incredible pressure and also felt completely unprepared. I knew that if Moore's testimony succeeded in disputing Dean's recollection of events, it would seriously undermine not only Dean but the committee's slowly building case. So much of our credibility was resting on him.

In finding a sympathetic witness, the White House probably could not have done better than Moore. It was hard not to like him. He was a friendly, older gentleman, and freely admitted that he had no real line of authority in the White House. At one point, he compared himself, endearingly, to the president's old shoe. He admitted that one of his first jobs for the administration was to create what he called a "warm, lovable" image for the austere John Mitchell. Moore told us all of this good-naturedly.

I knew the risk of hounding a pleasant, amiable witness, but I had no choice but to try to poke holes in his testimony wherever I could. Borrowing from my experience cross-examining Boyd Douglas during the Berrigan trial, I asked a series of questions to challenge his memory and put him off-balance. I noticed quickly that his answers were different from those he'd given me when I'd interviewed him formally before. Even more troubling, they varied from the answers he'd given me in the corridor just moments earlier.

Despite the White House's intentions, Moore's testimony soon began to falter. A litigator can feel when an examination is going his way. A kind of rhythm develops where the questions become rapid-fire and the answers from the witness become increasingly confused. I felt that now. At one point I asked him about a meeting held at the White House on June 30, 1972—a key date in Moore's earlier statements and just days after the Watergate break-in. "There is nothing about that date that helps me out," he confessed. After I caught Moore in a series of apparent contradictions over his various statements, Moore blurted out, "I'll let the answer stand, whatever it was," leading to laughter in the hearing room and, undoubtedly, groans over at the White House.

In terms of prosecutorial art, I felt it was a home run. You win encounters with a witness like Moore by watching his body language, observing him as he leans to his lawyer, asking for advice. You stare at his features to look for signs of uncertainty or deception. The audience, the cameras, don't matter. But it is one thing to win on points and quite another to win in front of a jury—especially if that jury consists of tens of millions of people.

The reaction to my encounter with Richard Moore ran the gamut. "As an answer to John Dean," the columnist Mary McGrory wrote, "Moore blew up on the launching pad." McGrory, who had found herself on Nixon's enemies list, congratulated me at the end of the hearing. In her column she called Moore "the white-haired bumbler." Talking about our exchange, McGrory wrote, "If it had been a prize fight, the referee would have stopped it." The reviews weren't all like that.

Until the Moore cross-examination, I hadn't understood the power of television to engage an audience. The hearings became their own kind of soap opera for the public, in which many viewers saw an aggressive young man picking on a nice old man, and they didn't like it. When I returned to my office, our secretary immediately asked, "What did you do?" She said the phones hadn't stopped ringing with complaints about how badly I'd treated Moore. The backlash was exacerbated in a *New York Times* column by William Safire, a former Nixon speechwriter, who accused me of unleashing "a vicious attack" on a kindly old man. Safire made some brutal charges: that I was "bedazzled" by my moment "in the limelight" and that my actions were "proof that the purpose of the Ervin Committee is not to bring out the truth but to bring down the president." Since Safire had recently left his job as a Nixon speechwriter, I shouldn't have been surprised by his diatribe. He was, in effect, still working for the White House. After Safire's syndicated column appeared in newspapers across the country, the committee was flooded with letters and telegrams. A surprising number disparaged me as a Jew.

The negative attention undoubtedly spooked Sam Dash, who became visibly excited whenever things became tense. But the most important verdict, at least for me personally, came from Senator Ervin. When my cross-examination was finished, he leaned over to me and whispered, "Terry, I'm glad we didn't get rid of you. That was a great job." However angry Americans might have been at me and my tactics, very few people gave Richard Moore any credibility by the time our encounter had ended. (Some months later, I received a transcription of the tape of Nixon's meeting with Moore when they discussed Watergate and Moore's impending testimony. Moore seemed far more familiar with the details of the cover-up in that conversation than he did in testifying before the committee. At one point, Nixon advised Moore to have a "hazy recollection" during his appearance. Moore certainly followed orders.)

Senator Ervin, meanwhile, was quickly becoming a household name, and a popular one at that. Across the country, people wore "Senator Sam" T-shirts and buttons. But a minority continued to disparage the hearings. The *Dallas Morning News*, for example, labeled the hearings "a show trial." Other commentaries defended Nixon and condemned what they called a Democrat-inspired witch-hunt.

My team of investigators was also getting some attention. One paper called them "Lenzner's Longhairs." Many members of my team, in turn, started to call me "Columbo." My appearance was generally described as "rumpled," like the eponymous TV character, and my desk and every other horizontal surface were piled with papers. Not everyone had an effusive view of our activities. A profile of the committee, published in *Rolling Stone*, offered my team and me a mixed review. "Lenzner runs the most dynamic group on the committee's staff, a group which has conducted well over half of all the majority's interviews and which has delivered most of the committee's thunderbolts," the article said. It then went on to quote an anonymous staffer, who said, "Everyone hates Lenzner and his crew because they think they're better than everyone else and let them know it." I hope that wasn't the case, but we were a hard-charging bunch, and sometimes that caused others of the committee to feel bruised in the process.

While Moore's testimony was concluding, another witness appeared before committee investigators in private session. Then administrator of the Federal Aviation Administration, Alexander Butterfield was a middle-aged man who had formerly worked as a White House aide and deputy to Chief of Staff Bob Haldeman. Butterfield's interview with committee staffers was uneventful until one of the Republican lawyers working for Fred Thompson took his turn to ask some questions. Familiar with what our investigators were asking in our interviews with witnesses, the lawyer borrowed one of our standard questions. He asked Butterfield, for example, if he was aware of a taping system in the White House. It was a clear demonstration of the bipartisan atmosphere on the committee that the question was asked by a Republican counsel.

Butterfield stunned everyone present with his reply. "I wish you hadn't asked that question," he said, "but yes, there is." He confided that Nixon taped most of his conversations surreptitiously. The president used the tapes, Butterfield said, "to record things for posterity, for the Nixon library."

Since Butterfield had not been considered a major witness, neither Sam Dash nor I was present when he divulged this. In fact, we were meeting in Dash's office after Moore's testimony concluded when

Scott Armstrong came running in. He was out of breath and exhilarated. "The hearings have exploded," he announced, telling us that Butterfield had confirmed the existence of a taping system. "We've got 'em by the balls."

I felt right then that this was a game changer. I went to my office and drafted a subpoena for President Nixon, directing him to turn over any tape recordings and other documentation in his possession related to Watergate. Our knowledge of the tapes allowed me to be bold and seize the opportunity. I never thought that Nixon would respond to the subpoena, but serving it would put further pressure on the widening cracks in his administration. Public attacks brought informants out of the woodwork.

The Republican staffers had a completely opposite response; they thought the existence of the tapes was a good thing because it would prove Nixon was telling the truth. Some Democrats were nervous about that possibility as well. At least one Democratic senator called to warn me not to pursue the Nixon tapes, believing that Butterfield must have divulged that for a reason. The tapes had to be a Nixon trap.

Shortly after Butterfield described Nixon's tapes in a public hearing on July 16, Chairman Ervin called a meeting of committee members and the staff. After some discussion, the committee voted to issue a subpoena for the tapes. I told the chairman that I'd already taken the liberty of preparing one and offered to pass it around. "Terrific," Ervin said. I thought fleetingly of the irony that I was involved in subpoenaing the titular head of government who had fired me as director of Legal Services of the poor.

Another day of hearings was under way when the final version of the subpoena was printed. Our plan was to serve the subpoena immediately, and I was in a rush to get Ervin and Baker to sign it. I went behind the rostrum and asked for their signatures. Baker looked at my version and hesitated over one line. As I had written it, following standard procedure, the subpoena stated to the president, "We direct you" to hand over the tapes and documents. Congress couldn't direct the president to do something like that, Baker said, any more than the president could direct Congress to do something. He asked me to change the word "direct" to "request." It was a crucial fix. If we had served that subpoena as written, Nixon could have turned the issue into a debate over the separation of powers—whether the Constitution allowed Congress to direct the executive to comply with its orders. That issue might have gone all the way to the Supreme Court before it was settled and might well have derailed the entire case.

There was a brief discussion about subpoenaing the president to come physically to Congress to testify before the committee. No one was confident that it was a good idea. Up to that point, media coverage and popular support for the committee's inquiry was mostly positive. No one wanted to test that by dragging the president in if we didn't need to.

I had been the one to draft the subpoena of the president—the first ever issued by a congressional committee—so I was tasked with presenting it in person at the White House. Dash's deputy, Rufus Edmisten, arranged to accompany me.

Once it was decided to issue the subpoena, the committee choreographed its service with the White House. No one on either side wanted a confrontation or any surprises. Chairman Ervin and Senator Baker were both intent on having the subpoena served professionally, civilly, and without any hint of partisanship. I agreed with that completely. This was a very grave moment for the country. Everyone seemed to understand that. I remembered when the White House tried, almost successfully, to keep me off the committee, which was an appropriate red flag not to allow "payback" to sneak into the scenario of serving this historic subpoena. I concluded that the only way to proceed was as low-key and off-the-radar as possible.

Unfortunately the press somehow caught wind of the timing of our arrival at the White House. Before the end of the transaction, I would be able to determine how that happened. Reporters were shouting questions. Rufus and I entered the side door of the West Wing and made our way to the White House counsel's office. As we walked down the hall, I spotted a few people I'd known during my tenure in the administration. They gave me thumbs-ups or whispered, "Keep it up." It was heartening to see that not everyone in the White House was proud of what had been going on there.

I knew and respected John Dean's replacement as White House counsel, Leonard Garment, whom I'd met informally on other occasions in Washington. He met us at the White House counsel's office, along with another Nixon attorney.

"Len," I began, "I'm sorry to see you in this situation. I appreciate your letting us in and making this work smoothly."

"I'm glad we're all doing this right," Garment replied.

I handed over the subpoena and the lawyers accepted it. The exchange was cordial and professional. Then, at that very moment, Rufus whipped something out from his suit coat pocket. I saw that it was a miniature copy of the United States Constitution. With a dramatic flourish, he handed it to Nixon's lawyers.

Not knowing how to react, the lawyers took it. But they were not happy. Nor was I. I was embarrassed and infuriated by Rufus's gratuitous flourish. It made us look partisan and small-minded, like we were rubbing it in. The honor I felt as a key player in this historic event almost vanished. And I realized that Rufus had tainted and threatened the committee's claim to bipartisanship. I figured Edmisten also had alerted the press to our activities. He wanted the coverage.

Once we were out of earshot of Nixon's attorneys, I snapped at Rufus. "You should have told me you were going to try to pull some crap like that." Rufus just laughed. He got that story into the next day's newspapers, which was all that mattered to him. As we left the White House, there was a crushing crowd of reporters waiting and I attempted to repress any sign that I might feel triumphant or gleeful.

I was incredibly cognizant of the responsibility, after being fired by a senior member of the Nixon administration, to be a part of the process that included the first-ever congressional subpoena of a president. But I also remembered some advice that Peter Fleming, one of John Mitchell's lawyers, had given me. "Just remember all this is going to end at some point," he said. "And you are going to be back with the rest of us. Don't get carried away."

Rufus was not similarly restrained. He was already running for office in North Carolina (and was elected attorney general in 1974). Members of the press were only too happy to help him, as long as he helped them.

Indeed, the Watergate hearings brought out the best and worst of the Washington press corps. Many reporters were enormously helpful to our investigation. But the competition between them to get the "big story" was fierce. Bob Woodward was not the only one who worked sources, or tried to. The few direct contacts I had with Bob Woodward and Carl Bernstein gave me a glimpse of how the duo operated.

In the early days, Bernstein called me at the committee and said something like, "Terry, I've heard such and such. I am going to count to five, and if you don't deny what I just told you, I'm going to assume that you are confirming it." I didn't operate like that, and I told him so. True or not, leaks could compromise the investigation and give advance knowledge to potential witnesses about what we knew or were examining. Some witnesses began citing the leaks as a way to avoid testifying. After a few such efforts, Woodward and Bernstein stopped calling me. They had plenty of other sources. In one instance the duo managed to get grand jury transcripts from a court stenographer—a major violation of the rules protecting grand jury secrecy.

Lesley Stahl of CBS News was a friend of mine and one of the few newswomen covering Watergate. As a diligent investigative reporter, she managed to get a number of scoops. We finally became fed up by the leaks she was receiving from within the committee and decided to do something about it. We told the suspected leaker, a member of our committee staff, that we were about to subpoena Nixon's longtime secretary, Rose Mary Woods, at a certain date and time. Sure enough, Lesley Stahl got the leak. She was at the White House for some time waiting in vain for the subpoena to be delivered. Finally, she called me at my office.

"Terry," she said, "I've heard that you are about to subpoena Rose Mary Woods. I've got two camera crews here. Where the hell are you guys?"

"Lesley, I'm sorry to tell you this," I replied, "but I don't know what you're talking about."

Another reporter friend was the journalist Seymour Hersh, who had won a Pulitzer Prize for reporting the infamous massacre by American troops of Vietnamese villagers in My Lai. Hersh, a neighbor, came over to my house for breakfast one morning without an invitation. "I know you are feeding stuff to the *Washington Post*," he told me. "I'm going to start sourcing you in my stories if you don't talk to me too." I replied that, first of all, I was not leaking to the *Post*. And then I asked him to leave my house. On another occasion, the columnist Jack Anderson called to ask me to confirm that Nixon's lawyer, Herb Kalmbach, had testified privately to the committee a day earlier. He told me exactly what Kalmbach had said and wanted me to attest to it. "If you want to confirm the story," Anderson said, "I'll meet you somewhere near 1600 Pennsylvania Avenue so I can attribute the leak to a 'source close to the White House.'" *How inventive*, I thought. "If you don't confirm it," he continued, "I'll source it to you anyway." I didn't bite—and he never sourced me to anything in his story.

The committee's subpoena of the Nixon tapes set off a long and public battle between Congress and the president—a battle that made it all the way to the Supreme Court before Nixon was ordered to turn over the tapes, a year later, on July 25, 1974. But when I walked out of the White House in the summer of 1973, I still didn't think any of this would lead to Nixon's resignation. Nor, as far as I knew, did any member of the committee. Three months after the hearings began, Senator Talmadge told the press, "You have to assume there's not enough evidence to impeach the president." The Georgia Democrat claimed that "the climate of the country would not support it." At that moment, at least, he might have been correct.

W hile all of this was going on, I was still collecting evidence in preparation for an eventual hearing on dirty tricks. "Dirty tricks" constituted something far worse than the usual political games that both parties play against each other. In this case, there was evidence that the Nixon team used fraud and misrepresentation to damage Democratic candidates in an attempt to alter the election process. I suspected that Nixon tactics were behind the unexpected collapse of Senator Edmund Muskie's campaign for the Democratic presidential nomination in 1972 and the subsequent selection of a politically weaker candidate, Senator George McGovern. The idea of one major party using dirty tricks to destroy the leading candidate of the other party offended me. Such actions undermine the electoral process and threaten the very foundations of democracy. No one knows who is pulling the strings. Voters are supposed to be able to choose between candidates on their merits, not have their choice made for them by the other party.

Early on, the counsel for Senator Kennedy's Administrative Practices Committee, which had begun an investigation in late 1972, gave me material on dirty tricks that they'd uncovered and suggested there was much more yet to be found.

I began the dirty tricks investigation by putting together a chart of all the people named as well as their subordinates, secretaries, and other associates. The first two names that came out of media reports were a young Nixon aide named Dwight Chapin and a Nixon supporter and employee of the Committee to Re-Elect the President named Donald Segretti.

Senator Kennedy's committee staff entertained a theory that the root of all the scandals in the Nixon White House lay in the hands of Segretti. When we met with him, I was surprised. Segretti struck me as far from being a mastermind. We learned that Dwight Chapin, a senior White House official and graduate of the University of Southern California, had put together a group—eventually led by Segretti—to help Nixon in 1972, adopting the dirty tricks tactics. He referred repeatedly to a man named Dick Tuck, a Democrat who had pulled various pranks on Republicans like Nixon for years.

When Nixon campaigned for the Senate from California in 1952, Tuck was a student at the University of California, Santa Barbara. One of his professors, unwisely, asked Tuck to advance a Nixon speech. Tuck rented a large room, made sure the crowd of attendees was small, and then delivered a long, boring introduction of Nixon, who was taken aback when Tuck claimed that Nixon would be discussing the International Monetary Fund. After the 1960 Kennedy-Nixon debate, Tuck hired an elderly woman to hug Nixon and tell him, in front of television cameras, that Kennedy had won. It was madcap stuff. Tuck's tricks had become legend in California and beyond, and Segretti thought he could employ them too.

Chapin didn't think he had done anything wrong in promoting the president's reelection efforts. He claimed the standard defense we heard from everyone involved in such activities, that "everybody did it," that the tactics they employed were not exceptional. Yet what Segretti and Chapin undertook for Nixon was significantly different. There were operatives performing some silly Dick Tuck–style pranks, to be sure, such as ordering pizzas to be delivered to a rival campaign. But much of what Nixon's operatives undertook deviated from those practices. They were not meant to be funny, or ever to be disclosed to the American people.

At the heart of these tactics were, once again, the president's paranoia and feelings of victimization. Richard Nixon narrowly lost his first presidential bid to John F. Kennedy in 1960, and then lost a bitter election for governor of California in 1962. When he finally won the presidential election in 1968, Nixon's margin of victory was one of the narrowest in American history—0.7 percent of the popular vote. Nixon's team expected with good reason that his 1972 reelection was likely to be very tough. The list of Democrats considering running against him was broad and formidable.

Increasingly, attention focused on Edmund Muskie, a well-respected senator who had been the Democratic vice-presidential candidate in 1968. Through much of 1971 and as late as February 1972, the Gallup poll had Nixon and Muskie in a virtual tie. In February the margin was Nixon by one point, 43–42 percent. George Gallup asserted at the time that "Senator Muskie, the current top choice of the Democratic voters for the nomination, represents the strongest challenger to Nixon." But after Muskie's campaign was attacked through a dirty trick, his candidacy lost traction.

When the dirty tricks hearings began in the fall of 1973, public interest was beginning to wane. The Watergate Committee had been in operation for nearly five months, and so much had been revealed that the American people were on overload. Though transcripts of some of Nixon's taped conversations had been released by the White House, the president was still holding on to the actual tapes themselves. People speculated what they might reveal about the president's role in the break-in and cover-up. At the same time, many observers, including those in the media, believed that dirty tricks were common in both parties' campaigns. The Republicans, in fact, were vowing to expose Democrat dirty tricks during the hearing—which noticeably spooked the Democratic senators.

Patrick J. Buchanan, a pugnacious Nixon speechwriter and a die-hard true believer, was to be one of our key witnesses. As a result of a subpoena, we'd received a series of memos from Buchanan that revealed what the Nixon campaign had decided to undertake—an organized, perpetual campaign to sabotage Senator Muskie.

When called before the committee under questioning led by Dash, Buchanan was brittle, unyielding, and belligerent. He responded to Dash's questions with sarcastic jibes that made the committee look foolish. Buchanan accused the committee of a "covert campaign of vilification" against him. He was on offense from the beginning, demanding to know how so many leaks against him had found their way into the press. Buchanan was so effective in complaining about news leaks that even Ervin and Baker expressed sympathy for him. When asked by Dash if he wrote attack strategy memos against the Democrats, Buchanan replied unapologetically in the affirmative. What else, he suggested, would you expect from a fierce Nixon partisan? He denied any role in illegal activities, denied that dirty tricks had been done in Senator Muskie's candidacy, and denied that the Nixon campaign forces had, in effect, selected McGovern as Nixon's opponent.

The reviews of Buchanan's testimony were brutal. One article called it the committee's "Buchanan fiasco." The columnists Evans and Novak called Buchanan's appearance a "humiliation" for the committee and "a meticulous demolition of Dash." I was named as "the Rasputin of the committee" who had gotten into a heated argument with Fred Thompson over the hearings, a charge that was not true. "Buchanan," another columnist wrote, "was the best witness for the Nixon administration to appear before the Watergate Committee." I could not argue with that.

Though not riveting television, the hearings did produce disturbing information about the Nixon campaign. In testimony, Nixon operatives admitted to a long series of subterranean actions expressly designed to influence the choice of the Democratic nominee. Donald Segretti and others admitted breaking the law.

One witness before the committee, Martin Douglas Kelly, was involved in the attacks on the Democrats. He said that what had started out as pranks became "more and more intense." He confessed to writing bogus letters and fake news releases, and distributing misleading posters and advertisements. Senator Muskie was "the principal target" from the beginning, he said.

Segretti admitted to anti-Muskie activities of broad scope, including paying for an advertisement saying that Muskie opposed a black vice president and distributing a letter on Muskie stationery accusing his Democratic opponents of sexual improprieties. Evidence strongly suggested that an infamous letter dubbed the "Canuck letter" that led to Muskie's withdrawal from the presidential primary race was one of the dirty tricks.* The anonymous letter was printed in the Manchester *Union Leader*, an influential New Hampshire paper, two weeks before the New Hampshire primary. It accused Muskie of using an ethnic slur, "Canucks," in referring to Americans of French-Canadian descent, many of whom lived in New Hampshire and Maine. And the paper reported unflattering attacks on the senator's wife. Muskie was so outraged by the smear campaign that he denounced it and the newspaper's publisher in a famously emotional speech the week before the primary. As he stood angrily in the falling snow, tears appeared to be falling on his cheek. Reporters claimed Muskie was crying, a charge of softheartedness from which he never recovered. Whether it was true or not—Muskie and his aides denied he actually had cried—this event swayed enough New Hampshire Democrats to vote for George McGovern, giving Muskie a much smaller margin than his campaign had expected. Republicans pounced on the implications of Muskie's outburst, with Republican chairman Bob Dole saying Muskie's tears revealed his "instability." To this day, "Muskie crying in the snow" is synonymous in political circles of a single incident destroying an otherwise promising campaign.

---

*It was later reported that the "Canuck letter" was written by Kenneth Clawson, a White House political aide.

Muskie's campaign chairman testified to a series of activities that he blamed on Nixon forces: vital documents were stolen from their offices, a rumor circulated that Muskie had fathered a black child, and Democratic voters were awakened by late-night phone calls from callers claiming to be from the Muskie campaign. But by the time this was the focus of the hearings, few people seemed to care.

Muskie himself charged the Nixon administration with "a systematic campaign of sabotage," citing the Canuck letter as Exhibit A. Senator Muskie was by far the most potent threat to Nixon's reelection, and I remain convinced that the dirty tricks activities fatally damaged his candidacy. Through an audacious and unprecedented campaign of slurs and misleading letters and advertisements, the Nixon forces chipped away at Muskie every day. It is one thing to attack a political opponent transparently with campaign ads and direct confrontation from surrogates. I felt it was quite another to mislead voters and make them believe the Democrat was making statements that he never made. It was also ingenious, in that by using a small amount of money to destroy their leading rival in the primaries, the GOP saved the more considerable cost of having to fight Muskie in the general election.

What would have happened if Muskie had not been seen as breaking down in New Hampshire as a result of dirty tricks? Might he have gone on to be the Democrats' nominee instead of George McGovern? As an experienced senator, a more centrist and certainly more seasoned campaigner than McGovern, might Muskie have been elected and denied Nixon a second term?

Though there was no smoking gun in the dirty tricks hearings— no secret tapes, no blockbuster revelations, no White House aide warning of a cancer on the presidency—I was surprised by the public and the media reaction. *Rolling Stone* magazine, for one, mocked me for calling "some of the dullest witnesses of the hearings." Only one network carried the testimony live, and then only for a day. And some newspapers dutifully reported that only one or two senators were in attendance during some of the sessions.

After the hearings, I sent around draft legislation to make some of the activities undertaken by Nixon forces federal crimes. We did not get a single senator's response. To this day, there are assorted dirty tricks being waged in an effort to turn an election. In 2000, for example, Senator John McCain was on his way to winning the South Carolina primary against George W. Bush when phone calls went around the state claiming that McCain had fathered an illegitimate black child. It is not clear if that allegation turned the election away from McCain, but it certainly didn't help. With the rise of super PACs, when any billionaire can fund a smear campaign, we will see more dirty tricks. The Nixon legacy continues. Just recently, we've learned of fraudulent voter registration cards in ten Florida counties that were submitted by canvassers hired by the Republican Party. And the *Washington Post* reported on September 25, 2012, that Virginia voters had received anonymous text messages accusing the Democratic Senate candidate of calling for a "radical new tax on all Americans."

On September 29, 1973, Rose Mary Woods disclosed in court testimony that as she was reviewing one of the tapes discussing the Watergate break-in in the Oval Office, she had, in her words, made a "terrible mistake." She claimed she inadvertently taped over about five minutes of the tape and then discovered a "gap" amounting to eighteen and a half minutes. For that period of time, all a listener could hear on the tape was a buzz.

Woods's legendary loyalty to Nixon is now well documented. But back then, she was uncharted territory. She was tough as nails when we interviewed her in an executive session to prepare for our committee hearings on a money trail leading to Howard Hughes. Her responses to questions were curt and barely civil. If we were even slightly imprecise in the wording of a question, she let us have it. She did not come across as a person who made "terrible mistakes." She also gave us no information that was remotely useful. When our interview with her concluded, I was glad to see her leave.

Based on my meeting with her, my instincts, and my own experience looking into the workings of the Nixon White House, I have my own theory about the eighteen-and-a-half-minute gap. I didn't then and don't now think it was an accident. I think the missing minutes included a discussion by the president ordering the break-in. I am convinced he ordered it, because I don't believe his aides would have done something like that without his approval. My sense is that Nixon himself, or perhaps Woods on his orders, deleted the material. And Woods felt protected as a woman and a close member of Nixon's staff. But we will probably never know the truth with absolute certainty.

The other lingering question asked by many at the time was why Nixon didn't destroy the tapes as soon as Butterfield revealed them. The president could have destroyed them before I served the subpoena. One theory is that Nixon—ever interested in accumulating wealth— kept the tapes in order to sell them after he left office and get a huge tax write-off. My impression is that Nixon was so delusional he didn't think we'd ever be able to get to them. He thought his "executive privilege" claims would hold up.

On October 20, 1973, President Nixon fired Special Prosecutor Archibald Cox and accepted the resignations of his attorney general, Elliot Richardson, and deputy attorney general Bill Ruckelshaus in what became known as "the Saturday Night Massacre." Cox's removal led to widespread outrage—as further evidence that Nixon was trying to cover up the scandal. The great irony was that had Archie Cox succeeded in his earlier efforts to keep the Ervin Committee hearings from being televised, Nixon might have gotten away with this. But because of the many disclosures emanating from the hearings, the public was well aware that the White House was involved in a series of illegal activities. They viewed the firing of Cox as yet another sinister act.

It was not until partial transcripts of Nixon's tapes were finally released on April 30, 1974, that I believed for the first time that the president might be impeached. There were bombshell revelations, such as a conversation between Nixon and Haldeman that discussed the use of the deputy director of the CIA to stop the FBI's investigation of the break-in. Nixon admitted, "You open that scab, there's a hell of a lot of things and that we just feel that it would be very detrimental to have this thing go any further." The mood at the White House, which for months had been animated and determined, turned to shock and bewilderment. I sensed this when I called the White House press secretary, Ron Ziegler, and asked if I could meet with him for an interview.

For more than a year, Ziegler had been loyally and fiercely defending Nixon on Watergate and insisting on his innocence. When I saw the press secretary that evening at the White House, he looked exhausted. The press had all gone home by the time I arrived, and the West Wing itself was largely empty and quiet. And dark.

"You know what?" Ziegler said. "Let's do this down in the press room."

I was accompanied by Marc Lackritz and Scott Armstrong. Ziegler took us to the press room and gestured for us to sit in seats where the reporters usually sat. Then he walked to the podium and waited for us to ask questions, as if this were one of his daily press conferences. It was utterly bizarre. One of the last Nixon loyalists still standing, he no longer had the energy for denials and obfuscation. I thought to myself, *These guys are falling apart.* One of the last great defenders of the Nixon White House was now sputtering out.

CHAPTER 4

THE SECRET IN HANK'S SAFE

R ichard Nixon was a man who saw enemies everywhere—among the elites he despised, the Democrats, the Kennedy family, the media, all the people who'd looked down on him when he was younger. He took office determined to be impervious to them and to get back at them. That was why he hired men like Caulfield and Ulasewicz—to be enforcers against those he thought wanted to do him harm.

Another motivating factor for the president was money. Nixon was intent on accumulating financial and material security so that he would never be poor or beholden to anyone again. This led him to become entangled with one of the most powerful men in the world. That decades-long relationship, I came to learn, was the real secret behind the Watergate scandal. It involved a third attempted break-in that the country knew nothing about.

Donald Nixon pursued success as much as did his slightly older brother, though without similar success. Only one year younger than Richard, and cheerfully ambitious, Donald was always just one venture away from the big score. He was used to being overshadowed by Richard, who at forty-three had achieved fame, power, and national celebrity as vice president of the United States. Donald hoped to reap some of those benefits for himself.

In 1956, Don hatched a new entrepreneurial scheme: a hamburger-joint franchise originating in his native Whittier, California. He had already opened a drive-in, followed by Nixon's Family Restaurant, whose racy logo featured a man in kilt and tam-o'-shanter riding a bicycle. Don had taken out costly loans by then and needed a wealthy patron. He was surprised and pleased by how quickly he found an investor. And not just any investor, but the wealthiest man in the country.

Howard Hughes proved to be remarkably enthusiastic about the prospects of the Nixon Burger chain, despite the fact that few people in California, or anywhere else for that matter, were clamoring for "the Nixon burger." Hughes, a self-made billionaire, movie mogul, aviator, and industrialist, offered Richard Nixon's younger brother a $205,000 loan (the equivalent of $1.6 million today). The loan was not only interest-free, it lacked a payment schedule (indeed, it would never be repaid). In return, all the Nixon family had to offer as collateral was a virtually worthless lot, valued at just $13,000, in their hometown of Whittier.

And so, on December 10, 1956, one month after her elder son, Richard, won reelection as Dwight D. Eisenhower's vice president, Mrs. Hannah Nixon signed over the deed to Lot 10 on Whittier Boulevard. In my career, I have seen many times how seemingly trivial events can have outsized consequences. And American political history is replete with ne'er-do-wells complicating the lives of their president brothers. In many ways, the document Hannah Nixon signed that day—coupled with his brother's outsized ambition—haunted Richard Nixon for the rest of his life.

Hughes's connection to the Nixon family surfaced several times in

Richard Nixon's career. In the final days of his 1960 election battle with John F. Kennedy, columnist Drew Pearson reported the existence of a "secret loan" arranged by Howard Hughes to Nixon's little brother in exchange for political favors. The revelations infuriated Nixon, who blamed them for his narrow loss.

Again, in 1962, when Nixon was leading in his campaign for governor of California, the "Hughes loan" emerged in the newspapers. Nixon lost that race too. In both elections—1960 and 1962—Nixon hurt himself by denying knowledge of the loan and making other statements that were later proved to be untrue.

By 1972, as Nixon sought reelection to the presidency, the office he had finally attained in 1968, Howard Hughes became something of a preoccupation. Nixon had good reason to worry about whether revelations about a secret Hughes loan might resurface. He knew that Donald was not the only member of the Nixon family to have benefited from the Hughes fortune. That was the secret lurking in Hank Greenspun's safe in Las Vegas—which I believe answers the last lingering question of the Watergate break-in: Why?

In August of 1973, the televised hearings were in recess, and I had a brief opportunity to catch my breath. Seated in my small office in the basement of the Russell Senate Office Building, I reviewed testimony, including John Dean's.

I was particularly intrigued by Dean's calm description of Operation Gemstone, a series of schemes to thwart the Democrats that was launched in the office of the attorney general and outlined by G. Gordon Liddy. Some of Liddy's proposals were ludicrous—such as kidnapping radicals and holding them in Mexico. More feasible ideas included breaking into the Democratic National Committee headquarters at the Watergate office building, and also breaking into the safe of a man named Hank Greenspun. James McCord, one of the

Watergate burglars, had testified that the idea behind the Greenspun break-in related to "blackmail-type information on Democratic
candidates."

Investigators sometimes operate on nothing but a hunch. A few
questions stuck in my head: Who was Hank Greenspun? And what did
he have that could possibly interest the top officials of the Nixon administration? I didn't recall any reporter or columnist asking these
questions. The press was focused on the cover-up, Nixon's tapes, and all
the other revelations of the hearings reported so widely in the press. But
letting news headlines decide the parameters of a case is a common investigative mistake that can prevent you from seeing the larger picture
and what's lurking on the periphery that may be significant.

When you encounter an unknown in an investigation, you run it
down. So I assigned a researcher to find out whatever he could on
Hank Greenspun. There was no Internet in those days, of course, so
our primary resources were old newspaper articles that were accessible
in print or on microfiche at the Library of Congress. We learned that
Greenspun was the publisher and editor of the *Las Vegas Sun* newspaper. He had been convicted of violating the Neutrality Act by providing arms to Zionists in Palestine in 1947 and had been pardoned by
President Kennedy in 1961. That was enough to give me the sense he
was something of a colorful character. I decided to give him a call.

"Mr. Greenspun," I said, "my name is Terry Lenzner. I am with the
Ervin Committee. I've been looking at this Gemstone plan, and you're
named in it as a target."

A forceful voice came through the other end of the line. Herman
Greenspun—everyone called him "Hank"—was eager to talk to a
Watergate investigator. In fact, he seemed puzzled as to why no one
had called him earlier. Greenspun knew all about the plan to break
into his safe. The Nixon people, he said, were putting out a "bogus"
story that their interest in the safe had to do with "blockbuster" information Greenspun supposedly held related to Senator Edmund

Muskie. Greenspun said that explanation was bullshit, or words to that effect. The only thing he knew about Muskie was that he'd paid a fine for a hunting violation. That's not what the Nixon people were looking for, he said. He indicated there was much more to this story than we knew.

I told him I wanted to fly out to Las Vegas to talk with him. I could not stay long, since I had to return to D.C. to prepare for the dirty tricks hearings.

"Great," he said. "Come on out." He gave me the name of a hotel near his office, and I booked a commercial flight from Washington.

The Vegas I arrived in was not remotely like the city it is today. In the mid-1970s, most of the large casino hotels that now line Las Vegas Boulevard had not yet been built. The first, the MGM Grand, was just opening its doors. The offices of the *Las Vegas Sun* were on Highland Drive, not far from the popular casinos of the day. I entered the building, walked past the newsroom, and met Hank Greenspun in his office.

Hank was seated at his desk in rolled-up white shirtsleeves. He was tall with narrow shoulders and had a large, expressive face. Like his hometown, he was exuberant and lively. Both the city and the man were known for betting big and taking sometimes dangerous risks. At the beginning of our meeting, Greenspun and I engaged in small talk, just as I had been taught to do in Mississippi—talking about the city of Las Vegas, the newspaper, the weather—to get our bearings. It didn't take long for him to decide that he was comfortable enough with me to open up.

As he regaled me with stories of his colorful life, Hank gave no indication that he was trying to glorify himself. He was open and forthright, and conceded things he'd done wrong. My impression was that Hank was a gutsy guy who knew everyone and everything going on in his city.

He was a Brooklyn-born Jew who served in the army under

General George Patton during World War II. After the war, Greenspun settled in Las Vegas, where he worked as a PR flack for the Flamingo Hotel, operated by Bugsy Siegel, a flamboyant member of the Genovese crime family and one of the architects of Las Vegas. When Bugsy was gunned down, Hank was out of a job.

After he bought the *Las Vegas Sun*, he saw himself as a crusader. He told me he went on trial for "inciting murder or assassination" when, in one of his typically pointed columns, he suggested that Senator Joseph McCarthy kill himself before one of the victims of his anti-Communist "smears" took on that job from him. Clearly not one lacking for a turn of phrase, in another column Greenspun labeled the senator "the queer that made Milwaukee famous." Senator McCarthy considered a lawsuit but shortly thereafter married his female secretary instead.

Greenspun proudly informed me that he had hired a private investigator to expose corruption in Nevada politics and had led the fight to desegregate the city's casinos. Black singers like Sammy Davis Jr. and Nat King Cole performed in front of packed white audiences in Las Vegas, but after the shows they had to leave by the back door and stay in black-only hotels on the city's segregated west side.

When our talk turned to Watergate, Hank became even more enthused. He had been watching the hearings and wanted to tell me all about his role in these events, a story he'd been hoping to have a chance to tell. He seemed annoyed that no one had yet sought to interview him about Operation Gemstone. "My name was in the damn plan," he said. He was eager to have his connection to the Watergate scandal known. If John Dean is an outsized character in the Watergate saga, Hank Greenspun is certainly the most underappreciated. There is scant reference to him in Watergate histories. Woodward and Bernstein's *All the President's Men* doesn't mention him at all.

Hank told me that in the late 1960s, he had become friendly with Howard Hughes, then the wealthiest man in America, who was looking at investments out west. Hank said it was he, in fact, who had invited Hughes to move to Vegas in 1966. By 1973, Howard Hughes was a living legend, frequently mentioned in tabloids and other press. Though I hadn't followed his story closely, I knew he was a pioneering aviator, owned an airline company (Trans World Airlines), was an early Hollywood film producer, and had romanced a long list of Hollywood stars. The origin of his wealth was his inheritance of his father's Hughes Tool Company, which held the patent on a drill bit that revolutionized oil exploration. I knew only bare outlines of Hughes's life, but Greenspun had been privileged to a front-row seat to the Hughes operations for years.

Greenspun made it pretty clear that he thought Howard Hughes was nuts. When Hughes retreated into seclusion, he left the management of his Vegas empire to an ex–FBI and CIA agent and close friend of Greenspun named Robert Maheu. The relationship between Hughes and his top aide was peculiar to say the least. Maheu was Hughes's closest confidant for nearly a decade, but according to Hank, the two had never met. They apparently communicated through long, mostly handwritten memos in which Hughes issued orders and threats, whined and complained, and charted out his strategic vision to expand his empire. Maheu in return followed Hughes's instructions and offered solicitous legal and financial counsel. Nevertheless, Hughes fired Maheu in 1970.

Around 1971, Greenspun had what he called "a chance conversation" with Herb Klein, a journalist who had been Nixon's communications aide in many campaigns. Greenspun believed this conversation led directly to the Watergate scandal.

"I told Klein that the breakup of the Hughes empire in Nevada was going to sink Nixon," Greenspun said in his firm, deliberate voice. Hank, a Republican, was a Nixon supporter because of what Hank appreciated as Nixon's fervent support of Israel.

"What do you mean 'sink Nixon'?" I asked.

He said, "The Hughes-Nixon relationship was going to be exposed."

"What kind of relationship did Hughes and Nixon have?" I wondered. At that point, I didn't remember much at all about the Hughes loan to Donald Nixon that had haunted Nixon's campaigns.

"There was a payoff," Greenspun said. Hughes, he claimed, had given the president $100,000 in exchange for political favors. The money had gone to Nixon through Charles "Bebe" Rebozo, one of Nixon's closest friends. Hank told Klein that he knew about that payment and asked what Nixon was going to say about it when it came out.

I wanted to be sure I was hearing all this right. "Holy shit," I said. "Are you telling me that Howard Hughes gave a bribe to the president of the United States?"

Hank leaned back in the chair behind his desk. "That's what I'm saying."

Hank had much more to say. He told me that after his conversation with Klein, Nixon's personal lawyer, Herbert Kalmbach, came to Las Vegas to ascertain exactly what Greenspun knew about the Hughes-Nixon relationship. "He didn't learn much from me," Hank said, "and he left dissatisfied." This, he asserted, was why the Watergate burglars decided to break into his safe.

He then told me about an article in the *New York Times* that reported that hundreds of Hughes's memos and documents, and possibly transcripts of tape-recorded conversations, were "readily available" in Las Vegas. "The biggest collection found is in the possession of Hank Greenspun, publisher of the *Las Vegas Sun*," the *Times* article noted. The date of this article's publication—February 3, 1972—was most interesting. It was the day before Liddy, Dean, and Mitchell met in the attorney general's office to talk about the Gemstone plan and discussed a break-in of Greenspun's safe.

"They wanted the memos," Hank said of Nixon's burglars, otherwise known as the "plumbers." "The *Hughes* memos."

Volumes of Hughes's handwritten documents were still locked up in Greenspun's safe, which stood only a few feet away. "Do you want to see them?" he asked.

Hank led me to a huge green safe in the corner of his office. Right above it was an autographed picture of Richard Nixon. Greenspun pointed to scratches on the safe's faceplate that he said were signs of an aborted break-in that had occurred the previous summer. He had told this story to the *New York Times*, which published a minor article on Hank's claim in May 1973.

I could see why Hank's charges might have been viewed with skepticism by reporters. Some of his suppositions sounded far-fetched. He suggested that Special Prosecutor Archibald Cox was part of the Hughes-Nixon conspiracy. He also claimed that Nixon's plumbers had planned to use a Hughes jet to fly to Central America after they broke into his safe.

Hank retrieved from his safe a stack of papers about a foot high and placed it on a nearby table. There were hundreds of legal-sized pages, most of them covered in a legible, distinctive, looped scrawl. It was unclear how he had obtained the Hughes memoranda. My impression from talking with Hank was that he had convinced Maheu to give him the documents for safekeeping. After Hughes fired him, Maheu was embroiled in litigation with Hughes; Hank had suggested that the memos would be less susceptible to subpoenas and legal scrutiny if they were out of Maheu's possession. He offered the memos to me like a long-hidden treasure. Clearly, Greenspun felt that he had undeservedly been left out of what was unfolding in Washington and was glad to have someone willing to listen to his story.

I sat down and started to read the documents, with Hank occasionally handing me those he thought I'd find most interesting.

By the time Hank and I met, Hughes had become known as a paranoid recluse obsessively focused on avoiding germs by collecting his
urine and watching his fingernails grow. But the memos I read reflected a savvy, impatient, and extremely hands-on business magnate.

Many of the memos shed light on the touchy, and ultimately
doomed, relationship between Hughes and Maheu, his trusted deputy.
Like an unhappily married couple, they often squabbled through the
memos over one thing after another—one's perceived slight, bruised
feelings, or miscommunications.

"Unfortunately no one has an exclusive to having a busy day," Maheu snapped in one letter—dated Valentine's Day, no less. "It is now
5:15. I've not shaved, showered nor have I had breakfast or lunch and I
have given you my undivided attention as I usually do. I cannot help
but get the feeling, Howard, that you are making a deep-seated effort
to find something about which you want to have a real deep-seated
argument." It ended with this complaint: "Last week you mentioned
to me that there are times you get the feeling I think you have been in
this world for 12 years instead of 62. I sometimes get the feeling that
you think I am still in my Mother's womb rather than being 50 years
of age."

No corner of his financial empire was too picayune for Hughes's
attention. There was, for example, memo after memo about whether
Jack Nicklaus and Arnold Palmer would play in a golf tournament at
one of his hotels. "You will remember that when we discussed this
before, I said I could persuade these men to come," Hughes wrote.
"That was what I had in mind when I asked you if everything had
been arranged to your satisfaction for the golf tournament. You said
yes, and you frequently get annoyed with me if I interrogate you in any
way that might possibly be considered as an expression of uncertain
faith and confidence in your administration . . . I think it would be
the very worst public relations for these two men to cancel out right
at the very time of our acquisition of Stardust."

On one of the pages, Hughes had drafted by hand the statement his wife would use in announcing their divorce. The attached press release, dated the next day, showed that she had sent it out in the exact wording.

There was a good deal of discussion of politics and Hughes's business interests. He obviously savored memos with nuggets of political intelligence. One included speculation about the likely chairman of the Republican National Committee in 1969.

The memos demonstrated Hughes's annoyance with the federal government's interference with his enterprises—about nuclear testing in Nevada that he believed would damage Las Vegas tourism, about the FCC objecting to his purchase of a TV station, and about problems acquiring Airwest. During the mid-1960s, according to his memos, Hughes seemed frustrated by his inability to bend President Lyndon Johnson to his will.

As the 1968 presidential election approached, Hughes welcomed the opportunity to influence the next administration. "I am determined to elect a president of our choosing this year," he wrote, "and one who will be deeply indebted and who will recognize his indebtedness."

The memoranda indicated that Hughes gave $100,000 to both major party candidates in 1968—to the Democratic candidate, Johnson's vice president, Hubert Humphrey, as well as to Nixon—in exchange for policy favors. Ever the shrewd businessman, Hughes was determined to cover his bets. "Why don't we get word to [Humphrey] on a basis of secrecy that it is really, really reliable that we will give him immediately full unlimited support for his campaign to enter the White House if he will take this one on for us?" This referred to his effort to halt nuclear testing in the Nevada desert.

Then Hughes turned his sights on Richard Nixon. "Since I am willing to go beyond all limitations on this," Hughes wrote, "I think we should be able to select a candidate and a party who knows the facts of political life."

The memos went on and on, covering a wide universe of Hughes operations. I knew I couldn't read them all in one sitting, even if I'd wanted to. But it was sensational stuff. I persuaded Hank to let me have copies of the documents. We had talked long enough that he seemed to trust me. I stayed overnight in Vegas while Hank had the memos copied.

At this point in my career, I had interviewed hundreds of potential witnesses, and believed I knew how to judge credibility. Hank was flamboyant, leaned to the conspiratorial at times, but was very self-assured. His answers to my questions seemed spontaneous—he didn't hesitate with his answers or grope for the truth. I had little doubt that what he said was true—or at least, that Hank thought it was true. Hank had no doubt about the documents' validity. He wanted to help his friend, Bob Maheu, escape more nasty litigation from Hughes. Greenspun also believed that his information could break open the Watergate investigation. With a healthy view of his own contribution to history, Hank Greenspun was certain he was going to be a star witness in the trial of the century.

When I returned to Washington the next day, I made sure to make multiple copies of the copies. I then debriefed Sam Dash, the senators, and the staff. The information I'd obtained was greeted with enthusiasm tempered by skepticism. Which was about what I was feeling as well. No one, including me, was confident that the Hughes documents were even real. I do recall Senator Baker saying at one point, "If this stuff checks out, it's a whole new can of worms."

Hank Greenspun, though likable and earnest, was a convicted felon who, at one time, had worked for a mobster. He also had a reputation for rabble-rousing. I needed far more than his word to charge that the president of the United States had been bribed by Hughes. Sensational as Greenspun's allegations were, we couldn't bank on them. We couldn't rely on snap judgments or preconceived notions. We had to gather and follow the facts. We had to talk to dozens of witnesses—some at the highest levels of the federal government. Each had his own motivations and differing recollections of events.

To begin, I asked researchers to delve through news reports and books to see if public records tracked with the events Hank had described. We soon learned that Howard Hughes had indeed located to Las Vegas in 1966, as Greenspun had said. There were numerous articles about Hughes's efforts to buy up the city's hotels and casinos. Even then, Hughes was a mystery. Included in what Greenspun gave me was an article, apparently exchanged between Maheu and Hughes, that claimed that the reclusive billionaire might in fact be dead. Our investigators also compiled a list of relevant Hughes personnel who might be familiar with Hughes's operations and his financial contributions. At the top of that list, of course, was the other correspondent in the memos: Hughes's onetime right-hand man, Robert Maheu.

From the summer of 1973 until the following May when our committee finished its work, I met with Bob Maheu many times in conference rooms in a U.S. Senate building. He was a cocky and confident middle-aged man who looked much more benign than he probably was, considering he had worked for both the FBI and CIA.

Maheu told us that Hughes hired him to manage his Nevada operation in 1966, the same year Hughes moved to Vegas, to provide "management services" for Hughes's hotels, restaurants, casinos, and other holdings. Maheu reported directly to the billionaire, rather than going through executives at Hughes's primary business entity, Hughes Tool Company. Maheu also acknowledged that Hughes consulted him on what political leaders Hughes should support. He stood by the accuracy of the documents Greenspun had provided, and verified they were genuine correspondence between himself and Hughes.

Because Maheu's lawsuit against his former boss was ongoing, he was reluctant to put anything on the record that might complicate it.

When I tried to lock Maheu down on specific dates or times of meetings and conversations, for example, he said he couldn't remember. Even when we presented him with easily verifiable information, he claimed memory lapses. But he did provide us with some useful information. He confirmed that he had approached Howard Hughes about making a $100,000 contribution to Richard Nixon's presidential campaign.

According to Maheu, Hughes was amenable to making the donation. He especially liked the idea of channeling the money through Bebe Rebozo because Rebozo presumably would provide ready access to Nixon himself. Maheu also told us, quite bluntly, that Hughes's contribution was meant to ensure favorable treatment by the Nixon administration for any problems that Hughes's operations might have with the federal government. He said the initial request for a contribution came from Richard Danner, a former FBI agent who was connected to Nixon.

Dick Danner had been with the bureau for about six years when he resigned to work on a congressional campaign in Florida. When I met with him, after tracking him down in Vegas, Danner looked like he'd stepped right out of J. Edgar Hoover's office. He was very FBI-ish—a nice-looking, clean-cut man in a starched white shirt, dark suit, and sober tie. Very serious and with an almost paramilitary demeanor, he was cast well for his role in this saga: as a front man for Nixon.

Danner told us he had known Richard Nixon since the 1940s. It was Danner, in fact, who first introduced the future president to Rebozo. During the 1968 campaign, Danner told us that Rebozo instructed him to contact a lawyer named Ed Morgan who was connected to the Hughes organization to ask for a $100,000 contribution to the Nixon campaign.

In February 1969, after Nixon was inaugurated, the Hughes organization offered Danner a job as general manager of the Frontier Hotel and Casino, one of Hughes's properties in Las Vegas. Danner admitted that he had no prior hotel management experience, and that one of his jobs was to serve as liaison to the Nixon administration. In this capacity, Danner said Rebozo often reminded him that Hughes had not given enough money to the Nixon campaign, and "needled" him about the large contributions Hughes had given to Democratic candidates. He willingly cooperated by answering all my questions in a straightforward manner. This was odd, perhaps, but I attributed this to his experience at the bureau.

Shortly after joining the Hughes organization in 1969, Danner said he met in New York with Rebozo and Ed Morgan to discuss Hughes's efforts to acquire more hotels in Las Vegas. At a subsequent meeting, they discussed the transfer of the first $50,000 of the $100,000 contribution Rebozo had requested. Danner said the transaction was blown when the hapless Donald Nixon showed up at the meeting, asking that he be the conduit for any contributions to his brother.

In almost all of my preliminary interviews on the Hughes-Rebozo connection, in fact, Don Nixon's name kept turning up. It seemed that Donald Nixon had learned nothing about the damage his business relationships with the Hughes organization might do to his brother.

Yet knowing how sensitive the Hughes-Nixon relationship had been in the past, the Nixon White House nonetheless went out of its way to assist Mr. Hughes's financial empire. As we started piecing it together, that assistance raised a number of red flags.

During Nixon's administration, Hughes received favored treatment from the federal government, winning no-bid billion-dollar contracts and obtaining federal licenses for TV stations with comparative ease. Hank claimed to have seen a memo from Hughes instructing Maheu to offer Nixon $1 million to stop atomic testing in Nevada that was deterring tourism and hurting business at his casinos. That memo was not in the collection Hank turned over to me.

One of the areas we examined closely involved efforts by Hughes to acquire the Dunes Hotel in Las Vegas—an effort that brought the Nixon administration into conflict with its own Department of Justice. It also revealed how Hughes dealt with the federal government.

After learning of the Hughes effort to purchase the Dunes, I met with attorneys in the Antitrust Division of the Justice Department. They told me that Hughes's efforts to buy up hotels and casinos in Vegas, going back to the late 1960s, had been the subject of considerable scrutiny by antitrust regulators who were concerned that Hughes was trying to build an illegal monopoly in Nevada.

During Lyndon Johnson's administration, the Justice Department had thwarted Hughes's efforts to buy the Stardust Resort and Casino. The Justice Department did allow Hughes to buy a second hotel, the Landmark, though that deal was watched carefully and Justice Department employees expressed misgivings. Undoubtedly the government's actions in both cases frustrated a man liked Hughes, who was accustomed to getting his way. It undoubtedly motivated the sentiments expressed in his memos of getting people in office who would be more malleable to his demands.

By 1969, with a new administration in power and a new attorney general in office—Nixon's former campaign manager, John Mitchell— Hughes set his sights on another hotel and casino: the Dunes. This time Hughes was determined to get his way. In his interview with us, Dick Danner said he was dispatched by Bob Maheu to meet with Attorney General Mitchell with regard to the purchase. According to Danner's records, he met with Mitchell three times in early 1970 to discuss the situation. In the first meeting, according to Danner, Mitchell asked for some statistics or data that supported Hughes's case and that would refute concerns that he was building a Las Vegas monopoly. In the second meeting, which Danner claimed took place on February 26, Danner gave Mitchell a one-page memo. Danner then quoted the attorney general as saying that he would "let the boys look this over and give you an answer later." On their third visit, on March 19, 1970, the attorney general said the department would approve Hughes's acquisition of the Dunes. Danner remembered Mitchell as saying, "From our review of these figures, we see no problem."

Richard McLaren, who served as the assistant attorney general in the Antitrust Division during the relevant dates, told a different story. He said that when Mitchell had asked him about Hughes's Dunes acquisition, he had told the attorney general that the purchase would violate department guidelines. On at least two occasions, McLaren said he urged Mitchell not to approve the deal. All the other staff attorneys who normally would handle the case said they had no recollection of hearing of the case at all.

I then spoke with John Mitchell to hear his recollection of these events. The former attorney general was now living in a hotel suite in New York, registered under a fictitious name. I came to know Mitchell quite well during the Watergate investigation. Nearly sixty years old by the time of the Watergate break-in, he had been a close associate of Richard Nixon for years. Since he had managed the 1968 campaign and was the head of the Committee to Re-Elect the President in 1972, some outside observers viewed Mitchell as a ruthless figure and savvy political genius. What I saw was quite different: a successful bond lawyer from Manhattan who found himself thrust in the middle of almost unimaginable craziness. During Watergate, his whole world imploded. His name was plastered on many damaging memos that John Dean had turned over to the committee. The attorney general was named in Dean's testimony as having been in all sorts of key meetings, particularly those discussing illegal schemes hatched by Gordon Liddy. Meanwhile, Mitchell lived with his notoriously flamboyant and unstable wife, Martha, who saw conspiracies everywhere and had thrust herself into the national spotlight after the Watergate revelations came to light. (They were to separate very soon afterward.)

The first time he came to Capitol Hill for interviews, Mitchell was pushed and shoved by the gaggle of press and spectators. He looked shocked. He wasn't scared, but had never been treated like that before. He was totally out of his comfort zone. Seeing him, I was reminded of scenes in movies where generals came up for interrogation before Congress and, to their astonishment, are treated without respect. When Mitchell testified in public hearings, the senators grilled him extensively about the Gemstone and Huston plans, and asked with incredulity why he had never quashed them, nor told the president about them.

Though Mitchell could be peevish and sarcastic when cornered on something before television cameras, in private he was usually cordial and cooperative. We subpoenaed his memos and his diary, which included his daily schedules, and he allowed us to copy and review them. On occasion he even steered us in the right direction. In fact, it was Mitchell who directed us to McLaren in the first place.

Some months earlier, before I met with Mitchell, I had interviewed his secretary to get a sense of him. She liked her boss and told me that he would get all these memos from the White House, glance at them, and then put them in a credenza, never looking at them again. Whenever someone came by for a meeting, Mitchell would ask her to fish the most recent memos out so he could remember what the latest plan was. I could visualize a man like Mitchell sitting in the middle of the discussion of the Gemstone plan, puffing on his pipe and nodding as if agreeing with everything being said. But it was equally likely that he either didn't understand what was going on or he didn't care. He never struck me as the ruthless strategist behind the Nixon administration. He was a figurehead.

Unsurprisingly, Mitchell had virtually no memory of Howard Hughes's attempt to acquire the Dunes Hotel or of his approval of the purchase. At best, he said he could vaguely recall one meeting with Danner on the matter, not three. He didn't seem sure about that one either.

McLaren, however, had a clear recollection of events, including a memo to Mitchell urging him to oppose the Hughes acquisition. Mitchell gave his approval to Dick Danner anyway. Knowing what I knew of him, this seemed typical of Mitchell. My guess was that he was told by someone higher up—likely Nixon or Haldeman—to approve the Hughes deal, and he did it with hardly a second thought.

What was interesting to those of us investigating the Dunes Hotel deal was not only its impropriety but its timing. The very day after Mitchell gave his approval, Dick Danner flew to Key Biscayne, Florida, Bebe Rebozo's hometown. Hotel records and Danner's own diary indicated that he stayed at the Sonesta Beach Resort. In an interview, Danner admitted that he met with Bebe Rebozo during that period but denied that he discussed contributions to the Nixon campaign or the fact that the Justice Department had just approved the Dunes Hotel acquisition. Both assertions seemed difficult to believe.

When I spoke to Hank Greenspun about all of this, he told me a different story. Greenspun said that Danner returned to Vegas with a piece of paper from the Justice Department signifying approval of the Dunes deal. Danner told Greenspun that the approval was conditioned on a contribution to the Nixon campaign, which would come six to twelve months later so as not to appear suspicious. And in fact, a sizable cash contribution did make its way from the Hughes empire to the Nixon campaign coffers a few months later.

We were building a circumstantial case indicating that Howard Hughes and the Nixon administration had, in fact, exchanged money for political favors. As this information began to be compiled, I knew I needed to talk to someone who was close to President Nixon on these matters—the man whose name was tied to the $100,000 contribution. I sought out Charles "Bebe" Rebozo.

Though Rebozo was well known in the newspapers as the president's closest friend and confidant, Nixon in fact had two best friends. The other friend, the man who spent probably as much time with him as Rebozo, who joined the president on vacations and hung out with Nixon at his homes in Florida and California, was named Robert Abplanalp. Abplanalp was the inventor of the aerosol valve and founder of the Precision Valve Corporation. He owned an island in the Bahamas, among other properties. Unlike Bebe Rebozo, who enjoyed the attention of being the president's BFF, Abplanalp preferred to travel beneath the radar. He was equally loyal to Nixon but was more discreet and stayed out of trouble. I thought of him as the smart one.

Bebe, by contrast, was a constant presence in Nixon family schemes, especially when they involved money. A sixty-year-old Cuban-American who had known Nixon for decades, Rebozo from the earliest days of the administration was a conduit for financial contributions to the Nixon slush fund. One document we obtained from the White House as a result of a subpoena was a memo from H. R. Haldeman to John Ehrlichman. The memo, marked "confidential" and dated February 17, 1969 (less than a month after the inauguration), stated that Nixon had asked Rebozo to solicit a contribution from billionaire oil tycoon J. Paul Getty, then living in London. Naturally, I suspected that Rebozo was also sent to procure funds from Howard Hughes.

Bebe Rebozo was not a cooperative witness. We had trouble subpoenaing him and had to work through his particularly obstructionist lawyer, William Frates. Sam Dash and I received a memo from one of my staff that said "there has been a continuous effort on the part of Mr. Frates to harass and insult [our investigators] and this entire operation appears to be a concocted scheme to obstruct the work of the accountants on this assignment." Rebozo was slow to release his bank records and the list of documents he produced in response to our subpoenas was never complete. When Rebozo finally did meet with us, he was smooth and arrogant. He acted as if he could get away with anything, that the committee couldn't touch him.

Rebozo grudgingly acknowledged that he had received two $50,000 cash payments from Hughes, one at Nixon's California retreat on July

3, 1970, and the second in Key Biscayne that August. But Rebozo insisted that he had not sought the contributions. Rebozo also assured us that he placed the money in a safety deposit box at Key Biscayne Bank and Trust, the bank he owned, and never touched it. We learned more about this from Nixon's personal lawyer, Herb Kalmbach.

Kalmbach was a fascinating witness. I had first questioned him at his Los Angeles law office with Carmine Bellino on April 28, 1973, early in preparation for the Senate hearings. That interview was about Kalmbach's role in paying Segretti for his "political espionage." At that time, he said Dean had asked him to raise funds for the Watergate burglars. Kalmbach had been Nixon's attorney since 1968, and he looked the part. He was groomed impeccably—there was not a hair out of place. He spoke calmly and measured his words. His daily schedule was printed in perfect, precise type on small cards that he carried in his suit pocket.

Kalmbach did not enjoy being the subject of inquiry by a congressional committee. He was used to representing witnesses, not being one, and he was not inclined to let his service to Richard Nixon jeopardize his successful legal career. His cooperation with the committee needed the cover of the appearance that he had no other choice.

Kalmbach tried to avoid answering questions about Bebe Rebozo and the Hughes payment by asserting attorney-client privilege. Chairman Ervin overruled that, concluding that Kalmbach was not serving as Rebozo's lawyer. In fact, I had asked Rebozo to name his lawyers, and he had not mentioned Kalmbach, although Kalmbach claimed that Rebozo had consulted him. Having demonstrated that he had tried to keep quiet, he then became quite talkative. He told us that sometime during the week of April 23, 1973, Rebozo contacted him and told him that the IRS was inquiring about contributions Rebozo received in 1970. "He said he had personally received $100,000 in campaign contributions from Dick Danner representing Howard Hughes," Kalmbach told us. "He said that he had disbursed part of the funds to Rose Mary Woods, to Don Nixon, to Ed Nixon [Richard Nixon's younger brother], and to unnamed others during the intervening years, and that he was now asking my counsel on how to handle the problem." Kalmbach said he told Rebozo to find the best tax attorney he could and he advised Rebozo to return the money.

After Kalmbach testified on March 21, 1974, Rebozo and his lawyer suddenly asked to meet privately with Senator Ervin. Despite their reservations, I was allowed to attend. We met in a small room in the Capitol as Rebozo's lawyer walked in with a briefcase. Dramatically, he placed the briefcase on a table and opened it, revealing what he identified as $100,000 in cash. The money was in stacks of $100 bills circled by rubber bands.

I remember Ervin's astonished expression—his bushy eyebrows fluttered up and down, and he gasped. The cash, Rebozo's lawyer announced, was the money Rebozo had saved to return to the Hughes organization. It was proof, they maintained, that the money had never been used.

According to testimony provided by Rebozo, Danner, Maheu, Kalmbach, and others, the money that Hughes gave to the Nixon campaign had been procured in 1968. We located two employees of the Sands Hotel in Las Vegas who told us that at least $50,000 was taken from the hotel cage, which we believed was the likely source of the Hughes contribution.

Our forensic accountant, Carmine Bellino, worked over several months to piece together what actually happened with money Rebozo received from Howard Hughes. If Rebozo had disbursed part of the money as Kalmbach said, where did the $100,000 he presented to Senator Ervin come from? Rebozo certainly knew that every dollar bill issued by the Federal Reserve has a serial number indicating the date of its release. Our working theory, then, was that Rebozo had spent considerable time collecting $100 bills with serial numbers that were consistent with his prior statements that he had kept the money unused for three years. Unfortunately, Mr. Rebozo, or whoever was helping him, was not very conscientious. We examined every one of those $100 bills and found more than thirty whose serial numbers did not match. Those bills had been issued after the money was said to have been given to Rebozo and thus could not have been part of the cash Rebozo claimed to have left undisturbed. Furthermore, the briefcase of cash presented to us had an extra $100 bill, adding up to $100,100. We prepared another subpoena for him, but Rebozo had left the country.

I flew to California to meet with Donald and Ed Nixon. I knew that we had to tread lightly and not appear to be harassing members of the president's family. I wasn't sure what we might learn, but, since Donald Nixon's name kept popping up throughout our investigation, I felt it was important to talk with him. The senators on the committee agreed, voting to subpoena the brothers to testify privately at a Los Angeles hotel and to provide relevant records.

Don Nixon garnered no more respect from my investigators than he did at the White House. "In the genetic roulette of the Nixon family," Marc Lackritz once quipped, "Don drew the blanks." Don was a constant irritant to the White House. It did not take us long to learn that, at one point or another, nearly every senior member of Nixon's White House staff had been tasked with babysitting Don Nixon—from John Ehrlichman and John Dean to Herb Kalmbach and Jack Caulfield. In fact, one of Caulfield's first assignments was to monitor Don's activities. That soon became the purview of the Secret Service, which tapped Don's telephones at the president's request. The Secret Service refused to be interviewed on this subject, on the grounds that it related to their protection of the president. My suspicion was that the use of the Secret Service to spy on a presidential sibling was probably illegal but maybe not uncommon.

I spent two days in November 1973 with Don and Ed Nixon at a hotel suite in California. I can't say I noticed anything resembling familial care or concern between the two. Ed Nixon, who was almost sixteen years younger than Don, worked for a phone company in Seattle. He didn't have affection for anybody, as far as I could tell. He started telling anti-Catholic, anti-Jewish, and anti-black jokes as soon as we sat down.

After one conversation with Don, I could see why the president kept a watchful eye on him. Don was more affable than the president, even if a bit clownish. He looked eerily like his famous brother. At one point, I glanced at his silhouette in the window and thought I was looking at the president with his often caricatured nose. Don's entrepreneurial skills had not improved from the days of the Nixon Burger. He was involved in all sorts of enterprises—for example, looking at financing a porn film with Johnny Meier, who claimed to be Hughes's business advisor. We learned from the president's tax lawyer, Arthur Blech, that Don had complained that the Hughes operation hadn't given him a "finder's fee" after the federal government approved Hughes's acquisition of Airwest. If Richard was Michael Corleone, then Don was certainly Fredo.

When we went downstairs to the hotel restaurant for lunch, the married Don nudged me whenever he saw a pretty waitress walk by. At one point he asked me for my autograph. I guess that Don figured this was a historic event, so I obliged him.

Don and Ed both professed to know nothing about the Rebozo money, and claimed they received no payments from Hughes. When I asked Don whether he knew his telephone lines were being tapped by the White House, he said that he did know.

"Why do you think the president wants to bug your phones?" I asked him.

Don shrugged and said only, "He's my brother."

As it happened, the president addressed the issue at the same time. He held a press conference that very evening near Disneyland and was asked about newspaper articles, based on leaks from the committee, that he had bugged his brother's phones. The president said he had ordered the phone taps. He said he did so for security reasons to protect his brother.

Based on their body language and tone, I didn't think either Don or Ed had any more relationship with the president than they had with each other. If anything, they seemed resentful that their powerful brother hadn't done more for them. My glimpse into the inner workings of the Nixon family was brief, but it was scary. These totally unimpressive figures shared DNA with the most powerful man in the world.

There was still one other person the committee had to interview, the one person other than Richard Nixon who could tell us everything about the Hughes money. It was time to subpoena Howard Hughes. I drafted a subpoena for the billionaire, asking him to testify and provide documents relating to Bob Maheu and Bebe Rebozo that might fill out the missing details of those relationships. I also asked for information about his license to acquire Airwest, a charitable tax deduction he had received for his medical foundation, and the federal government's role in his attempt to buy the Dunes. Preparing the subpoena was relatively easy; serving Mr. Hughes with it was another matter. No one was ever sure where he was.

With the help of the Federal Aviation Administration, we obtained the tail number of Hughes's private plane and tracked its flight path. In early 1974, we learned that the plane was landing at an airstrip in the Bahamas. A United States marshal was sent to the airport to serve a subpoena the moment that Hughes emerged from the plane.

I didn't expect Hughes to comply with the committee even if served with a subpoena, but we had to make the effort. I was in my office in Washington when the marshal's office called to tell us Hughes's plane had touched down on the tarmac. As the plane rolled to a stop, we awaited word. But the doors never opened. The plane sat in place for a moment. Then the engines revved up again and the plane returned to the air. We sent him a letter requesting information, but that was never

answered. We also subpoenaed his company's vice president, his pilot, and a slew of his employees. I don't think anyone complied.

On June 6, 1974, I drafted a letter for the Ervin Committee to send
to the president. It included substantial evidence that Rebozo used
cash funds to directly benefit the president and offered to give the
president "an opportunity to comment on this material prior to the
filing of this report." The White House never responded to the points
raised in the letter. The Senate hearings were over, and the House
of Representatives was considering impeachment. It was clear that Nixon, Hughes, and anyone else I had hoped to hear from believed our
committee had run out of time, so their strategy was to delay, delay,
delay.

Our investigation was hampered throughout. But it did help me
understand why the burglars were sent to the Watergate office complex that June night in the first place. And it highlighted a central
figure in the Hughes firmament, at least as the Nixon White House
saw it. That person was Larry O'Brien.

O ne of John Dean's first disclosures to the committee was the operation code-named Gemstone. This appeared to be the successor to some of the earlier schemes—Operation Sandwedge and the
Huston Plan, for example—that never got fully implemented. The meeting over Operation Gemstone, Dean told us, ultimately led to the Watergate break-in to bug the office of Democratic National Committee
chairman Larry O'Brien and search his files.

Jack Caulfield gave us a memo he had prepared for Nixon officials
in the fall of 1971 that proposed a sweeping operation, code-named
Sandwedge, to counter what he believed the Democrats were up to
under O'Brien. As I examined White House documents and spoke to
witnesses, I learned that O'Brien was a particular and constant target
of the Nixon team. "The presence of Lawrence O'Brien as Chairman

of the Democratic National Committee unquestionably suggests that the Democratic nominee will have a strong, covert intelligence effort mounted against us in 1972," Caulfield wrote.

In 1971, memos exchanged between Haldeman, Dean, and Caulfield tried to establish what relationship O'Brien had with the Hughes operation. Some of the memos were labeled HUGHES RETAINER TO LARRY O'BRIEN. Nixon aide Robert Bennett, a future U.S. senator from Utah, reported that O'Brien's lobbying firm had been retained by Hughes and "the contract still exists."

The infamous Gemstone meeting in Mitchell's office on February 4, 1972, concerned two targets—Hank Greenspun and Larry O'Brien. I was confident that there was a relationship between the attempt to open Greenspun's safe and the Watergate break-in. I assumed the plumbers were looking for the Hughes memos. My theory was that the president and his senior advisors believed O'Brien had evidence that Hughes's $100,000 contribution was connected to administration favors, and they assumed that O'Brien was just waiting for the right time to put out that information. They feared the secret Howard Hughes loan was going to ruin Nixon politically again, just as it had in 1960 and in 1962.

Watergate conspirator Howard Hunt substantiated this. He testified in late September 1973 that he obtained the plans of Greenspun's office in early 1972 from a Hughes associate. Just as Greenspun had told me, Hunt testified that he had asked the Hughes people to provide him with a plane to take him and the other burglars to Central America after they had breached Hank's safe.

Jeb Magruder, then special counsel to the president, testified that Mitchell asked Liddy to survey Greenspun's offices in Las Vegas to determine if entry was possible. Magruder also said that Chuck Colson told him to get moving on Liddy's budget requests because information on Larry O'Brien was needed.

We obtained further corroboration from Ralph Winte, the director of Hughes's security. He told us that he met with Nixon's aide Robert Bennett in Washington and that Bennett introduced him to Howard Hunt, saying Hunt was with the CIA. In February 1972, Winte and Hunt met at the Beverly Wilshire Hotel. Hunt proposed to break into Hank Greenspun's safe to steal the Howard Hughes memos. Winte said that after the theft, Hunt proposed to use a Hughes plane to fly him to Central America.

Tony Ulasewicz told me that Dean and Haldeman had asked him to look into O'Brien's associations, especially his relationship with Robert Maheu. Tony added a new piece of information: that Nixon campaign officials blamed O'Brien for leaking the information about Hughes's loan to Donald Nixon that infected Nixon's 1960 and 1962 campaigns. Speaking of O'Brien, Nixon campaign advisor Murray Chotiner told Ulasewicz, "His turn is coming."

Tony believed what I did. As he put it later, "The genesis date of the Watergate break-in was not 1972, but 1969." He said it began with the Nixon group's decision to target Larry O'Brien to find out what he knew about Howard Hughes.

My view, then and now, was that the break-ins at the Watergate and Greenspun's office in Las Vegas were parts of the same quest. Nixon wanted to find the Hughes memos and prevent them from destroying him.

I went to see O'Brien in New York in December 1973. I expected he'd be glad that committee investigators were interested in him and his connection to the Watergate scandal. But that was not his attitude.

From the beginning of our meeting, O'Brien was frosty and defensive. He indulged no small talk to break the ice. He showed no interest in who we were or what we wanted. At one point he questioned why we were interviewing him at all. "I'm the victim here," he said.

"Do you think that the Watergate break-in and cover-up was related to your work for Howard Hughes?" I asked.

He wasn't going to discuss that, he said. It was none of my business. It was clear that he thought I was no different from the Republicans who disparaged him.

I had prided myself on not being surprised by what a witness said. But here I was taken aback. O'Brien was a significant figure in Washington then, and I had expected him to appreciate what we were trying to learn from him. We tried to push him on a few specifics, but we got nowhere. It was strange.

I finally realized that O'Brien was afraid that we might be investigating him. He didn't want his own activities as a lobbyist for Hughes to come under scrutiny. It's not a stretch to imagine that Hughes treated O'Brien the same way he treated other politicians: using his money to get what he wanted. The biggest irony may have been that Nixon was right to be paranoid about O'Brien.

There were, as Senator Baker used to say, a lot of animals crashing around in the forest. He believed the CIA was lurking in the shadows of the Watergate break-in. I learned inadvertently that he may have been right. When you pull on a loose thread, sometimes something bigger unravels.

During the Hughes-Rebozo investigation we periodically checked John Mitchell's diaries from when he was the attorney general. These showed dates and summaries of various meetings. One of my investigators came across a meeting in February of 1971 between Mitchell and Bob Maheu. No subject was indicated, and I wondered about it.

I knew Mitchell couldn't remember much, so I asked Maheu about it over the phone. There was a pause on the other end.

"I got a subpoena to talk about organized crime in Vegas," he said.

"So I got Mitchell to have me debrief the people who were interested so I could get rid of the subpoena."

There was something about it that didn't seem right to me. "What did you talk about?" I asked.

He didn't remember.

"What was the focus of their questions? What was the name of the primary questioner?"

"I don't remember any of that stuff," he said.

Unsatisfied, I called Will Wilson, the head of the Justice Department's Criminal Division who was at the meeting with Maheu and Mitchell. I told him Maheu's story and asked him if it checked out.

No, he replied. It didn't.

"That meeting was about the wiretap on the McGuire sisters that we came across," he said.

I was confused. Why was the government interested in the popular singing trio? Wilson told me that the sisters associated with Sam Giancana and Johnny Roselli, two powerful organized crime bosses. The wiretaps picked up conversations between the Mafia figures about their work with the Kennedy administration to plan the assassination of Fidel Castro. Wilson told me the mobsters were brought into the plot through Bob Maheu. Wilson said the White House had copies of these wiretaps, and he believed that Nixon intended to use this information against Ted Kennedy if Kennedy ran for the presidency in 1972. Mitchell had met with Maheu to get corroboration that the Hughes organization had been involved, which may have been an effort by the Nixon White House to get information on Hughes they could use to control him.

I was stunned. Not only by Wilson's story, but also by his complete candor. I had no idea that the U.S. government was behind a plot against Castro. I felt I had no choice but to bring this information to Sam Ervin directly and see how he wanted to proceed.

By the spring of 1974, the House of Representatives' Judiciary Committee was about to begin its impeachment inquiry of President

Nixon—led by the Judiciary Committee's chair, Representative Peter Rodino, who hired John Doar as chief counsel.

Ervin was intrigued by the information I brought to him. He asked question after question about it. He seemed genuinely interested in the players and the story, and how it might play into our existing investigation. Ultimately, however, time ran out and he decided it was not relevant to Nixon campaign activities in the 1972 election. He felt the country had had enough drama and disruption. We didn't need to throw another stick of dynamite onto an already burning pile.

I disagreed. I told the chairman that this information could be directly relevant to Watergate if, as I believed, it showed the Nixon team tried to use the plot against Castro to blackmail political opponents. Possibly Nixon wanted to use Hughes's involvement to get more money from him and keep him in line. There were unanswered questions, and I wanted to keep looking for answers. Reluctantly, Ervin allowed me to keep going.

I subpoenaed Giancana and Roselli. I knew of them from the U.S. Attorney's Office in New York, since they were members of the Genovese and Bonanno crime families that we targeted. They both agreed to come in and speak with us, accompanied by their attorney, an organized crime lawyer from Chicago. His manner was smooth, and I remember that peaks of a carefully folded, flamboyant handkerchief emerged from his breast pocket.

As they assembled in one of our committee rooms, neither Giancana nor Roselli seemed to take any of this seriously. I figured they had been through so many subpoenas and interviews by law enforcement and spent so much of their lives under surveillance that my questioning was not going to faze them. I was right. When I broached the subject of Hughes or the assassination plot, they declined to answer, their lawyer citing a national security exemption that he claimed prevented them from responding. I was frustrated, but I couldn't help but laugh. I knew these guys from my work prosecuting organized crime, and now they told me they were involved in national security? It seemed ridiculous.

Ervin declined to overrule their exemption, and as a result, we didn't go any further. In a sense the chairman was right. Whether or not Hughes and the mob were involved in a plot against Castro had no relevance to whether Richard Nixon had committed any crimes. But it sure as hell was interesting. It would be several more years until the full scope of those activities was exposed in Senator Church's hearings to investigate the CIA.

L ooking back, it was a miracle that the Watergate Committee suc-ceeded in uncovering as much as it did. The people involved had conflicting (sometimes shifting) loyalties and at times evasive responses filled with hidden meanings and agenda. Herb Kalmbach, for example, once told me that he had agreed to help the Nixon White House cover up its financial activities only if Nixon promised to protect Herb's family. "My family needed to be safe," Kalmbach said. His lips quivered, his voice broke, and I saw tears in his eyes. I was moved. But then Kalmbach said the exact same words to others on our committee—quivering his lips, breaking his voice, summoning tears at that precise moment. Then on television, he did the same thing again—the minute he mentioned his family—with almost identical words. I was less moved. Another time, Scott Armstrong and I inter-viewed a Nixon administration official, Egil "Bud" Krogh, who had headed the White House plumbers group. He recruited Liddy and authorized the break-in of Ellsberg's psychiatrist's office. When we interviewed Krogh, he was at the Department of Transportation.

Krogh was a serious guy with a reputation for scrupulousness. He struck me as an unusual choice to oversee the plumbers. Armstrong and I met with him and conducted a rather inconsequential interview. At the end of it, I thanked Bud for his time.

Armstrong, realizing how useless the interview had been, made a joke. "Well, we definitely got the big guy today," Scott said, implying the president.

I knew Armstrong was being sarcastic, but Bud didn't. The color drained from his face. He looked stricken.

Once we were out of earshot, I chided Armstrong. "Scott, I don't think you can joke around with these people," I said. "There is so much nervous tension here. We have to be serious." In fact, after months of questioning Nixon people about the scandal, we became accustomed to what I called "the look." It was a sort of contained panic, as if everyone was waiting for one more shoe to drop, for one more person they knew to be carted off to jail.

It turned out Krogh hadn't told us the truth about what he knew. Late in November 1973, he pleaded guilty for his part in the break-in of Ellsberg's doctor's office and agreed to cooperate with the prosecutors. He ended up serving four months in prison. Ehrlichman, in his memoir, said Krogh "materially contributed to the demise of the Nixon administration."

The major players in the Watergate saga—even the "good guys"— sometimes had an agenda that I didn't appreciate or understand. For example, in executive session during the Hughes-Rebozo investigation, I questioned General Alexander Haig, who had replaced Haldeman as Nixon's chief of staff. Senator Weicker swore Haig in and, in fact, was the only senator in attendance.

I asked General Haig a series of questions about what people in the White House actually knew about the Hughes-Rebozo money as well as about the administration's efforts to prod the IRS to investigate Larry O'Brien. I expected that, as chief of staff, Haig would have a great deal of information about Nixon's activities. But the interview failed to uncover any new revelations. The general was a reluctant witness and invoked "executive privilege" at least forty times in response to our interrogation.

At the close of the encounter, I followed Senator Weicker and his aide out of the committee room and then went back to my office. Almost immediately the phone rang at my desk. It was a reporter from the *New York Times*.

"Terry, can you confirm that General Haig took the executive privilege exemption forty times today?" the reporter asked.

I didn't answer the question. Committee rules said I couldn't comment, and it went against my nature to disclose that kind of information. I was certain only one other person could possibly have been the source of that information. I rose from my desk in a fury and made my way directly to Senator Weicker's office.

Weicker was seated behind his desk when I was shown in to his private office. "What can I do for you, Terry?" he asked.

I had long suspected that he and his aide had been leaking to reporters throughout the hearings and I was going to let him have it. I told him about the phone call I'd just received. "Senator," I said in full umbrage, "we can't run an investigation with everything being leaked instantly to the press."

Weicker listened in silence as I went on.

"These leaks are going to give people a reason not to talk to us," I said, "and they will also allow potential witnesses to know what we are doing and what our next questions might be."

Finally, Weicker had had enough. The senator was six feet six and standing up behind his desk, he was an impressive, even intimidating, figure. As he looked down at me, a frown lined his face. "Terry, let me ask you something," he said. "Who elected you to the United States Senate?"

Until that moment, I'd felt totally justified in marching into the office of a United States senator and chewing him out for screwing up my investigation. It never occurred to me the hubris I was exhibiting or, for that matter, that the senator might have had a good reason for his leaks.

Weicker went on to explain to me that he felt it was his duty to inform the public about what we were learning. I knew that his leaks also helped Weicker maintain useful relationships with the press, but I hadn't yet realized that his purpose was larger than that, and valid. Leaks from the committee helped keep the story going—making it harder for the White House to conceal information or get away with telling only part of the story.

When President Nixon fired special prosecutor Archibald Cox in October 1973—as part of the so-called Saturday Night Massacre when Attorney General Richardson resigned—the administration might have tried to claim the firing was the outcome of a legitimate internal struggle. They might have succeeded in arguing it was not a big deal. But because the public was more aware of the full story—not just from televised hearings but from press reports from many sources, including leaks—the White House's dissembling had far less credibility.

To me as a former prosecutor, the Watergate investigation was about following leads, assembling facts, and preparing a case in confidence. But it was just as much a battle for public opinion. Senator Weicker got that. I didn't.

O n June 23, 1975, Richard Nixon appeared before the grand jury to testify on the Watergate scandal that had ushered him from office the summer before. Although President Ford's pardon of the former president excused Nixon from criminal prosecution, the pardon did require him to cooperate with the special prosecutor.

Reading the transcript of his statements to the grand jury is a fresh reminder of the demons that haunted Richard Nixon—paranoia, suspicion, bitterness. When asked to discuss his efforts to turn the IRS against Larry O'Brien, Nixon characteristically turned the tables.

"So, in other words," the former president interrupted, "the special prosecutor's office is only interested in the IRS harassment activities insofar as it deals with Mr. O'Brien? It is not interested in any harassment that the IRS may have done or is doing or has done with regard to, say, me, my friends, or anything like that?"

Nixon's fixation on O'Brien was apparent. He noted "as public knowledge" that Larry O'Brien and Hubert Humphrey's son-in-law were both on retainers of "the Hughes organization." He questioned whether these retainers were "for services rendered" or "for the purpose of being funneled into political campaigns." He accused the Hughes organization of "payoffs" and claimed O'Brien "had his hand in the till there." Clearly lost on Nixon was the fact that he was accusing the Democrats of receiving Hughes money when in fact he had been receiving it all along.

Nixon then went into a long, self-pitying discourse. He said, "If you were to look into Larry O'Brien's activities politically over the years, and into the activities of the Democratic senators and others, including some Republicans who are taking on this sanctimonious attitude about the cleanliness of their campaigns, if you would put them to the same test you have put us, you would find that we come out rather well."

That was nonsense. Mostly. But penetrating the fog of his typical obfuscation, partial truths, and self-serving accusations was one unnerving thought: Nixon was right. At least, in part. There *was* a lot of activity with respect to Howard Hughes that few people wanted to untangle. And so we never did.

In December 1973, Sam Dash, responding to leaks about the Hughes-Rebozo investigation, faced reporters. "Both Senator Ervin and I feel the Hughes investigation is as important as anything we've produced thus far," Dash told them. He noted that more than a hundred witnesses had been interviewed in the case, mostly by me. Dash's support and statements were encouraging. And it seemed that we were really making some headway. By February 1974, I believed we had compiled enough information to justify reopening the Watergate

In front of the U.S. Capitol with my Trinity School classmates.
I am fourth from the left in the front row, 1951.

I played guard at Harvard College and was captain of the football team in 1960.

With coach Bill Clark, one of my first mentors, at Exeter Academy, where I was captain of the undefeated football team in 1956.

Bloody Sunday at the Pettus Bridge in Selma,
March 7, 1965. Photographs were used to identify
patrolmen and posse when indictments
were sought.

Robert Morgenthau swore me in as an assistant attorney in
the organized crime unit at the U.S. Attorney's Office for
the Southern District of New York, January 1967.

My OEO boss, Don Rumsfeld, introduced me to
President Nixon at the White House in 1969. Richard Cheney,
Rumsfeld's special assistant, is seen behind me.

As head of the Legal Services
Program, I presented the White
House with a petition signed
by thousands of law school
students opposing the Murphy
Amendment. With Donald
Rumsfeld, Pat Moynihan, and
several law school students.

Meeting with my Legal Services senior staff, pictured clockwise from left:
Hugh MacMillan, Kimba Wood Lovejoy, Mickey Kantor,
Troy Overby, me, Roger Detweiler, Mathea Falco,
Bruce Kirschenbaum, and Frank Jones.

(© Jan Faul, 2013)

OEO senior officials meeting at Camp David, 1969.
I am standing third from right, having been held
hostage briefly by a group of law students
demanding a grant earlier that day.

After Hurricane Camille devastated
the Gulf Coast in August 1969,
I flew to Mississippi to present the
governor with an emergency grant
for legal services. Left to right:
Boyce Holleman of the Mississippi
Bar Association, Mississippi
governor John Bell Williams in
post-hurricane attire, and me.

Conferring with Edgar Cahn,
a co-founder of the Legal Services
Program, and John R. Kramer, another
advocate for antipoverty programs,
about strategy to prevent Congress from
emasculating the program in 1969.

Frank Jones and me, holding a press conference the day after our dismissal from the OEO in November 1970. We held it in a hotel meeting room rented for $85, donated to us by former Legal Services colleagues.
(Bettmann/Corbis)

Reviewing with Senator Howard Baker during a Watergate hearing the subpoena that I had drafted for President Nixon's tapes, 1973.

Conferring with Nixon's lawyer, Herbert Kalmbach (center)
and his lawyer at the Watergate hearings.

Viewing the Watergate complex with Tony Ulasewicz
from the Howard Johnson's hotel across the street, where
Tony had left money for the burglars on a ledge.

Leaving the White House with Rufus L. Edmisten (left) after serving the president with the Ervin Committee subpoena, 1973.
(George Tames/ The New York Times/ Redux)

With my client Dr. Sidney Gottlieb, after his testimony to Senator Kennedy's subcommittee about his work for the CIA, 1977.

To Terry,
Good thing you changed up!
Best,
John Kennedy

With John F. Kennedy Jr. and my son, Jonathan,
at a 1997 reception for *George* magazine.
Jonathan is now executive vice president of IGI.

hearings to publicly explore how the federal government had been infiltrated by one of the most powerful industrialists in the world. I also thought there was a chance that television hearings would create public pressure on Mr. Hughes and others in his organization to cooperate with the investigation and maybe appear at the hearings.

On February 15, I drafted a memorandum to Chairman Ervin, formally requesting him to reconvene the hearings. I noted we had assembled evidence of a "clear pattern of involvement by the President with regard to the contribution of $100,000 in cash carried by Richard Danner to the President's friend Rebozo." I made the case that these revelations, and others, merited full disclosure to the American people.

After Senator Ervin read my memo, he called me into his office. "Terry, this is good work," he said, "but I don't think we'll hold another hearing." He said he had thought the matter over carefully. The timing, he indicated, was the problem.

By early 1974, the Watergate scandal had become the center of attention in the House of Representatives, where the Rodino Committee would soon prepare preparing a bill of impeachment against President Nixon. Ervin said he'd turn over the information we compiled to Leon Jaworski, the new special prosecutor who had been appointed to replace Cox. He also said he would allow us to draft a section of the committee's final report, revealing the evidence about Hughes we had obtained to date.

I respected and admired Senator Ervin, but I was disappointed by his decision. A written report would certainly not have the impact of a televised inquiry. His decision also assumed our investigation was complete. We would not be able to subpoena any more witnesses or garner any new information. I had believed that new hearings would shed light on the central question behind Watergate—why the break-in was ordered, what Nixon had been trying to hide.

Over time, I began to wonder if there might be other reasons that the Hughes-Rebozo hearings were scrubbed. During the investigation of the Hughes network, it quickly became clear that the billionaire's reach was not limited to Richard Nixon. We had interviewed dozens of witnesses in many major agencies and departments that had dealings with Hughes—from the Department of Justice to the CIA to the IRS to the Atomic Energy Commission to the Federal Reserve.

Mr. Hughes was a bipartisan ATM. Robert Maheu claimed that, before Nixon took office, Hughes had instructed him to take $1 million to the LBJ ranch in Texas—a bribe to get the president to halt nuclear tests in Nevada. Maheu said he did go to the ranch and stayed there for four days. But it was never made clear to me what happened to the $1 million.

There was another allegation that Hughes gave money to Johnson's vice president, Nixon's 1968 opponent, Hubert Humphrey. This was early 1974, when Humphrey was considering another run for the presidency. Maheu claimed that, holding a briefcase filled with $50,000, he had entered a car with the vice president and gotten out a block later without the briefcase.

One could assume that Howard Hughes's money had found its way even to senators on the Ervin Committee. While the committee was quick to denounce the Nixon White House for financial impropriety, it was unlikely the Democratic senators were all that interested in exposing possibly illicit contributions to their own campaigns or those of other Democrats. Senator Talmadge, for one, had financial skeletons literally in his own closet.

While tracking the Nixon campaign's money trail, we came across the name of a wealthy donor from the South, A. D. Davis, an owner of the Winn-Dixie grocery stores. Davis had given a $50,000 contribution to Bebe Rebozo. I decided to interview Mr. Davis to see what he could tell us about that contribution as well as about Rebozo's fundraising.

According to committee rules, whenever investigators interviewed a witness in executive session, at least one senator had to be present to swear in the witness and act as arbiter of the questioning. While preparing for the Davis interview, I was called by Senator Talmadge's aide, who said that his boss wanted to preside over the session and asked that it be held in Talmadge's office. Since the witness came from Talmadge's home state of Georgia, the senator felt a proprietary interest in the matter. Chairman Ervin agreed to the request.

I knew something was amiss when Davis entered Talmadge's office. One of the first things Davis said was, "Herman, I've got my plane here. You want a ride back to Georgia?"

We got little from Davis. Every time I raised a sensitive question about the $50,000 contribution he'd made, his lawyer objected. And Talmadge, as the presiding officer, upheld every objection that was raised. I found that remarkable, and presumed Talmadge had decided to do a favor for a prominent constituent to shield him from embarrassment. But there was more to it than that.

Later, Talmadge's aide was arrested for taking a bribe from Davis. The bribe apparently was made the day before Davis testified. No evidence linked the senator directly to this. However, when Talmadge and his wife later divorced, she found bundles of cash hidden in her former husband's shoes while cleaning out one of their closets. On October 11, 1979, Talmadge was denounced by the Senate for "improper financial conduct." One of the last segregationist Southern Democrats, he was defeated for reelection in 1980 by a Republican. But he never faced criminal charges.

Hank Greenspun, one of the only people willing to finger Hughes, described the billionaire industrialist as "the biggest despoiler of the American political system." Curiously, Greenspun had also benefited from Hughes, who had given Hank a loan to buy his newspaper. Even the crusading journalist was tainted by money from Howard Hughes.

Hughes got away with it all. He was never questioned about his attempts to influence the American political system through bribery and intimidation. No one ever uncovered how much money he had given to elected officials and candidates of both parties in exchange for political favors. To this day, no one knows exactly how much his influence impacted decisions by the federal government.

Post-Watergate, Congress tried to constrain financial influence on candidates. New campaign finance laws limited individual campaign contributions and provided a formula for public funding of presidential campaigns. Those limits were upended decades later by the Supreme Court's decision in *Citizens United*. Super PACs now funnel unlimited funds without transparent attribution to benefit political campaigns. In fact, the checks on someone like Howard Hughes are as lax today, if not more so, than they have ever been.

I n retrospect, the Watergate investigation and public hearings served the American people and our democracy extremely well. Elected officials—in both parties—our federal judges, and many members of the media worked to bring many revelations to light. Nixon's impeachment for "high crimes and misdemeanors" proved the enduring strength of our Constitution. That America's elected representatives could peacefully depose the highest elected representative in the land was a remarkable feat, one that spoke to how well and deliberately Congress approached Watergate. Over the decades that followed, I've been interviewed by many foreigners seeking to learn from the successful outcome of our Watergate experience. Other countries faced with entrenched corruption, including Afghanistan recently, have hoped to use Watergate as a model for cleansing their political systems without violence.

Watergate's successes could not have happened, it must be said, had it not been for men like Sam Ervin, Dan Inouye, and other Democrats committed to working in a bipartisan way to uncover the truth. That is also true of Howard Baker, Fred Thompson, and his investigators, most of them Republicans who followed the facts and were willing to implicate a president of their own party, a man they'd voted for and likely admired. The bipartisanship, the comity, on display during those months was an impressive example of America at its best. Unfortunately, Washington wouldn't always work that way.

CHAPTER 5

THE TRIBES

On November 28, 1953, the doorman at Manhattan's Statler Hotel slipped away from his post for a quick drink. Returning to the job, he saw a shadowy figure in the sky, grasping the air as he fell. His body smashed against a piece of metal as he landed, making a loud thud before coming to rest on the Seventh Avenue pavement. The doorman rushed into the hotel in search of the night manager, who became witness to a grisly scene. The man's head was bleeding. His legs were mangled at unnatural angles by the impact. Bone protruded from his arm. After a brief attempt to form a few words, he died.

Dr. Frank Olson was identified as an army microbiologist, a husband and father, who had last been seen alive on the hotel's tenth floor. He was forty-three years old. Olson's death was ruled a suicide. But his family never believed it.

For years, the Olsons had believed that Frank had been in the army, until it was revealed that he actually served in the CIA. After a CIA semiannual retreat in the Maryland woods, Olson returned home to his wife and children "a different man," as they put it. He was with-drawn, depressed, and angry; something had happened to him that weekend—what, exactly, they couldn't know and he wouldn't say. Over Thanksgiving in 1953, he had traveled to New York ostensibly on busi-ness. His family never heard from him again.

Two decades later, the relatively forgotten story of Frank Olson resurfaced, and in a big way. It came to light when the country was still reeling from the Watergate revelations, Nixon's resignation, and his subsequent pardon by the new president, Gerald R. Ford. The pardon infuriated many Americans, some even believed the new presi-dent was himself part of a criminal conspiracy to help Nixon cheat the justice system.

New revelations about secret federal government activities threat-ened to further erode the public trust. In December 1974, Seymour Hersh authored a front-page story for the *New York Times* that impli-cated the Central Intelligence Agency in a host of illegal activities go-ing back to the Eisenhower, Kennedy, and Johnson administrations. The paper unearthed a massive archive of classified documents, the CIA's so-called "family jewels," which revealed the agency's involve-ment in attempted assassinations of foreign leaders, surveillance activi-ties in the United States, and drug experiments conducted on American citizens without their knowledge. Prominent on that list was Frank Olson. Twenty-one years after his fall, Olson had effectively come back from the dead, threatening to tear apart the institution that he had served his entire career.

The CIA had come under some scrutiny during Watergate. Senator Baker, for one, was convinced to the very end that the agency had played a larger role in the scandal. I never thought there was much to that. It was true that some of the Watergate burglars, like Howard Hunt and James McCord, were former CIA agents. I came across one

CIA agent who apparently provided false IDs, fake glasses, and other disguises to one of the plumbers. And then there was Hughes's Bob Maheu, of course, who was involved in the CIA plot to assassinate Fidel Castro. But I never believed that the agency as an institution was involved in crimes because I assumed the president had approved these activities. If Nixon's men needed operatives who could run a clandestine operation, it only made sense that the first people they called were some agency retirees.

The disclosures about the CIA shocked Americans who wanted to believe in their government's good intentions, and confirmed for others their long-held suspicions about the agency. College campuses banned CIA recruiters. Liberal members of Congress proposed legislation to bar the agency from being involved in covert activities, which would have gutted the agency and put an end to an institution that was effectively the nation's eyes and ears against the Soviet Union.

I didn't agree with any knee-jerk reaction. It didn't surprise me that there were unsavory skeletons in the CIA's closet, but I needed more information before judging, and much more was soon to come out.

In the wake of the Hersh article, hearings were quickly convened on Capitol Hill, led by Senator Frank Church and Congressman Otis Pike. The two Democrats promised live testimony from witnesses about the abuses within the intelligence community. The Ford administration, joined by Republicans in Congress, tended to be more deferential to the CIA and its officials, complaining that the hearings risked exposing national security secrets that might aid the Soviet Union.

At the time, I was working for a small law firm that I'd joined in January 1975: Truitt, Fabrikant, Bucklin, and—now—Lenzner. As the CIA revelations mounted, a friend who was special counsel to CIA director Bill Colby asked me to go to agency headquarters in Langley, Virginia, to talk to the officers and advise them about their legal rights. Some would be subpoenaed to testify, and many were encountering investigators who showed up at their homes to ask questions. Expecting to encounter sophisticated operatives trained in how to respond to public inquiries, I instead found a group of earnest, dedicated people utterly clueless about what was happening to them—relatively unaware that they could face jail time if they said the wrong thing to a congressional panel.

These were people who spent most of their lives in a bubble. Because of their sensitive jobs, they couldn't talk to anyone else about what they knew. They ate lunches and dinners together; their families socialized together. During the Cold War, congressional oversight of the CIA was usually appreciative and always highly confidential. I was surprised by how unprepared they were. That an agency whose assignment was to gather sensitive intelligence would leave the holders of those secrets without any advice about how to respond to questions seeking high-security information and susceptible to prosecution was troubling. They were completely vulnerable to some hard-nosed attorney on the Church Committee who would be looking to rattle them, catch them in a small lie that would lead to a charge of perjury, and expose their secrets. Many didn't even seem to understand that they needed lawyers—and that their lawyers would talk to Congress on their behalf.

On July 22, 1975, President Ford disclosed that Frank Olson had been the unfortunate victim of an experiment that had secretly given LSD to unsuspecting subjects in order to gauge the effect the drug might have in interrogations. The circumstances of Olson's death returned to the headlines as the family pressed for more answers about how the United States government could have allowed this.

As preparations for hearings progressed, attention focused on Sidney Gottlieb, whom the media referred to as "Dr. Death." He was the scientist who oversaw the drug experiments as chief of the chemical division of the CIA's technical services staff. According to some accounts, he had destroyed documents to cover them up. He was retired from the agency, unavailable to the press, and living abroad. Gottlieb's former deputy at the CIA, Robert Lashbrook, who had shared a hotel room with Frank Olson on the night of his death, publicly implicated Gottlieb in the episode. Lashbrook said Gottlieb was present when Olson was given LSD in a drink. Separately, the United States Commission on CIA Activities Within the United States, led by Vice President Nelson Rockefeller—an independent blue ribbon commission tasked to examine the entire array of allegations against the CIA— reported that Gottlieb had defied orders by President Nixon to destroy the toxins he had helped develop. A CIA laboratory was found to still possess illegal stockpiles of poisons such as cobra venom and shellfish toxin.

A few weeks after Ford's admission that the CIA had been involved in Olson's death, the lawyer who'd asked me to talk to the folks at Langley contacted me again. He said a former employee of the agency, Sid Gottlieb, needed legal representation and wanted to know if I might be interested.

"Sure," I replied. "Have him give me a call."

A day later I was in contact with Dr. Death himself. Sid Gottlieb's husky voice had a pronounced stutter, but he came across as confident, not nervous. Considering that he had spent decades in the CIA with a portfolio that included devising ways to eliminate enemies of the United States, I suspected it took a lot to get him rattled.

Sid told me he'd be interested in meeting and underscored his desire for discretion. I suggested we meet in a small park in Northwest Washington called Rosedale, around the corner from my house. There it would be more difficult for anyone to plant listening devices. It was certainly not out of the realm of possibility that he was under surveillance by his former employers.

Anyone who read the coverage in the newspapers would have expected some sort of devilish monster to arrive on the scene. Instead, as

I sat waiting on a park bench, a man with a limp came toward me. He was casually dressed, and his clubfoot dragged behind him. He approached cautiously, casting furtive glances around him—subtly enough that it was clear to me he had been well trained in the art of countersurveillance.

Once he took a seat beside me, he offered his hand. "I'm Sid Gottlieb."

"Terry Lenzner," I replied. "I'm glad we could get together in person."

Dr. Gottlieb told me that he and his wife had recently flown back from India, where they ran a hospital for lepers. He said he had learned of the allegations against him and the agency and was troubled and angered by them. A lot of the accusations, he hinted, were untrue. What especially bothered him were the attacks on the CIA, which had been his home for decades.

"The agency is devoted to the defense of this country," he said. This was not a man who appeared frightened or defensive, or desperate for guidance to get him out of a legal jam. This was a fifty-seven-year-old guy who was ticked off. It's fair to say I liked him right away.

"If we work together," Gottlieb said, "the first thing I want to do is hold a press conference and rebut these charges one by one."

I'd heard few ideas as counterproductive as that one. All he would accomplish from going public would be to put an even larger target on his back.

"I think that may be a little premature," I replied with uncharacteristic understatement. "If I'm to represent you, we'll need to talk through everything before considering our options."

He pondered this for a moment and decided that it made some sense. "Well, I am going to need legal counsel," Gottlieb said. "But before we work together, I'm going to need a sample of your handwriting."

"Why is that?" I asked.

"I have someone at the agency who can analyze it and tell me whether I should trust you."

No one had ever asked me for that before. But considering his line of work, it seemed reasonable. I knew that handwriting analysis was commonly used in many other countries to assess a job applicant's character and veracity. Besides, I was kind of curious about what they'd find out. He asked me to jot down some miscellaneous sentences on a piece of paper and then placed it in his pocket.

"I'll get back to you," he said. "Nice to meet you." Then he was gone.

Sid Gottlieb's return to the United States was significant news, making headlines in the *Washington Post* and other papers. The *Post* also noted that he had retained me as his legal counsel. Meanwhile CIA officials confirmed that Dr. Gottlieb was one of the scientists present when Olson and other army personnel were experimented on. I assumed that if the agency was looking for a scapegoat, they might well choose Sid. If he chose to work with me, I would suggest he fight for immunity.

A few days after our meeting, Gottlieb telephoned. "You checked out," he told me. "No character defects." The woman who analyzed my handwriting had told Sid that I would fiercely defend him. We arranged to meet again.

As my involvement in the Gottlieb case became known, many of my liberal friends were bewildered, even aghast. "How can you defend a man like that?" I was asked. They were the same kinds of questions people on the other side of the political spectrum had asked me earlier when I defended Phil Berrigan. My answer was the same: Why shouldn't I? In both cases I represented clients who were considered villains by many Americans, and in some sense scapegoats for people's discomfort with the larger issues their activities raised. Both men impressed me with their ideals, commitment, and courage, which played major roles in my decision to represent them. It wasn't my job to pass moral judgment on either man. My job was to help give them a sound legal defense. In retrospect, two of the cases I am proudest of are my representation of Sid Gottlieb and defense of Phil Berrigan and his colleagues.

I didn't think it made sense to push a man like Sid Gottlieb, trained in secrets, to share information any sooner than he was ready. Instead I began our conversation talking about the more innocuous subjects, such as his background and personal life. He told me he was the child of Hungarian immigrants and, as was often typical of first-generation Americans, deeply grateful for the privileges that this country offered. After earning a Ph.D. in biochemistry, he joined the agency in 1951.

Sid had wanted to fight in World War II, but his clubfoot made him ineligible. He was earnest in his belief that America was engaged in a life-or-death struggle against Communism. He wanted to play his part. In his mind America could do no wrong. Though neither man would welcome the comparison, Sid reminded me a lot of Phil Berrigan—one was distrustful of the government, the other willing to risk his life for it, but both shared a certain quality. In simplest terms, I think it was an absence of cynicism.

I watched Sid carefully as he spoke—studying his movements and gestures, listening for any hesitations or pauses. Just like Berrigan, there didn't appear to be an ounce of deviousness in him.

Retired from the agency since 1972, Gottlieb pursued a quieter life. When he was not in India, Gottlieb and his wife lived in Washington, Virginia, a sleepy town nestled in the foothills of the Blue Ridge Mountains, a ninety-minute drive from D.C. He told me he raised goats and grew Christmas trees, which he sold at a roadside stand during the winters. He had taken up folk dancing. In his spare time, he volunteered to help children overcome stuttering. Having abandoned his Jewish roots, he explored Zen Buddhism. And he still felt deeply patriotic and appreciative of his country. As I said, it was hard not to like him.

Eventually, as Sid became more comfortable, our discussion turned toward his work. Small and informal in its nascent years after World War II, the CIA had been more of a club than the complex organization it has since become. Its senior ranks were filled with dashing, well-heeled men of Yale and Harvard. With his stutter, clubfoot, and immigrant roots, Sid did not fit into that crowd. I could sympathize. After all, I had similar feelings of separateness when I was at Harvard.

Because of his expertise in poisons, Gottlieb told me he was put in charge of assassination programs for the agency. He managed several operations to attempt to assassinate foreign leaders. The agency, for example, considered giving President Sukarno of Indonesia a sexually transmitted disease through an airline stewardess working for the agency. Gottlieb conceived ways to send various James Bond–like poisons to Fidel Castro: a monogrammed handkerchief dipped in poison, exploding cigars, poisoned wet suits. In contrast to newspaper accounts and widespread suspicions, which depicted the CIA as an efficient killing machine, Sid pointed out that none of these plans were either implemented or successful.

Gottlieb described one executive action in which he had been deeply involved. In the summer of 1960 his boss, CIA deputy director Richard Bissell, ordered him to select a poison to be used against a leader in Africa. He was not told at the time which leader, only that the plan had been approved by the "highest authority," presumably President Eisenhower. Sid presented Bissell with his pick of various poisons: rabbit fever, tuberculosis, anthrax, smallpox, sleeping sickness, and undulant fever. They selected one that was indigenous to the region and certain to be fatal. Bissell then revealed the agency's target: Patrice Lumumba, the prime minister of the newly independent Congo. The U.S. considered Lumumba a Communist, the Castro of Africa and a fervent ally of the Soviet Union who had to be neutralized.

Sid described to me assembling hypodermic needles and rubber gloves, and arranging his flight to arrive in the Congo that September. His plan was to have a vial of poison injected into Lumumba's toothpaste or food. After flying to the capital of Léopoldville, he handed the deadly toxin to the CIA station chief there. But before the plot could be implemented, Lumumba was captured by his domestic rivals, imprisoned, and shot by a firing squad.

Surprisingly, much of Sid's work did not focus on U.S. enemies abroad. The CIA also conducted experiments on American citizens. Sid was not at all defensive about the LSD program in general and indeed thought it was essential to American security. During the Korean War, Gottlieb recalled, CIA officials had observed what the North Koreans did to American POWs. Eyes glazed, mumbling, they had been drugged during interrogations to give up information. Some thought they had even been brainwashed. (This would be the basis of the 1959 novel *The Manchurian Candidate*.) In 1951, George Kennan, a senior American diplomat in Moscow, had given a press conference where he delivered notably undiplomatic remarks and seemed to have lost all judgment. Sid and others at the agency believed Kennan had been drugged or exposed to something that controlled his mind. He told me that the CIA had information that the Soviet Union had secured a large quantity of LSD in Switzerland. The agency feared the Soviets were trying to buy up the world's entire supply. They believed the Soviets had developed an advantage in mind control, and America would have to make up the difference—fast.

Sid said that he had supervised LSD experiments on more than twenty unsuspecting people. He had experimented with LSD on himself too. When we discussed individual cases—subjects or victims of the program, depending on your point of view—he seemed pained. As an academic exercise, Sid could go on confidently about the rightness of his activities. But he wasn't so comfortable talking about individual cases or real people whose lives were affected. Not surprisingly, he wasn't enthusiastic about talking about Olson. His deranged suicide had occurred when Olson was receiving treatment for the effects of LSD, but because Sid had directed the use of the drug, he felt responsible.

As he recounted this, one thing became perfectly clear—at least to me. The press conference he had proposed was now off the table. From my perspective, it had never been on the table. That is, if he wanted me to represent him. "And before you talk to any committee or anyone else," I told him, "we're going to ask for immunity from prosecution."

Sid was troubled by my insistence. "I'm not going to do that," he snapped. "I'm not going to hide behind the Fifth Amendment." He thought it was un-American. He believed he was totally in the right— if only he could explain himself, the senators and the country would understand. I thought our relationship might be over at that point.

"Look, Sid, the goal here is to keep you out of the newspapers and, at a minimum, out of jail," I said. "You don't understand how this works. You could very well become the fall guy in this whole investigation." There was another investigation into Olson's death under way, led by the Manhattan District Attorney's Office, and Sid was a ripe, juicy target. He was no longer a senior official in the agency. He had few defenders.

"They could try to pin Olson's death on you," I advised him.

He considered my words. For the first time in our conversations, he seemed to fully understand his potential legal peril.

Evidence suggested that the agency did plan to scapegoat Gottlieb. Of the documents the CIA released to the press and federal investigators in response to the growing scandal about its activities, most were heavily redacted, with individual operatives' names crossed out. But Sid's remained plainly legible. He stood out alone.

Scapegoating Sid might have been the CIA's intent, but I figured the Church Committee might have bigger aspirations. Church and the Democratic majority were hoping Gottlieb would provide information that would supplement what they'd already gathered on the agency, and ultimately incriminate higher-ranking officials in these activities. For these reasons, I figured they'd grant Sid's immunity request.

Fortuitously, the immunity negotiation dragged on for weeks. This gave us a chance to look over all the documents the committee had that involved Sid and prepare him for his testimony. The delay also kept us out of the spotlight when the Church hearings were going full bore. By the time Sid's immunity request was granted, the hearings were winding down. Public attention had waned. This of course was what we'd hoped for in our slowdown strategy.

As part of our immunity deal, Sid's testimony was closed to the public and conducted in a secure room that was outfitted to prevent electronic surveillance. Unfortunately, on the day of his testimony, the news that Gottlieb had requested immunity was leaked to the newspapers. This was a violation of our agreement and very unprofessional. It looked like Sid was trying to hide something, or was afraid to appear before the crusading committee, when in fact I was the one who had insisted on the agreement.

When the hearing commenced, I was so upset that I addressed the senators directly. "I want to put on the record my objection that this committee has disclosed my client's request for immunity, despite our agreement to the contrary," I said, looking at the assembled senators one by one. "Leaking that information is reminiscent of the character assassination that Senator Joseph McCarthy specialized in." I stated that Sid had sought immunity on my advice, and that he had wanted to talk without any protection.

As I anticipated, the reference to Senator McCarthy touched a nerve, especially among liberals on the panel. I don't think Gottlieb was comfortable with it either. Senator Walter Mondale, who was a neighbor of mine and who had been a supporter of mine in Legal Services, went ballistic.

"Terry, I think that's overstating things," he snapped.

"Well, I don't," I replied.

As payback, I assumed, the committee's chief counsel asked Gott-lieb to state his residence for the record. We had reached an agreement before the hearing that this information would not be asked for or re-leased. I whispered to Sid to give him my office address. I could tell Gottlieb was uncomfortable with my approach and my references to McCarthy. Sid was used to being forthright and respecting authority.

In testifying, Sid defended the drug experimentation programs. Under the instructions of CIA director Allen Dulles, the agency had initiated a program in 1953 to explore the frontiers of the human mind. Sid said he was charged with implementing a project code-named MK-ULTRA. Researchers focused on the psychedelic drug LSD as a potentially powerful tool in espionage. Sid described his belief that the USSR was ahead in this quest and that U.S. experimentation was es-sential to maintain comparable capability.

Under MK-ULTRA, funding was provided for these experiments—mostly on prisoners, mental patients, and others who weren't in posi-tions to object, like the customers who frequented two brothels run by the agency in San Francisco and New York. The agency, sometimes working with the military, also conducted experiments abroad, slip-ping various pills and lozenges of LSD into the drinks of strangers and misfits. Gottlieb denied that he was the one who had failed to destroy illegal toxins found in CIA laboratories. Throughout he was calm and measured, always defending the agency as the guardian of the coun-try's security. The hearing was going along fine, without any surprises, until Senator Richard Schweiker, a Pennsylvania Republican, handed us a heavily redacted document.

"Dr. Gottlieb," the senator asked, "can you tell me what this memo is about?" The memo had an ominous title: "Health Alteration Com-mittee." Gottlieb had written and addressed it to senior CIA officials. I'd never seen it before, even though the committee had agreed to give us all memoranda in their possession prior to the hearing.

Sid, however, clearly had seen the memo before. He looked distressed. A silence fell over the room.

Putting my hand over the microphone, I leaned in toward my client. "What's up, Sid?"

"I need to talk to you about this," Sid whispered.

Sid suffered from a heart condition, so I turned back to the microphone and addressed the committee members. "Mr. Chairman, my client isn't feeling well," I said. "Can I request a brief recess?"

Sid and I then retreated to a small, empty office. I shut the door behind us.

He was breathing heavily, his face still drained of color. He closed his eyes and then began what looked like a slow dance, his arms extended. What on earth was this?

As if reading my mind, Sid said, "Tai chi. Helps me relax."

"Sid," I prodded again, "help me out here. What's in that memo?"

He was still in tai chi mode. "That's the one," he said. "The one that worked."

He told me the memo referenced a Communist official in an Arab country whom the CIA "wanted to get rid of." According to a State Department document, the Iraqi colonel was "extremely aggressive . . . anti-Western to the point of hatred . . . and has given important support for the success of Communism and Soviet policy in Iraq." Sid had arranged for a scarf to be mailed to the colonel from a "fan club."

I shrugged. "What kind of scarf?"

"One infected with tuberculosis," he said. "He died after a couple of weeks."

Allowing Gottlieb to reveal a successful CIA assassination at this point in the Church hearings had the potential to ignite an entirely new inquiry and put him smack into the spotlight. Fortunately for Gottlieb, the senators didn't appear to know what they had in their possession. The memo was too vaguely worded for anyone else to decipher.

Sid and I sat down and devised a careful answer to avoid revealing this new information without committing perjury. When he returned to the hearing room, Sid said that the agency had sent a handkerchief "treated with some kind of material for the purpose of harassing that person who received it." The senators didn't know enough to ask the right follow-up questions, and Sid made it through the hearing relatively unscathed.

As a condition for Sid's testimony, I had requested that his name not appear in the Church Committee's final report. In response, the committee basically told me to bug off. They had granted immunity to get Sid to testify, but they had no interest in acceding to any further requests.

Consequently, I filed a lawsuit on Sid's behalf, asking a federal judge to do something rather unorthodox for the courts—namely to order a Senate committee to keep my client's name out of its final report. Substantial legal precedents held that courts could not censor congressional publications. But I thought I'd give it a try, if only to vindicate Sid's handwriting analyst.

Through a friend at the agency, I contacted Bill Colby, then the director of the CIA, who agreed to testify in court that naming Sid Gottlieb in the final version of the Church report would pose a danger not only to Sid but to his family. Colby noted that Sid had relatives all over the world who could conceivably be targeted for reprisal attacks.

Predictably, the federal judge who heard the case—Gerhard Gesell—would not dictate what the legislative branch could say. But he was persuaded by my arguments. In making his ruling, on November 17, 1975, he added an additional "finding of fact" stating that should the Church Committee go forward with their plan to name Gottlieb, then the United States Congress would knowingly place Gottlieb and his entire family in danger. In other words, the judge told the Senate—if anything happens to this guy, you've got blood on your hands. It was a brilliant move, and it scared the senators. On November 18, 1975, the Senate Select Committee on Intelligence voted to delete Dr. Sidney Gottlieb's name from its report.

Sid and I had one more hurdle to overcome. Although Richard Helms, the director of the CIA in 1973, had ordered MK-ULTRA files destroyed to avoid discovery during Watergate, a cache of files was found in 1977 in response to a Freedom of Information Act request. That same year Senator Edward Kennedy, a talented politician who knew how to seize a good story and turn it to his political advantage, scheduled a hearing of his Subcommittee on Health and Scientific Research to examine the U.S. government's experimentation with drugs in the Cold War, focusing especially on the most salacious aspects of those programs—ones involving soldiers and prostitutes. Specifically, Kennedy intended to grill Sid on accusations that he had doctored and destroyed many of the CIA's reports. Sid still had immunity from prosecution, but as his lawyer, I was concerned that he might perjure himself or incur more scrutiny.

I worked with Kennedy's staff to ensure there would be no surprises during Sid's testimony. I insisted that the hearing be held in executive session behind closed doors, and that the witness be protected from exposure to the press and the public. I told them that Gottlieb had a heart condition and that TV cameras and a crowd of spectators would be too much for him. Sid's cardiologist helped us out with a note warning against overexcitement. Most important, I said, for the safety of his family, it was imperative that Gottlieb's name not be leaked nor a picture of him taken. Knowing that Sid's testimony would be vital to the headline-grabbing hearing they wanted to present, Kennedy and his staff agreed to these stipulations. We had arranged for Sid to testify from a private room via a closed-circuit camera—which would allow committee members to see him but the press in the committee room to only hear his voice.

A few minutes before the hearing was to begin, the door to the room burst open. In marched Kennedy, with a smile across his face and a photographer in tow, already snapping pictures. The senator marched over to shake Sid's hand.

In a fury, I instructed Sid not to stand up—I didn't want to make the photo any easier for the senator. In the picture, Kennedy is shown standing awkwardly over the witness. Not only did Kennedy violate his express promise, Sid's picture was almost certain to dominate the front pages of newspapers. I did worry that Kennedy's publicity stunt would endanger Sid and his family.

After Kennedy left the room, and just before the hearing was to begin, I pulled Gottlieb aside. "Sid, is there anything you can add to your opening statement that reporters can focus on? Anything that would make news?"

He thought for a moment. "Well, there is one thing," he said. "I think that it's classified, though."

"What is it?" I asked.

He told me a story that I had never heard before. Nor, I was certain, had members of the press corps. I knew it would be a dramatic distraction from Kennedy's effort to put Sid's activities on trial.

"Well, we are going to declassify it right now," I replied.

As Kennedy banged the committee gavel and brought the hearing to order, Sid spoke to the senators through the closed-circuit camera.

After Sid was sworn in, I gestured to him. He looked at me and nodded. "At this point, with your permission, I would like to interject two or three incidents," he told the senators. "I did not write them here [in my opening statement] because they were not recalled." Kennedy told Sid that he could proceed.

Gottlieb then told the committee what he'd just shared with me. In 1971, the Nixon White House contacted the CIA asking for help. One of the president's physicians had become disoriented and had difficulty remembering the names of friends and acquaintances. The symptoms arose immediately after a trip with Nixon to what Sid called "a hostile country," which everyone assumed, correctly, was the Soviet Union. The president's personal physician also had odd symptoms, Sid revealed, including "inappropriate tears and crying." Sid said the "foreign country" was known to have stockpiles of LSD, which led the White House and the CIA to consider whether this foreign government had given mind-altering drugs to two men in extremely close proximity to the president of the United States.

I could tell from the silence in the room that Sid's revelation had floored everyone. Senator Kennedy was not at all prepared for this issue.

"Are you suggesting that the presidential party was drugged?" Kennedy asked, incredulous. He added solemnly that the allegations had "extraordinarily grave" implications.

"I'm suggesting they wanted us to review and determine whether that ever happened," Sid replied, saying the CIA never conclusively proved it. He added that there were at least twenty other instances in which U.S. military or diplomatic officials were thought to have been administered drugs by foreign agents. Sid told the committee about a courier carrying U.S. documents who was staying in a hotel room abroad when a pipe was slipped under the hotel room door. An odorless gas was transmitted into the room, rendering the courier unconscious while classified papers were stolen. It was a riveting story, James Bond stuff.

Gottlieb used that story to make an important point, one that cast his experiments in a different light. Use of mind-altering drugs by America's enemies on our officials had posed a grave threat to the U.S. He said the CIA was woefully behind in its own knowledge of the drugs and their effects. During the Cold War, this lack of knowledge posed "a threat of the magnitude of national survival." Sid also admitted that he did in fact destroy some documents related to these programs. He did so, he said, to protect the agency, because "this material was sensitive and capable of being misunderstood."

Sid's testimony changed the focus of Kennedy's hearing. After it was over, I could see the senator was not happy. "Drugging of Aides Feared by CIA" was one of the numerous headlines in the next morning's papers. One reporter described poor Sid, sympathetically, as a man in "precarious" health. Whatever point, or headlines, Kennedy had wanted to make was lost.

What struck me the most about the Gottlieb case was the knee-jerk reaction that people had depending on their assumptions. Many were determined to believe what the CIA did was justified, using "national security" as a cover for all manner of sins. On the other side were those who believed the very worst about the CIA's operatives, including Sid, without knowing them at all.

The Washington tribe mentality was brought home to me again in 1981, after Ronald Reagan unseated President Jimmy Carter and moved into the White House. At the time, I was working for a different law firm—Wald, Harkrader, and Ross—which had merged with the small firm I had joined after Watergate.

Reagan nominated Alexander Haig, who had been Richard Nixon's last chief of staff, to be secretary of state. As the Nixon White House crumbled under threat of impeachment, Haig was widely regarded as the person in control. To many Democrats, Haig was still considered an unindicted co-conspirator in Watergate—one of the Nixon people who'd gotten away unscathed. It was curious, maybe gutsy, that Reagan appointed him to such a prominent post.

Claiborne Pell was the senior Democrat on the Senate Foreign Relations Committee and a powerful figure in Congress. His committee was responsible for holding confirmation hearings on the Haig nomination. As the hearing date approached, Senator Pell asked me to visit him in his spacious Senate office.

From behind his desk, Senator Pell, a lean, slight man from Rhode Island, looked at me through his dark-rimmed glasses. "Mr. Lenzner, I want to talk to you about becoming my counsel in the hearings for Al Haig," he said.

He knew some of my background, specifically that I'd worked on the Watergate Committee. That was what interested him. "I want to look at General Haig's involvement in the scandal," he said. "I figure you're the best person to help us do that."

I knew that Haig had been only tangentially involved in Watergate. I had questioned him specifically about his knowledge of the Hughes loan and the audit of Larry O'Brien. But no evidence ever implicated him in any improper activity. I knew nothing from the Watergate investigation that was at all relevant as to whether Haig should be confirmed as secretary of state. It bothered me that Watergate might be dredged up now without real merit.

After giving it some consideration, I expressed my concerns to Pell directly. I understood that the nomination of the secretary of state—the most senior official in the cabinet—deserved a thorough examination. But I believed that the confirmation hearings should be conducted with care and fairness so as not to compromise the nominee's ability to carry out foreign policy. I recalled that the Senate Foreign Relations Committee had a history of bipartisanship—in line with the adage "politics stops at the water's edge"—and traditionally gave broad deference to a president's nominees, particularly those intended to implement U.S. foreign policy.

"With all due respect, Senator," I said, "I don't think this is a good way to do this." I said I didn't think it made sense to revisit Watergate and put the country through that all over again with a new president and a new administration coming into office. I said that in my view the only issues relevant to a hearing like this were the capabilities of the nominee.

I offered him an alternative. "What I'd like to do is make this a nonpartisan inquiry," I said. "I'd like your permission to go see Howard Baker"—Baker was the new majority leader of the Senate—"to see if we might work together to avoid an ugly, partisan hearing over the nomination."

Pell smiled politely, but he looked skeptical. "Fine," he said. "Go ahead and see what you can do."

I hadn't seen Senator Baker since the Watergate hearings. The new majority leader was, as always, friendly and gentlemanly. I told Baker that Pell had asked me to be minority counsel. I presented my idea that the Republican and Democratic committee staffs work together to prepare for the hearings in a bipartisan manner, a replication of our work together on the Watergate Committee. What was even more perfect was that Baker had assigned Fred Thompson to be his lead counsel for this confirmation. It would be a grand reunion. Or so I thought.

Baker said he liked what I was saying. "I'm not gonna stand in the way," he said in his soft Tennessee accent. Then he added, "Of course, it's all going to be up to Fred. Why don't you go talk to him?"

Since Thompson and I had gotten on well during the Watergate hearings, I was pretty confident he'd agree to collaborate on the Haig nomination. When I met with him in his Senate office, I suggested that we work together and pool our information during the hearings. We would share witness lists, conduct interviews together, and discuss our strategies, just as we had during the Ervin Committee hearings.

Fred seemed amused by the suggestion. He even laughed. He seemed excited to head up the defense of Haig. During Watergate, Fred was a member of the minority and was eager for Democratic assistance and collegiality. But with the Republicans now in the majority in the Senate, the power dynamics had shifted. Fred was now in charge, and that made a big difference to him. I had the sense that Thompson was understandably ambitious and hoped to make a name for himself. Also, he clearly wanted to protect President Reagan and his nominee.

"Terry, if you were in my shoes, would you agree to do it this way?" he asked.

"Of course I would."

"No, you wouldn't," Fred replied. "You're asking me to do somethin' you wouldn't ever do." I think he thought I was trying to take advantage of him, or it was some kind of Democratic trick.

"That's not true," I said. "In fact, if you don't agree to this, then I won't take part at all."

He laughed again. "Come on, Terry, this is high profile. You'll do it anyway."

He was wrong. I went back to Senator Pell and said I wasn't going to be involved in the hearings because of my concerns about their partisan flavor. Pell seemed surprised, as I'm sure Fred Thompson was, by my decision. It was a big disappointment to me—I would have enjoyed the break from my law practice. But I wasn't interested in playing political games with something this important.

As it turned out, Pell's effort met unexpected resistance from the outgoing Carter White House. When the senator asked the Carter people for White House files on Haig and any information they had related to Watergate, Carter's national security advisor, Zbigniew Brzezinski, refused. He said Carter would not be part of a "witch-hunt" or be used to create a "spectacle" in the confirmation hearings. It was a classy thing for the Carter people to do. The next day Pell told reporters on the new CNN cable network that he expected Haig to be confirmed. That didn't stop a contentious battle over the release of some of the Nixon tapes—a battle that did little to stop Haig's confirmation.

Neither party learned much from that exchange. I was observing the closing of the Washington political mind—hardened behind partisanship and distrust. With the Vietnam War over, and the cleansing provided by Senate Watergate and CIA hearings past, this should have been a period of greater political bipartisanship. But more and more, people who involved themselves in national affairs were taking one side or the other. As one who bridged that divide, I was becoming an anomaly, though I hadn't quite realized it yet.

CHAPTER 6

WHERE THERE'S A WILL, THERE'S A WAY

I continued working at my law firm, sometimes on cases requiring investigation that helped hone my skills, but they were relatively straightforward and kept me close to home. But soon enough, three cases came along that took me beyond Washington for weeks at a time. The first was a case requiring good old-fashioned shoe leather—and in this case, I mean that quite literally.

In June 1975, I received a phone call from David Mugar, whom I had met through a friend now working in the Boston Police Department. David was the son of a prominent Armenian-American businessman in Boston who had founded the Star Market grocery chain and owned several other properties.

From the outside, Mugar's Boston office looked like many of the red-brick buildings that dotted the New England city. But inside, it looked as though it had been designed for the next century. The modern office had all kinds of gadgets, and David seemed to use every single one of them. Certainly, his office proved that he was unique. He also was generous, thoughtful, and smart.

When we sat down, David told me he wanted to branch out into television; he wanted to own one of Boston's network affiliates. He had his eye on Channel 7, which was owned by RKO General, a subsidiary of General Tire and Rubber Company. The Ohio-based company had purchased RKO Radio Pictures from, of all people, Howard Hughes in 1955.

In Mugar's view, Channel 7 was airing pretty dull programming and failing to produce intelligent, challenging entertainment. Unfortunately the station wasn't for sale, but it was time for it to seek renewal of its license with the Federal Communications Commission. The Mugars filed a bid with the FCC to challenge reissuance of the license.

The Mugar family claimed that they should be given precedence over RKO for the license because they would broadcast higher-quality programming, which was in the greater public interest. It was a weak argument, and they knew it. As a general rule, the FCC did not strip licenses away from one company because their programming was inferior. One guy's *Masterpiece Theatre* is another person's *Jerry Springer Show*. Not surprisingly, the commissioners denied the Mugar challenge.

Mugar's lawyer had advised that the only way the family had a chance to win the station was to find something "blockbuster" about RKO or its parent company that would change the commissioners' minds. I had no idea how to approach this, but figured that there might be something significant hidden in RKO or General Tire's operations. No one expected me to have much luck, but David really wanted me to try. The Mugar family did not make a fortune in America by giving up whenever they encountered an obstacle.

Clearly, the case required more than good lawyering. It required another critical quality for an investigative firm: good instincts. The first thing I did was pull together all the business records and reports I could find on RKO and General Tire and Rubber. We assembled annual stock reports and SEC filings, but there wasn't likely to be anything in them that was sufficiently dramatic. Additionally, I searched on microfilm for news about the companies and their executives and employees. This was a painstaking process too—you never know what small, seemingly insignificant thing may have a big impact.

I came across an article that mentioned two midlevel General Tire and Rubber executives, Howard Swires and Bob Curtis, who had retired to a small city in Mexico called Morelia. That piqued my curiosity. For one thing, the men seemed too young for retirement. Also, I wondered why two midlevel executives would choose a location so far from home. Retiring to Mexico may be more common for American executives today, but it was unusual in the 1970s. On nothing more than curiosity and Mugar family funding, I decided it would be worth a trip to Mexico to see what these guys might have to offer.

I hired Scott Armstrong, my former Watergate investigator, to accompany me. Scott was good at getting information out of people. When I called David to let him know I was following a hunch to Mexico, he decided to come too. I had one of my investigators call General Tire and Rubber asking how to contact Swires and Curtis in Mexico for a delivery. We got a phone number, and the day before we were scheduled to fly out, I called the number and asked for Howard Swires by name. When he came to the phone, I asked if he was going to be home the next day.

"What's this about?" he asked suspiciously.

"I have a package for you," I said. "I'd like to deliver it tomorrow if you will be home." I did have a package for him, though certainly not what Swires expected. All I could give him were documents related to my client's bid. But Swires seemed interested enough in this mysterious package, and gave me his address.

I had no idea how this trip would turn out. It could have been the proverbial wild-goose chase. But I figured that at the very least, they could tell us something about General Tire's internal operations.

When we arrived at the address in Morelia, we found a compound surrounded by barbed wire, with a Mexican police officer standing outside. It looked like these guys were in hiding. We gave the officer twenty dollars, and he opened the gate.*

H aving satisfied the guard, we walked to the door and knocked. The casually dressed middle-aged man who answered looked like he could be one of the executives we sought. Another fellow came to the door behind him. I made introductions and explained the real purpose of our visit—that we were looking for information that might help Mugar's bid for an RKO TV station in Boston. RKO meant little to them, even if they knew it was a subsidiary of General Tire and Rubber. They had no interest in RKO's success or failure and no reason to be defensive on its behalf.

It soon became obvious they didn't get many visitors. I could see they were desperate to talk to other Americans. They were cooped up in the middle of nowhere with nothing to do, completely bored. What I was telling them was the first mildly interesting thing that had happened to them in who knows how long. They invited us to come inside.

"We'll either kill you or we'll talk to you," one of them said. I decided to take that as a joke.

Howard Swires and Bob Curtis had come to Morelia with their wives, who didn't seem any more content than their husbands were.

---

*Some years later, I was on an assignment in Mexico City on behalf of the U.S. State Department to help train Mexican police officers on investigative tactics. I met with the police commissioner there and spelled out my agenda. I told him that one of the seminars was going to be on internal department corruption. Everyone knew that Mexican police officers were subject to bribes and other forms of influence. "Oh, no," he said. "You're not going to do anything on corruption. We've got that taken care of." His solution to the problem, he told me proudly, was to house new police cadets in a separate building from the old, tainted police corps. One day I went out with the police commissioner and some cadets on a raid to shut down unlicensed vendors in a town square. The cops were pushing the vendors and telling them to shut down their illegal operations. Out of the corner of my eye, I saw one of the vendors hand a camera to a police officer. The cop took the camera and walked off. That vendor did not get shut down. The commissioner was standing right next to me. He saw this happen too, and did nothing.

The men had occupied many days drinking and playing poker. I figured the only way to engage with them was to go where they were. So I asked them to deal us in.

Scott, David, and I spent two days hanging out with Howard and Bob in Morelia. They seemed happy to have us as long as we wanted to stay. They took us to their club for lunch, where we sat outside overlooking the city, then we returned to their compound for more poker and drinking. They poured drink after drink. Eventually I started pouring the drinks. I'd pour them glasses of beer or tequila and tried to avoid drinking much myself. We talked football, politics, movies, anything and everything for hours on end. And then they started to talk about what we had traveled two thousand miles to find out.

Swires and Curtis had been middle managers at General Tire and Rubber, so they didn't care about the people at the top. It's not surprising that middle managers sometimes harbor grievances against higher ups—especially when they believe themselves to be smarter and more competent. Many are confident they would have been better leaders than their bosses if only they'd gotten the right breaks. I sensed our guys had been forced to retire and were pretty pissed about that. If they loosened up enough, they might reveal something "blockbuster" that we could use.

They described all sorts of schemes they had hatched for General Tire and Rubber. They bragged about padding expense reports for trips they took. They told us they'd had to flee Chile after the company's trendy whitewall tires turned out to be frauds. After heavy rain, white paint washed from the tires, leaving telltale pools on the streets. The tires weren't actually whitewall at all, but only painted to look that way. They had been paid by the company to relocate to Mexico, and in effect to disappear.

I was pleased when they opened up to us, but I didn't dare to make any obvious effort to take notes. They threatened to kill us more than once. They seemed to get a charge out of saying it, and although I strongly doubted they meant it, I didn't want to antagonize them. And I figured note-taking would make them more guarded. But Armstrong was wearing shoes with white soles. In a stroke of spontaneous brilliance, he discreetly started jotting names and shorthand notes on the bottoms of his shoes with his foot rested casually on his knee. When we returned to the hotel we quickly wrote up more complete notes from our recollections, jogged by what Scott had written on his shoes.

Whenever I had the chance, I painted a picture of the Mugar family as an example of American entrepreneurial success—decent, hardworking immigrants who really wanted to improve their community. Since they couldn't get control of a TV station on the merits of their intentions, I suggested they needed a "bombshell" of derogatory information about the license holder. Swires and Curtis listened intently and, eventually, sympathetically.

When I thought the time was right, I asked, "You guys have any thoughts?"

They looked at each other and smiled. In fact, they did have some thoughts. Boy, did they ever.

They told us about a secret bank account in Akron, Ohio, where the company was headquartered. It had accumulated money from skimming profits from General Tire and Rubber, including a company in Chile, which is where they had worked. They had closed that account to open a new one in Liechtenstein, used as a political slush fund.

"Why did you need those accounts? What's the money in those accounts for?" I asked, trying to skirt a line between uninterested and too interested.

"For bribes," they said. When I heard that word, I knew our trip to Mexico had been worthwhile.

"Bribes?" I asked.

The men told us that money in the accounts was used to pay off foreign government officials all over the world to obtain contracts for

General Tire and Rubber, in violation of the Foreign Corrupt Practices Act. They spoke about this knowledgeably, even finishing each other's sentences. I had no reason to doubt their veracity.

They also said that the chairman of the company, M. G. O'Neil, had a safe in his office at the company headquarters in Akron that contained cash for senior executives to contribute to Republican political candidates.

Jackpot.

Our two new friends identified people who they said could support their allegations, and gave us hundreds of pages of documents. Perhaps they had been waiting for an opportunity to pay back the company that had taken away their pensions. But they weren't going to sign affidavits themselves or testify under oath. Telling these facts was as far as they were willing to go.

Armed with this information, we left Mexico as soon as possible. The Mugars' impossible dream might just be possible after all.

As we checked out the information we'd been given and followed various leads, it became clear that what we'd learned in Mexico was true. David and I flew to Frankfurt to talk to someone involved in the General Tire and Rubber schemes and got him to sign an affidavit. We then learned of the bank account in Liechtenstein from which $160,000 had gone to bribe officials in Chile, Morocco, and Romania. The bribes were used to block competitors, such as Goodyear Tires, from getting government contracts. We traced money to government officials in Morocco: the secretary of state for finances, the minister of commerce, the minister of tourism, and a number of others.

But time was running out. The FCC was in the process of finalizing the decision on the Boston license, and we were still scrambling to assemble all the information we had discovered. Thinking quickly, the Mugar family's lawyer and I did some research into the backgrounds of the FCC commissioners. We managed to find a very attenuated connection between one of the commissioners and the law firm representing RKO. We decided to file a request asking the FCC to decide whether this connection was a conflict of interest. Since the commission had to consider the merits of our allegation before making a decision about the license challenge, the delay gave us more time to amass our evidence. I remember telling RKO's senior lawyer about this request at his office on Christmas Eve.

When the FCC hearing began in December, we had given Mugar's communications lawyer more than enough evidence—six hundred pages of documents—to support accusations of fraud and bribery on the part of General Tire and Rubber. He argued that evidence of the parent company's moral turpitude was so great that RKO should not be allowed to maintain its license. General Tire simply denied the allegations. But we sent a copy of our submission to the Securities and Exchange Commission too, which opened its own investigation. The SEC required General Tire and Rubber to conduct an internal investigation, which corroborated the claims we had made. The SEC determined that the company had violated several U.S. criminal statutes, including bribery, financial fraud, and perjury.

Ultimately, the FCC found that the company lacked the requisite moral character to have the radio and television licenses. After appeals that went all the way to the Supreme Court, the case finally concluded, seven years after our visit to the retired executives in Mexico. Denied the licenses, RKO went out of business as a broadcaster and sold its thirteen radio and television stations, one of which the Mugar family had waited so long to obtain. At midnight on May 21, 1982, RKO signed off its Boston station for the last time. David Mugar was now the owner of Channel 7. It was a huge victory, a landmark case, and a great boon to my investigative career. Obtaining a network-affiliated television station in a major market for simply the cost of its physical assets was an extraordinary accomplishment.

For me, the Mugar case demonstrated that investigative skills were needed on business cases as much as they were needed for political ones. Instead of resigning myself to becoming yet another typical attorney, I began to wonder how I might apply my skills to other matters.

When I was in Mississippi working on civil rights cases in the sixties, I once drove a white woman to testify in a grand jury in Biloxi. I was struck by something she said about racial conflict. "Wait till this gets up north," she said. She believed the South would solve racial problems before the North did—because the North had racial inequities that hadn't yet risen to the surface. I encountered proof of her prediction in the city of Boston, the cradle of the American Revolution.

In 1963, the local NAACP demanded that the Boston School Committee recognize the de facto segregation of Boston's public schools. Thirteen of its schools were at least 90 percent black, although the city's black population was small. The independently elected school committee refused, and its chairperson, Louise Day Hicks, became an enormously popular politician among Boston's large Irish-American population. In 1965, she led opposition to desegregation of Boston schools that had been mandated by the state legislature to achieve racial integration. In 1967, Hicks lost narrowly to Kevin White in her bid to be mayor, but controversy over school desegregation continued to haunt Boston for several more years, bedeviling Mayor White's efforts to revitalize the city. In 1974, when busing of students was mandated to balance the racial demographics, widespread violence erupted, especially in South Boston's Irish-American enclave.

Boston was troubled by racial tension. Minority citizens perceived hostility from city officials, and the city was under court decree to desegregate public housing and revise hiring policies, particularly in the police and fire departments, whose forces were almost entirely white. Mayor White was getting flak from the NAACP for the mistreatment of blacks in formerly all-white housing projects in South Boston—and the seeming indifference to the matter by the Boston police. "Southie" was notorious for anti-black sentiments and resistance to integration. The few minorities who dared to move into the housing projects were harassed, threatened, and sometimes assaulted by their white neighbors.

Knowing of my experience in the South in the 1960s, Mayor White hired me to come to Boston to look into the situation and see what actions I might suggest for his administration to ease racial tensions. There was resistance to this idea internally. Bureaucrats, especially in the police department and housing authority, didn't like outsiders coming in to scrutinize their work and offer direction. But I liked and respected Mayor White a lot, and wanted to help him as much as I could. He was an energetic, optimistic, blunt, and charming guy. At one point, when I put forward a controversial plan to address racial violence in a housing project, the mayor was supportive—to a point. "If things get screwed up," he said, "I'm going to go out on the steps of city hall and announce I hired an a—hole for a lawyer." I laughed, but I didn't doubt it.

Racial tension in parts of Boston was in some ways worse than in the Deep South, where blacks and whites had lived together forever, however unequally. One of my first assignments for the city of Boston was to investigate the shooting of a young black man by three white youths in 1979. The now paralyzed victim, Darryl Williams, was a football player, and the white boys who shot him claimed they had been on the roof of a housing project aiming at pigeons. I doubted that was true. Boston public schools had been integrated four years earlier with enormous conflict, and tensions were still running high. I did what the Boston police should have done. I went up to the project's roof and checked out the angle the boys would have had in relation to the football field below. It appeared to me that the shooting could not have been an accident. I told the police that I didn't believe the white boys and that we had to reconstruct the scene. I also asked to examine the victim's clothing to determine the angle of the bullets' penetration. The police blithely replied that they'd already destroyed the relevant evidence. Eventually, two of the three boys pleaded guilty to assault and battery with a deadly weapon and each were sentenced to ten years in a state correctional facility.

The police were of equally little use in protecting minorities who integrated the housing projects. They were going to do little more than what was required to enforce desegregation. We had to devise more unorthodox approaches.

One case involved the harassment of minority tenants at various projects. At the Mary Ellen McCormack housing project in South Boston, for example, I was put in charge of helping a Hispanic woman move into an apartment. Tensions among whites, blacks, and Hispanics were so intense that the woman was a target of demonstrations, threats, and outright violence. In order to help her survive, I had police put bulletproof glass in her apartment windows. We installed a panic button connected to the police department. Officers were stationed in a squad car near her residence twenty-four hours a day.

On the day of the move, flyers were distributed on car windows in the neighborhood calling for a rally against her. Fearing a violent confrontation, I urged the police to move her in ahead of schedule. The officers refused. "We have batons if there's a problem," one told me. Finally I moved her in with my own people. The woman didn't stay for long. After her car was burned, she moved out.

I also remember a housing project in East Boston where the tenants being harassed by white gangs were reluctant to talk with investigators. For understandable reasons, they distrusted the police, city officials, and most strangers. So I came up with the idea of having some of my investigators move into the projects for several weeks. I hoped that, as neighbors, they would earn the tenants' trust and encourage them to talk. Eventually this worked. We learned the names of the white neighbors who were causing trouble and making threats. But the witnesses were reluctant to say anything publicly. They were afraid the police would not protect them from retribution, and I feared their concern was justified.

I turned to a sympathetic federal judge and asked him to examine the statements of an anonymous list of witnesses. I asked the judge to have the police escort the white residents named in the anonymous complaint into his courtroom, almost as if they were under arrest. The judge confronted the tenants and informed them of the law and the consequence of any further harassment of black tenants. That scared the hell out of them and made a big difference. I heard of no more complaints of racial threats or violence in those buildings.

In 1976, I received a call from Monroe Price, a friend I'd first met in Washington in the 1960s. He was a brilliant and creative lawyer who had set up a legal services program in the Navajo Nation while I was at the Office of Economic Opportunity. He was now teaching at UCLA Law School and still deeply involved with Native American issues.

When Price called me, he was working with a native group in Alaska. He brought me onto a case that not only consumed every ounce of energy I had for seven months, it also changed my life. In fact, the idea for the company that became Investigative Group International originated on the frozen tundra of Alaska, thanks to a good-natured troublemaker.

Price was working with the Cook Inlet Region, Incorporated, one of the twelve regional native corporations created in 1971 by the Alaska Native Claims Settlement Act. Though initially poor, Cook Inlet was becoming a major corporation whose shareholders, members of a group of native tribes, benefit from its landholdings and financial success.

In 1974, construction began on the Trans-Alaska Pipeline, which when completed would transmit oil eight hundred miles across the state, from Prudhoe Bay to the port at Valdez, much of it across native Alaskans' land. Before construction could begin, complicated land exchanges between federal, state, and tribal lands had to occur to ensure fairness for the native corporations. Monroe introduced me to the Cook Inlet group to help them with an internal legal matter. It was reasonably straightforward work, but it led to a much more significant and complex case.

Alyeska, a consortium of eight major oil companies—including BP, ExxonMobil, ConocoPhillips, and Unocal—was authorized to build the pipeline. In order to oversee the massive project, the state legislature created the Alaska Pipeline Commission. The commission was specifically responsible for regulating construction, safety, and protection of the fragile environment.

The commission came to me with a serious problem. After the 1973 oil shortage sharply increased oil prices, oil exploration in Prudhoe Bay was fast-tracked. The original budget for the project ballooned—from an $800 million estimate in 1969 to $8 billion in 1976, by which time construction had begun and I came onto the case. This rate seemed incredible—a 1,000 percent increase. And costs would have a major impact on the citizens of Alaska. Through a complicated formula, costs of constructing, maintaining, and operating the pipeline would be deducted from the portion of annual oil revenue owed to the state of Alaska. In other words, if the $8 billion figure withstood scrutiny, the Alaskans risked losing a fortune.

The state legislature had no reason to know how much it should cost to build a pipeline. Most of the Alaska legislators were earnest libertarians more interested in passing laws to legalize marijuana than in micromanaging such a complex project. The pipeline commission had access to Alyeska's proposed budget, but they lacked the resources and expertise to second-guess the oil companies' projections. They had deferred to Alyeska until they began to fathom the astronomical costs, and began to wonder if the oil companies were bilking the host state. The oil companies tried to defend the cost estimate and dissuade criticism by claiming that the pipeline was "the most expensive privately financed project in the history of the world." The commission asked me to investigate. My task was to see whether that boast was a point of embarrassment or pride.

The Alaska Pipeline case is an interesting study in how corporations often take advantage of circumstances—in this case, an oil shortage—to shortcut careful planning and cost consciousness in order to reap profit as quickly as possible. Without adequate planning, greed and hubris ruled the day.

Our charge from the commission was to go over all the major costs associated with the pipeline's construction and identify areas in which money was imprudently spent. Our findings would be reported to the Alaska Pipeline Commission, who would then turn it over to the Federal Energy Regulatory Commission, the Washington agency responsible for determining the formula for allocating revenue to the oil companies and to the state of Alaska. If we could document cost overruns, the state would get more revenue from the pipeline. We had about six months to conduct an initial investigation and draft a report, with a budget of around $100,000.

There was no doubt that the Alaska pipeline was a feat of engineering. It was the largest ever constructed in the United States—measuring four feet in diameter. It spans eight hundred miles of Alaskan wilderness and carries two million barrels *each day* to Valdez. From Valdez, oil is then loaded onto ships and sent down to the lower forty-eight states. The pipeline crosses mountains, valleys, and one of the most active earthquake faults in the world. In addition, it is built over Alaska permafrost. The permafrost posed unique challenges because steps had to be taken in the construction to ensure that the heat of the oil pumping through the 48-inch-diameter pipeline would not melt the ground beneath it, crack the pipeline by shifting its supports, and cause an environmental catastrophe.

I didn't know anything about oil pipelines at the time. I also didn't know much about Alaska, how business was conducted there, the unique weather conditions, or its unusual culture. That would change over the course of the investigation. I flew from Washington to Alaska and back on dozens of occasions, coming home jet-lagged to a busy family. In Anchorage, I fell into a routine: I would check into a hotel, prepare questions for depositions, and then travel, usually in small aircraft, all over the state for interviews. The entire southeast coast of Alaska, including the state capital of Juneau, is landlocked between the sea and a mountain range. As a result, flight is a common mode of transportation. And everybody seemed to like flying in Alaska, including a number of pilots who probably should have stayed on the ground. One of the first times I landed at the Anchorage airport, I noticed wrecked planes off the runway, which was not terribly encouraging. Some weeks later, as I was in a taxi headed to the airport, the driver told me he'd just dropped off a passenger who was drunk and about to pilot a transport plane filled with livestock. The next morning the *Anchorage Daily News* reported that a plane had crashed on takeoff, scattering animals all over the tarmac.

Everything I heard about the quirkiness of the state rang true in my experience. I remember reading an article about an Alaskan who had sailed or windsurfed from Little Diomede Island in Alaska to Russia, where he was arrested by Russian border guards. On one of my first trips when I was staying at the Captain Cook hotel, I was awakened by a loud noise. The next day I learned that a Teamster had blown up his wife's car in the parking lot.

While assembling my team, I encountered some very unusual and interesting people. One of the smartest lawyers was Jeff "Mad Dog" Lowenfels, who had moved to Alaska from New York City after he had been mugged and shot in the head in Central Park. After recovering, he didn't like being in crowded cities. He was incredibly smart and competent with a great sense of humor. Once, while in court, the judge asked why he had a toothbrush in his breast pocket. He replied that he expected the judge to be perturbed by the oil companies' lack of compliance and that someone might have to spend the night in jail.

I found an Alaskan to serve as our forensic accountant. He was a graduate of Dartmouth's business school who had taken to the Alaskan frontier with the zeal of a convert. He lived in a cabin about twenty miles outside of town, beyond the end of the road. The cabin had neither electricity nor a telephone line. We had to call him on the bush radio whenever we needed him in town. He would go to the railroad track with his two Siberian husky dogs to flag down the train, which was required to stop for such passengers. When he came into the office, he brought the two dogs, who would lie on the floor all day. On one occasion, he contacted us and said he wasn't coming in because he was in the process of moving his entire cabin. He had seen a snowshoe print in the vicinity, which had apparently ruined his sense of isolation.

I worked with Terry Bird and Vince Marella, former assistant U.S. attorneys with a practice in Los Angeles. I hired them to head up the Anchorage office. We worked closely with Alaska's attorney general, Will Condon, who had grown up in Yellowstone National Park and had been in my class at Exeter Academy.

Back in Washington, my law firm, Wald, Harkrader, and Ross, wasn't equipped for the extensive investigative work required in this case. In addition to analyzing thousands of documents, we needed to interview people in Alaska and across the country who could tell us about various aspects of construction. The firm's lawyers could have learned how to do this, but they had their own cases, and they would have been costly. They billed by the hour, which meant that time spent going to and around Alaska and interviewing various pipeline workers would quickly add up. I needed people like those I'd worked with at the Justice Department and on the Watergate Committee—investigators first and foremost who knew how to ascertain people's credibility, who had good instincts and knew how to develop leads. They had been paid on salary, not by the hour. So I found people who could be good investigators and brought them into the case—former FBI agents and lawyers, for example. Some were journalists; several were recent law school graduates who loaded information from oil companies, contractors, etc., into computers (then fairly primitive). Marc Lackritz and his wife, who had both worked with me during the Watergate investigation, had come to Wald, Harkrader, and Ross with me to work on the case.

With teams in place in D.C. and Anchorage, we began to piece together the facts. Alyeska oversaw the pipeline subcontractors through a web of committees and subcommittees. Making things more complicated, the pipeline was divided into five different geographical sections, each managed by a different set of contractors. An audit during the planning stage had already revealed early problems with inventory organization, architectural plans, and general management. Consultants who'd been brought on board to address those problems had made a number of suggestions to improve efficiencies, most of which were ignored. The audit also suggested hiring one outfit to oversee the whole project, and even recommended a particular company: Bechtel. The giant engineering and construction firm had built the Hoover Dam and had done pipeline projects all over the world. They had a sterling reputation.

Still, it was three years before Bechtel was finally hired in October of 1973, with construction set to begin the following April. Six months later, the Alyeska's owners' committee abruptly demoted Bechtel. When I began the investigation, I figured that Bechtel people might be good sources of information.

At the very beginning, I recommended that the Alaska Pipeline

Commission issue subpoenas to Alyeska and all the oil companies, contractors, and subcontractors for any and all documents relevant to the construction of the pipeline. I wanted those documents locked down fast. The Pipeline Commission had no jurisdiction outside Alaska, and I was afraid that if documents left the state we'd never be able to get them.

I met personally with the CEO of Alyeska, an arrogant oil executive named E. L. Patton, to deliver the news. He wasn't happy. Not surprisingly, the oil companies blew off the subpoenas. On my strong recommendation, Attorney General Condon filed suit on the commission's behalf to ask a state court to order compliance with the subpoenas. The judge agreed. This was a major step for us. It sent the message that we weren't going to be rolled over and had the full weight of the state government behind us.

With the subpoena secured, the very next day I took my team en masse to the headquarters of the Alyeska Pipeline Service Company in Anchorage. I wanted to demonstrate that we had the resources and the will to complete our task. I told them to read every document they came across and to copy anything at all that reflected sizable expenses. We walked out of those offices with boxes of material and a number of leads for interviews.

One of the most obvious places to look for incriminating information was with the people at Bechtel. Ex-employees are always gold to an investigator, most especially those who had been terminated. Their demotion from the project had been embarrassing and left bad feelings all around. Bechtel executives told us they had wanted more time to plan the project, but found themselves under intense pressure from the oil companies, who wanted the pipeline operating as soon as possible. Their relationship quickly deteriorated, which Bechtel attributed to the oil companies' micromanagement. They cited continual reworking of the construction plans because of "constantly changing criteria," lack of expertise shown in creating plans, and lack of timely decisions.

The oil companies had created a huge bureaucracy where decisions had to be vetted and approved. Delays and confusion proved almost inevitable. The construction had begun without a cost estimate in place and without any kind of inventory system.

What happened over the next two years in the construction of the pipeline was a stunning example of financial mismanagement. Alyeska farmed out the construction projects to various contractors. They avoided doing necessary studies of the unique conditions in Alaska. As a result, they were unprepared for Alaska's challenges. Because of the harsh temperatures and shifting permafrost holding up the pipeline, it was prone to splitting and cracking. To fix the cracks, they used a tape called Royston, which didn't work at all. When, two and a half years later, it finally was decided to stop using that tape, one of the executives working with the oil companies tried to destroy all evidence of its use. Unfortunately for them, they didn't destroy everything. A memo we obtained through the subpoena included the following: "It might be well to destroy this report so there will be nothing in your files that indicated any expected trouble with Royston tape."

In addition to speaking with Bechtel employees and others still working on the project, we identified various outside experts and people with other pipeline experience. At one point I flew up to Calgary, where the Canadians were building a pipeline of their own. There was near unanimity that one of the biggest mistakes the Alaska pipeline folks made was beginning construction in March, still winter in Alaska. Dealing with terrible Arctic weather and setting up camps for workers was enormously expensive and—it doesn't take an expert to know—dangerous. But the oil companies' interest was in getting the project completed as fast as possible, costs be damned. The Alaskan taxpayer would eventually take the hit for the costs once the oil began flowing.

The Canadians also told us that one of the most crucial aspects to building a long pipeline was to adopt a "conveyor belt" approach. Efficiency could be maximized if all the tools, equipment, parts, and support staff were stored at the warehouse near the point of construction and moved along the route at the rate of construction. That way, they could avoid delays and regain all the lost time and energy spent on looking for tools and parts. That was not at all how the Alaska pipeline was working. Most pipeline workers didn't even know what was in the warehouse closest to them. Without any inventory control, construction brigades couldn't find the tools they needed. So when a contractor needed something desperately, he would charter a large plane to pick up equipment and bring it to the working site—if they could figure out where the equipment was being stored. This often meant buying parts at unreasonably high prices because they needed them quickly and paying more to have them flown in.

Sometimes the tools that were missing in the winter would be found where they were supposed to be when the snow melted in the summer. Lack of effective management meant that the workers were being paid without having work assignments.

The workers brought their own laundry list of problems. They were unionized by the Teamsters. The Teamsters also unionized the Alaska police force, which undoubtedly added to the difficulties for the oil companies in dealing with the pipeline workers, since they'd be the ones who would have to break up strikes or involve themselves with slowdowns. When the pipeline began, the union promised not to strike at any point in exchange for premium wages, which were 25 to 30 percent higher than normal wages in the lower forty-eight. So what the Teamsters did instead was to practice slowdowns and work stoppages based on the slightest pretext. We documented workers sitting in buses or sleeping on the job for excuses that ranged from lack of driving directions to bad weather to inadequate equipment or materials to poor scheduling. In all, we counted at least fifteen work stoppages and hundreds of slowdowns.

Without adequate planning or oversight, the management had

brought this nightmare on itself. But they didn't seem to worry about cost overruns. We found numerous examples, through reports and memos, of workers receiving paychecks for far more money than they were entitled. There was man-hour abuse on every single crew. Time card abuse overall, by our calculations, totaled 2.5 *million* man-hours and nearly $85 million. One pipeline worker was paid for working twenty-four hours a day for twenty-seven consecutive days. The screening of personnel also had problems, especially when it came to welders. To ensure the safety of the pipeline, the welders were required to X-ray a sealed pipeline section at various points to make sure that everything had been welded shut. The contractors had found a novel shortcut around this regulation by taking one X-ray and copying it, passing it off as X-rays of other sections that they never checked.

Greed undoubtedly played its part in the rush to construct the pipeline, regardless of considerations of safety and efficiency. Yes, the corporations cut corners to get oil pumping quickly to generate revenue quickly. But it was also in their interests to make sure the pipeline functioned properly. In their defense, building a pipeline across eight hundred miles of the most unforgiving terrain in the world was a massive challenge, and one that would inevitably entail cost overruns. They were undertaking a difficult enterprise with a rule book that didn't take into account the terrain and climate, no real supervision, and a whole host of problems they should have foreseen. The oil companies knew what they needed to be doing, had the time to prepare for it, and yet did little to do so. The corporate people at headquarters had no idea how to run an efficient pipeline operation, and didn't bother to find out.

Many people tend to extol the business world for their ruthless efficiency in turning profits. Maybe there's truth to that. But not always. In this case, these major companies, some of the biggest and most profitable in the world, proved just as bad at running a bureaucracy as the federal government ever was. The oil companies had few incentives to make sure that they were being cost-effective. The state of Alaska was not blameless in the situation either, which the legislators recognized. Their regulators were "fish and feathers" guys who cared more about the wildlife and landscape than about cost overruns. As a result, the oil companies were left to their own devices. They knew they would get hefty revenue checks no matter what. The federal government too was entrusted with monitoring the pipeline's construction. They lacked either the resources or the ability to do so, leaving the oil companies and their contractors with a free rein.

Our final report for the commission, officially entitled "The Management, Planning, and Construction of the Trans-Alaska Pipeline System," was 598 pages long. The report's completion coincided, as it happened, with the delivery of the first barrel of oil through the pipeline to the port at Valdez in July 1977. So the pipeline worked, but it was not without issues.

We submitted our report to Alaska Pipeline Commission chairman Harry Donahue on August 1, and it became public a week later. The report cited three main problems: 1) a lack of an effective inventory system; 2) not enough warehouse space; and 3) a procurement program without procedures. Overall, the themes of the report were poor management and inability to get things done in a timely manner, the combination of which bred many other problems. We estimated a cost overrun of $1.5 billion over the $8 billion expended. This figure too demonstrated the complexity of the investigation. Our goal wasn't to damage the oil industry but to protect our clients, the citizens of Alaska. In fact, we found that the vast majority of the sums spent on construction—or $6.5 billion—seemed to have some legitimacy.

Nonetheless, the pipeline's CEO, E. L. Patton, immediately blasted me and the investigation for bias, despite having told me he'd reserve comment on our findings. Yet even he recognized that our facts were unassailable.

During our presentation to the Federal Energy Regulatory Commission in 1977, the oil companies capitulated. They agreed to negotiate with the state to determine how much of the construction costs were legitimate. That new calculation decreased the portion of revenue that the companies could recover and raised considerably the portion of revenue the state would receive. The settlement ultimately allotted Alaska an additional $1 billion in revenue from the pipeline's oil production. Through the Alaska Permanent Fund Corporation, which manages the state's oil revenue for the benefit of current and future generations, every state resident receives an annual dividend—as much as $2,069 in 2008.

The pipeline case was challenging and invigorating. It taught me the value of having a team of investigators on the payroll with skills to navigate the complexities and surprises of these sorts of projects. Using highly paid lawyers to retrieve and analyze documents, interview scores of witnesses, and follow leads would have been far too costly. There was no way in the world a bunch of lawyers could have undertaken something so complicated without billing the state a fortune in legal fees. Investigators could do this job not only cheaper but better. They were trained to ask the right questions and discern a witness's credibility. They were paid on salary, and we charged the client much less per hour for an investigator than a lawyer would have billed. I figured our law firm might be able to keep a functional investigation office as part of our legal practice for cases just like this.

I spent a lot of time with the full-time investigators on the pipeline case. I was fascinated by the forensic accountant, who could analyze various aspects of construction and then reconstruct how the money had been spent—much as Carmine Bellino did with the Howard Hughes money in the Watergate investigation. I liked interviewing the executives, watching them answer questions, and getting a sense of whether what they were telling me was true. A lawyer doesn't always have the time to follow his instincts in a case, especially if it leads to a dead end. But an investigator lives on instinct. He may run into a half-dozen dead ends before he finds a payoff.

These cases impressed upon me the virtue of persistence. David Mugar got the television station he wanted because he didn't accept lying down the rejection the FCC first delivered. The state of Alaska, refusing to accede to Alyeska's demands, received the compensation from the oil companies that it deserved, revenue that still benefits its citizens. And Kevin White was able to lead the city of Boston through a very difficult time of racial conflict with creativity and judgment.

When I left the Wald, Harkrader firm in 1981 to join Rogovin, Huge, and Lenzner, I took my cases with me. I brought the investigators along to continue with the pipeline case before the Federal Energy Regulatory Commission. They were not part of the law firm but operated out of separate offices nearby working on my cases and for other partners. In 1984, when we founded Investigative Group International—with me as chairman and Jim Mintz as president—I was still a partner at the law firm but was soon spending about 50 percent of my time on IGI matters.

As IGI prospered, I supported the investigators' eagerness to conduct investigations for their own clients as well as for the firm's. The law firm benefited because my IGI clients had to retain and pay the firm for my time, but this cohabitation wasn't easy. The other partners didn't share my enthusiasm for the investigative operation. Too often, the investigators were told they couldn't work for a client who came to IGI because of conflicts with the law firm's clients. And I was annoyed that my investigators weren't paid nearly as much as the first-year associates. I really enjoyed working with the investigators, and I realized how important private investigating can be to the practice of law. But my law partners felt I wasn't sufficiently committed to the partnership. My allegiance was split.

Eventually one of the other partners came to me.

"Terry, this isn't working," he said. "You need to either be a full-time partner here or become an investigator. You have to choose."

For me the choice was pretty easy. I left the law firm and moved my office around the corner to work with the investigators full-time.

CHAPTER 7

CONDUCTING INVESTIGATIONS

The founding team of what became the Investigative Group consisted of me and three other people, all of them former investigative reporters. John Hanrahan and Jim Mintz had come from the *Washington Post*, and Kathy Kadane was a journalist and former congressional investigator. From observing reporters like Woodward and Bernstein in Watergate, I recognized the superb investigative skills some had, and quickly discovered that with them IGI could add a critical ingredient to the practice of law. Reporters are agile and effective at getting information from people in an informal setting. In contrast, lawyers asking questions in depositions or in court are not apt to get as much. And former FBI and other government investigators are used to a different environment, where they can depend on search warrants and subpoenas to gather facts.

I learned early on to pay close attention to what my clients know about the people they want us to investigate for them. They surely knew better than an outsider the personalities in a case—their strengths and weaknesses and their habits. Clients' instincts about their case situations are also valuable, and often right. When I worked for the Cook Inlet native corporation in Alaska, for example, my clients told me that they believed their business and investment manager was cheating them. I initially pooh-poohed the suggestion. After all, I thought, the native Alaskans were corporate novices and distrustful of anyone who came from the "lower forty-eight." The manager at first struck me as an accomplished professional. But it turned out that my clients were right. The manager *was* cheating them. That was a good lesson I never forgot.

We continued to work for some of the Rogovin firm's corporate clients, and built up a reputation for due diligence in mergers and acquisitions cases. During the 1980s, the time of the takeover craze and leveraged buyouts, mergers and acquisitions law firms provided a lot of work for us. By the middle of 1987, IGI had been involved in more than forty friendly mergers or hostile takeovers. Law firms negotiating friendly deals hired us to investigate the target companies and their executives, to discover their financial status and uncover any potential regulatory problems or reputational risks. On the other side of a case, when working for a company that was threatened with takeover, we tried to help them resist the raider.

The work IGI did on behalf of companies that were targeted for hostile takeover was multi-dimensional. We uncovered negative information about the raiders to feed to the lawyers to enhance their legal maneuvers, as well as to the public relations firms and proxy solicitors who were hired to develop strategies to discourage shareholders from supporting the takeovers. We navigated our way through webs of dense financial data and complex transactions to ferret out irregularities and governance issues. We found, for example, instances of illegal self-dealing among major shareholders, and sometimes insider trading, that damaged the raider company's reputation. Our success in this line of work contributed to building IGI's reputation and proved to be a lucrative practice for us.

IGI has evolved over the years. At one point I was convinced that we needed to have a physical presence in many places in order to look credible and attract clients. We had as many as a hundred people spread across offices in Boston, Chicago, London, Los Angeles, New York, Seattle, Tampa, and Washington, D.C. That proved to be a bureaucratic and quality control nightmare. Managing offices, leases, payroll, and personnel in many locations required a costly layer of administration, which distracted me from the hands-on work I enjoyed. Overseeing cases, clients, and staff in multiple locations wasn't what I wanted to do, and I worried that all our offices might not be delivering consistently high-quality products.

Eventually I realized I didn't need the headaches of such a large operation. The increasing access to information via the Internet and the easy use of computer communications meant that we didn't need offices and support staff in many places. I could depend on a core group of expert and reliable employees and a number of independent contractors with whom we worked regularly. We could surge with additional investigators as needed.

IGI has been fairly lean in recent years, with no more than twenty-five people on staff for our day-to-day operations. Most of our work is done in Washington, though we retain small, one-person offices in nine places, including Seattle, Tampa, Los Angeles, and Boston. These investigators are my own version of Doar's "fast ponies." The indefatigable Bob Mason in Seattle, for example, is available to travel as needed. The arrangement has returned IGI to what it was in the beginning—a small, aggressive, competent group of investigators without a lot of overhead. This mode is cost-effective and gets results.

We have a bench of foreign contractors to call on for work that has to be done overseas. We learned to cultivate former employees of U.S. embassies who have connections with government officials in foreign countries, and draw upon a loose network of retired FBI and intelligence professionals for a variety of assignments. Since the Cold War ended, these have included former agents from the CIA and KGB, who sometimes work together on various cases.

I once used them in a case for the magician David Copperfield. While he was on tour in Russia, seven trucks full of equipment he used for his magic act were confiscated. Before beginning the tour, the illusionist had secured the permits he needed to transport his equipment throughout the country—but the documents "disappeared" after his final show. Without them, he couldn't leave Russia with his equipment. When the U.S. State Department proved useless, one of Copperfield's team came to IGI. I asked the most obvious question: "Can't he just magic the trucks back?" Copperfield's team didn't think that was very funny.

Eventually we learned from our contacts that the trucks and equipment were in the hands of a company linked to the Russian Mafia. They would return the trucks only after Copperfield paid a six-figure "fine." So my client forked over the money, and the trucks were allowed to cross over to Finland. Most of this work was done by subcontractors who weren't on my permanent staff—and they did the job well.

When IGI was larger, I hadn't hesitated to hire some well-known people when I could. For example, Larry Potts was a big help to us when he came to IGI. Larry was a career FBI agent who had served as deputy director of the FBI in 1995. He trained a lot of intelligence and law enforcement personnel from other countries at the FBI facility in Quantico. I had heard of Potts years earlier—I was told by one of his colleagues that Larry was one of the best agents the FBI ever had. I knew he'd be a terrific get. He was actually even better than advertised.

When I approached Potts in the mid-1990s, he had just left the FBI. As a senior agency official, he had supervised from Washington a deadly standoff at Ruby Ridge, Idaho, over several days in 1992 between law enforcement officials and a man named Randy Weaver who

was wanted on weapons charges and allegedly had links to white su-
premacists. In one exchange of gunfire, a U.S. marshal and Weaver's
fourteen-year-old son had been killed. In another, a sharpshooter, believing he saw somebody threatening coming out of the cabin, fired
his weapon and killed Weaver's wife while she was holding the couple's
baby. When Congress investigated Ruby Ridge in 1995, Potts, who'd
been named deputy director only ten weeks before the tragedy, stoically took the fall and left the FBI shortly thereafter.

I expected that Larry was chafing to get back to work. In part to
fill some of his time, he was volunteering to be a coach at a local high
school. Mutual friends suggested that I might like him. I invited him
to lunch—he told me his entire story. I found him to be smart, careful,
and a person of great integrity. At the end of lunch I said to him, "I
want you to come work for us." I think he was surprised. He hadn't
expected anyone to hire him at that point. "We'll put you back together again," I said. Which is what we did. He proved to be one of the
most insightful, competent, and careful investigators I ever worked
with.

While he worked for us as chief operating officer, Potts helped IGI
cultivate relationships with intelligence and law enforcement personnel around the world, including some of the people he'd helped train
at the FBI. Potts left IGI in 2004 for a corporate position in New York.

Another invaluable addition to our office was Ray Kelly, who had
been the police commissioner of New York City—a job he would regain later under Mayor Michael Bloomberg. After Rudolph Giuliani
was elected mayor in 1993, I heard that Kelly was going to be replaced
by Bill Bratton. So I went up to New York City to talk with him.

Kelly had worked in the NYPD for decades. He was very well respected, known as a thorough investigator and a good leader. He was
a terrific guy—funny, clever, and energetic. I told him I heard that he
was leaving and suggested he join IGI to run our New York office.
After thinking it over, he decided to join the team. Kelly's connections

in the law enforcement community were impressive and valuable. He brought us some big-name clients. With him on board, IGI contracted with the U.S. State Department to train international police monitors in Haiti. We were hired by lawyers representing Brown & Williamson, the tobacco company, to investigate whistle-blower Jeffrey Wigand. After Michael Bloomberg became mayor of New York City in 2002, he reappointed Kelly as police commissioner, where he currently serves.

People occasionally ask me how one becomes a good investigator. Surprisingly, fact-finding is rarely taught in a law school's curriculum. In 1987, I wrote a book for the Practising Law Institute, *Conducting Complex Fact Investigations*, and have taught seminars on the subject at law schools and for law enforcement. Most of the people who come to work at IGI as investigators have had some comparable experience—as an investigative journalist or in law enforcement. Some have come soon after graduating from college, bringing useful research skills from academia. The personal character traits we value are curiosity, persistence, objectivity, and intuition, as well as imagination. They have to be able to connect dots that aren't readily apparent. They also need to develop some discrimination. Separating the wheat from the chaff isn't easy, but this skill can develop with experience. I have a high regard for those who can write well. Organizing material and presenting it clearly in written documents is an essential part of our work. Interestingly, I find that people who apply to work for IGI are self-selecting to a considerable extent. If they know about us and are interested in working with us, they generally tend to be good at what they do.

I especially appreciate the women on our staff. In some respects, female investigators have an advantage over men. They are viewed as more empathetic and less threatening, so interview subjects are more likely to disclose information to them.

My own version of movie heroine Erin Brockovich worked for me on a toxic chemical case in Woburn, Massachusetts. We were hired by lawyers representing the families who sued chemical conglomerate W. R. Grace & Company and two other corporations after a number of children were diagnosed with leukemia. The lawsuit was prompted after the townspeople learned that the companies dumped raw chemicals that contaminated the town's water supply. When IGI was called into the case, the trial was just about to start. (The trial is depicted in the film *A Civil Action*, based on the book by Jonathan Harr.)

I could tell we were brought late to the game, and that hurt us. Little real fact-finding seemed to have been done on my clients' behalf. With little time to waste, I sent two investigators into Woburn, both of them women, and one of whom was pregnant. They had worked for IGI for years, were both mothers and terrific investigators, and I expected that the residents would be especially sympathetic and cordial to a pregnant woman. Indeed, residents almost unfailingly invited them in, asked them to sit down, and appeared happy to share what they knew. Our investigators got lots of good information, but, unfortunately, the case was dismissed by a judge who sided with the company's scientists. (Belatedly, the EPA found evidence of the company's culpability.)

In general, I don't turn down a paying client who has an interesting and reasonable case. The usual problem for me is thinking that nearly *every* client's case is interesting. I am attracted to the mysteries, like most investigators. But as busy as I am, I can't adequately oversee cases for all the clients who ask for IGI's help. So I have to be somewhat selective. Not all cases, or clients, are reasonable. And some have trivial concerns. Every once in a while, for example, I hear from a rich guy who met a pretty woman on a ski lift or on an airplane and got only her first name. He wants us to track her down. Sometimes he claims it was love at first sight and he can't get her out of his mind. I tell these guys that we don't invade people's privacy. If that woman wanted him to contact her, she would have made it possible.

I start every case with whatever the client brings to IGI. I am open to trusting their initial inclinations but I try to avoid prejudgments and biases. When a client first calls, we find out briefly what their problem is. If we've worked for them before, we can agree to get right to work without a meeting. But if it's a new client, I try to find out as much as I can over the phone and schedule a meeting, asking them to provide relevant documents. We do some preliminary background checking on the Internet before we meet with them. We always ask how they found IGI; if another client referred them, that gives us another way to check them out.

I ask a lot of questions, some of which may seem irrelevant to the client. But I know that too narrow a focus can overlook important details a broader beam might shed light on. Some of my questions are designed to help me evaluate clients by observing their body language and the style of their responses. Are they consistent in the quality of their replies? Do they avoid answering certain questions? Do they dissemble? After the meeting, we review documents they may have given us and do some simple research to assess what more needs to be done. Then we make a proposal including the scope of the investigation that we recommend and a budget estimate. If the case is complex, the investigation is separated into phases, and we ask for an "evergreen" retainer that recognizes more to come after the initial payment has been exhausted for the first phase.

The range of interpersonal and business relationships that I encounter constantly fascinates me. I suppose families at every income level have conflicts, but I hear from the wealthier ones in cases that often involve money. In such situations, IGI is usually retained by the lawyer who needs facts to document his client's case.

I'd like to say that I approach every case with complete objectivity, but I've come to realize that's not exactly true. It's pretty hard to serve clients without putting myself in their frame of mind. Most think they have been abused—by another person, by a business, by a process, or by the system. They want us to help them right the wrong.

On the business side, a number of clients have been corporations under attack by short sellers who try to drive down the value of the company's stock so they can buy more shares for less money. Basically, they've "rented" the stock by pledging to pay for it at a fixed share price that's much lower than the stock is selling at. Some employ devious techniques—sometimes planting erroneous stories about the company's leaders, operations, or prospects—to drive the price down temporarily. Identifying short sellers is not easy. Even the existence of a large short position is not publicly known until the Stock Exchange's monthly report indicates it. In one case, our client hadn't been paying attention to his company's website, which invites comments on a message board. After a short seller posted a fraudulent letter, ostensibly from the company's chairman, saying that quarterly revenue would be down 50 percent below previous predictions, the share price plummeted and the stock lost considerable value.

Our clients are usually in a hurry—they are desperate for help and want results yesterday. Sometimes I can offer suggestions for how they might create more time for themselves through delaying tactics. Then we respond by gathering facts as quickly as possible. Speed was of the essence in the case we had for United Way of America, which is described here in chapter 8. When the client learned of impending critical news stories, they asked IGI to investigate the organization's leaders and operations so the governing board would know how to respond. We were able to analyze reams of documents and conduct interviews with more than thirty people in little more than a month that included Christmas and the New Year's holidays.

Some clients are surprisingly naïve. Even sophisticated people who should have known better can do some pretty stupid things. One client came to me about an investment he had made in an oil and gas development in Oklahoma. He had made a fortune with a mortgage company he founded during the housing boom, and President George W. Bush made him an ambassador to a European country. He had learned about the venture from the developer's son, whom he'd met at a ski resort. He made a huge investment but, curiously, had no legal documents to prove it. He hadn't received normal reports of the expenditures made with his money nor of the results of drilling activity. We investigated extensively and got some results, including witnesses to his payments. But the lawyer who was advising the ambassador questioned the value of our work, since we hadn't found all that his client was looking for. The ambassador died shortly after we sued for payment, and his widow refused to pay our fee or that of the consulting lawyer. In the end, we settled for a fraction of our costs.

When IGI first started, we used computers with rudimentary databases that we leased on an annual basis. At the time, we could pull a person's Social Security number and date of birth and get a slew of information. (It's much harder to get Social Security numbers today.) LexisNexis had started a database of legal actions and public records in the 1970s that allowed us to see if a person or entity or the targets of various investigations had been involved in legal actions. But we also still had to do old-fashioned research.

Some years ago, for example, a member of an East Coast family came to me with a dilemma. After the family patriarch died, a woman claimed to have had an affair with him and given birth to his child. She demanded a significant monthly allowance to dissuade her from going public with the story. The family was very upset and also very skeptical. But because the woman was someone in their social circle, they recognized the remote possibility that her story could be true. Before deciding how to respond, they asked me to check it out.

Sometimes clients make suggestions for an investigation, based on an approach or tactic they might have seen on a TV crime show, that aren't exactly kosher. In this case, they suggested that we surreptitiously get hold of the child's toothbrush to obtain her DNA—which presumably involved breaking into the mother's home. That was too absurd for me. We don't break into private property, nor do we steal.

I came up with a simpler idea. I had an investigator go to the library to search local magazines and the social pages of area newspapers for photos of events that occurred around the time the woman claimed her child was born. Since these were high-society people, I thought there was a reasonable chance we could find pictures of the woman and see if she looked pregnant at the time in question. The investigator found a picture of her, dancing at a benefit just days before her love child was supposedly born. She was visibly not pregnant, and my clients thought I was a genius.

Now confident that the woman was trying to extort, my clients had another request. They asked me to get the toughest-looking guys I could find to meet with the woman privately. The former FBI agents we hired delivered the family's message: We know your claim is unfounded. Don't ever contact us again. As far as I know, she never did.

I found a creative way to help another client in the case of James Thornwell, an African-American from Oakland, California, whose life had become a disaster. He had been given LSD covertly years before while serving in the U.S. Army, and learned of this only after the Church Committee hearings when the surgeon general issued a report naming individuals who had been subjected to drug experiments. When I had advised Sid Gottlieb, I represented a client who was responsible for CIA experiments with LSD. Now I was on the side of a victim of a similar program in the army. There was no conflict because Gottlieb had no role whatsoever in the Thornwell case. Thornwell's lawyers were preparing a lawsuit against the army, and they hired me to help get information about what happened to him.

One of the first things we did was to file a Freedom of Information Act (FOIA) request for all of the government's files on Thornwell going back some twenty years or more. Getting a response to an FOIA request can take months, even years, so it was something we had to move on early. When we finally received documents, we had to locate all of the individuals named in the files—a list of several dozen people whose addresses were decades out of date. We sent each of them a registered letter. If the address was wrong and a forwarding address was on file, the post office forwarded the letter and sent us a return receipt so we could see where it was redirected. And so as not to tip off these potential witnesses, the envelopes we mailed were empty.

What I remember most vividly from the Thornwell case was my meeting with a senior official of the United States Army. I told her why I was representing Thornwell, that he had been given LSD covertly, and since then was married and divorced and unable to hold down a job. "The army pretty much ruined his life," I said. I told her that I'd like her to say on behalf of the army that she would provide the resources needed to help Thornwell through the rest of his life.

She looked at me, and I'll never forget what she said. "We don't have any legal or moral obligation to this guy," she said coldly.

"Well," I replied, "I think you are going to regret saying that." Thornwell's lawsuit was filed shortly thereafter.

Some time later, a producer from *60 Minutes* called my office. They wanted to do a story on Sid Gottlieb and his experiences at the CIA. Sid was leading a quiet life and certainly didn't want any publicity. I thought of a way to help Sid and get useful publicity to help Thornwell. "You don't want to do that old story," I told the producer. "I have a better one for you, one that's new." When *60 Minutes* broadcast a segment on Thornwell, the case garnered national attention. The army was roundly criticized and Secretary of the Army Clifford Alexander deplored publicly how badly Thornwell had been treated. In the end, South Carolina senator Strom Thurmond got a private bill through Congress to set up a trust fund of $700,000 for Thornwell, who was his constituent.

IGI uses pretty straightforward investigative techniques, but I know that unorthodox ones are sometimes tried in very difficult cases, like the Atlanta Child Murders case. Between 1979 and 1981, more than twenty African-American children between the ages of seven and sixteen, as well as four young men, disappeared or were found murdered in a particular geographic area of Atlanta. When national media focused on the Atlanta murders, attention became so great that all sorts of people were calling in tips and offering to help. IBM sent the Atlanta police something novel for an investigation at the time: computers. None of the cops knew how to use them, but they were trained to create and maintain a database of leads to follow. Unfortunately, realistic leads were few. Authorities assembled what was then the largest task force in U.S. history.

Lee Brown, the Atlanta commissioner of public safety, brought me into the case as a special advisor to the task force—which consisted of the FBI and state and local police. With few promising avenues of inquiry, the task force made a profile of the kinds of people who might be even remotely interesting. One by one, the task force tracked many potential suspects who had been incarcerated or charged with child abuse. They found a lot of awful pornography, but no new information. Because some of the bodies were found with dog hairs on them, the task force started tracking people in the area who owned dogs. No luck there either.

Under increasing pressure to find the killer, the task force became desperate. They brought in a famous psychiatrist from Harvard to try to analyze the killer. We consulted criminal profilers. Then came the psychics and people who claimed the murders could be tracked against the lunar tides or some nonsense. Then experts came in to hypnotize potential witnesses.

I was in the task force's war room when an elderly security guard was brought in. He had been guarding a building near where a child had been abducted and remembered seeing a car in the vicinity. He was seated at a table across from a hypnotist while a large group of us observed. Once he was in a hypnotic state, he was asked to visualize the car and its license plate number. Eventually, the man said he could see the number. It was clear as day. Then he recited it. The cops around me scribbled down the number and ran out of the room to issue an all-points bulletin so they could track down the car.

It was an amazing thing to see. I was impressed. Since I was left in the room with the guard, I decided to strike up a conversation.

"It was amazing that you could recall the license plate number like that," I said.

"Yes," he said, but he looked preoccupied.

"What are you thinking?" I asked.

"Those numbers," he said. "Now that I think about it, I think I saw them written down somewhere."

He reached for his wallet and looked through it. Then he pulled out a slip of paper with the exact same license plate number he'd conjured up under hypnosis. The number he'd remembered was on the license plate of one of his cars.

I went out to look for the police officers. "Uh, you might want to put a hold on that bulletin."

Investigators need to operate not only at the direction of their clients, but also within ethical limitations. There are some things we don't do, even if a client requests it. These are activities that fail what

I call the "throw-up test." Admittedly it's not the most elegant phrase, but it makes the point. We never want to do anything for a client that would disturb a judge or jury that hears about it. That kind of information ends up being useless for our clients, so why should they have to pay for it?

As an example, my office almost never offers the promise of a remuneration—cash, stock, gifts, trips, or anything else hinting of a bribe—in exchange for information. That undercuts a witness's credibility. Information that appears to have been the result of a payoff will very likely be discounted by a court.

There are some exceptions to this. I once worked on a case involving Microsoft on behalf of one of its rivals. The Oracle Corporation was trying to persuade the Justice Department to go after Microsoft for antitrust violations, and Microsoft was being publicly defended by supposedly independent analysts. Microsoft leased offices in a building that housed other occupants. The various companies all shared a common outside area for their trash. We paid one of the building's janitors to gain access to Microsoft's discarded trash. Unfortunately, we were so successful at getting information this way that somebody on our team bragged about it and the story made its way into the newspapers. This was embarrassing to Oracle—they'd hired investigators to go through a competitors' garbage. But in this case I thought what we did was perfectly defensible. These documents were in a public area. Their ownership had been abandoned. We did not trespass on Microsoft's property or obtain anything illegally. And what we recovered proved enormously invaluable. Microsoft had been citing the conclusions of independent analysts to buttress their position. But in the discarded trash we found invoices and receipts showing that Microsoft had been paying these analysts and reimbursing their expenses. This was a very significant revelation that we would not have otherwise uncovered. My advice to companies wanting to protect sensitive information is always keep it secure or destroy it. Don't dispose of it intact for prying eyes. A standard shredder usually is not good enough for this purpose. I've had some cases where shredded documents have been meticulously pieced back together. In Microsoft's case, the company's carelessness was good for Oracle.

Another redline is to misrepresent ourselves to others or use another pretext to gather information. Pretexting—in other words, pretending to be someone or from somewhere that you are not—is a widely assumed investigative practice. It is fraud, and not a technique that IGI approves of. The perpetration of a fraud is legally actionable and can undermine a client's case in a court of law.

Contacting someone and asking questions without fully identifying yourself or your purpose is not pretexting. In the Mugar case, someone at IGI called General Tire and Rubber Company and got contact information—a landline phone number and a physical address—for the retirees in Mexico. Getting such information so easily seems hard to fathom today, but it wasn't so difficult in 1975.

In one IGI investigation, a man who had raided the bank account of an art school in Washington where he worked was found dead in Florida of natural causes a few weeks after he vanished. (He had a heart attack in the bathtub and was holding a drink in his hand.) An IGI investigator went to the decedent's memorial event to try to learn about his secret life. The art school hoped to find his assets and reclaim paintings he had "bought" but never paid for. She posed as a mourner and chatted up random friends and associates of his—until they became suspicious of her and asked her to leave. This required chutzpah and charm, but was not a pretext; the investigator never claimed to be someone she wasn't.

Though it is not unethical or illegal, I decided early on that I didn't want IGI to take part in divorce disputes where we'd be asked to conduct surveillance on a cheating spouse. Conducting surveillance in general is an expensive, time-intensive task. Just following someone around in the hopes they'll get caught doing something is not a great use of time. There are also ethical boundaries involved. For example, in many jurisdictions we can tape-record or eavesdrop on conversations only where there is no expectation of privacy—such as at a bar or a restaurant. When you do conduct surveillance and follow the guidelines carefully, every once in a while you can score a big payoff.

IGI once was hired by a company that was selling chewing tobacco in vending machines in gas stations all over the country. My client was convinced that a competitor was paying off gas station attendants to replace my client's products with his own. We interviewed one of the gas station attendants, who admitted that he was receiving money from the competitor. And not just from anyone, but from the CEO of the company. We then set up a sting operation, planting cameras in the gas station to record the CEO the next time he came by with a bribe. When the CEO saw the tape of his action in court—right after testifying that he'd never participated in such activities—you could practically see his shock. The case led to a $1 billion settlement for our client.

In one situation where we did hire someone for surveillance, we got a welcome result very quickly. A corporate client called when his daughter thought she was in love with a man her parents had good reason to distrust. After visiting the daughter in rehab, the boyfriend, whom the girl insisted was good for her because he was not a drinker, flew home. We were told what flight he would be on, and e-mailed a photo of him to an investigator we hired for this one-time assignment. When the boyfriend was driving from the airport parking lot, he was captured on film gulping from a quart bottle of vodka.

An interesting aspect of investigations has been the themes that have emerged over time. The search for truth against the reluctance to see the facts or, in some cases, to re-create the facts. And the many opportunities I've had to see the human condition in its various forms—greed, jealousy, courage, and ambition. The diversity of my cases makes for an ever-changing scene, and gives me a uniquely broad spectrum of experience and perspectives to draw from. I've loved nearly every minute of the job and never regretted making the decision to abandon a lucrative law practice to give it a go.

CHAPTER 8

SEEING NO EVIL

In June 1993, university secretary Sheila Wellington was in her office at Yale University when a colleague ran in with startling news. A bomb had gone off at nearby Watson Hall. Rushing to the scene, she found a long trail of blood, extending down the block, marking the trail of a victim in search of medical help. As she recounted in the *Yale Daily News*, she was soon joined by New Haven police, the FBI, and eventually the Secret Service in sharing the horrific thought that her school was under attack.

Rushed into Yale's university health service clinic, David Gelernter, a Yale computer science professor with an international reputation, had a blood pressure rating of zero. Gelernter had been in his office, opening the mail at his desk. When he opened a package that he believed was a Ph.D. dissertation, he saw a flash and then smoke.

Dr. Gelernter, then thirty-eight, was injured in the face, chest, and abdomen. The bomb tore off part of his right hand and blinded an eye. He ran from the office immediately, wearing only one shoe, his shirt in tatters. Had he not received medical assistance quickly, he almost certainly would have died.

Police linked the bombing to another package that exploded two days before. Charles Epstein, a genetics professor at the University of California in San Francisco, lost several fingers and sustained other serious injuries. The FBI believed that Epstein and Gelernter were just the latest victims in a series of similar attacks since 1978 that they believed were committed by someone they called the Unabomber. Sixteen package bombs had injured nearly two dozen people and killed three. The FBI had been trying for years to identify the mysterious perpetrator in the Unabomb case—so called because the early bombs targeted universities and airlines. To the bureau, he was "one of the most creative and elusive bombers ever encountered."

Since the Watergate hearings, I had been asked to appear on news programs from time to time, as a private investigator who could talk about various newsworthy cases. I was an occasional guest for Geraldo Rivera, who had held me hostage only two decades earlier when he was a radical law student. In the fall of 1995, I was invited to discuss the latest surfacing of the Unabomber. In April, he had sent a letter to the *New York Times* and a taunting one to Dr. Gelernter. The same week, Gilbert Murray, head of the California Forestry Association, was killed when he opened a package bomb. In June, the bomber sent a lengthy typed "manifesto" titled "Industrial Society and Its Future" to major U.S. newspapers and demanded that it be published in full. Failing to comply, he warned, would lead to more bombs "with intent to kill."

Prompted by the interviewer, I surmised that the Unabomber was "obviously a brilliant psychopath. He could not have gotten away with twenty-some bombings, killing three people, if he wasn't extraordinarily careful, working by himself, and also by the way he's been improving his technology as the years have gone on."

"Do you think he will ever be caught?" I was asked.

I nodded. "I do think he will be caught."

The executives of the *Washington Post* and the *New York Times* who had received the manifesto hesitated to allocate print space for this deranged thirty-five-thousand-word diatribe. I appreciated their reluctance, since accommodating one such irate tirade, under threat, could encourage others. But in this instance federal authorities pressed the publishers to agree. The FBI and U.S. Postal Service inspectors had been searching for the Unabomber for seventeen years, and hoped that someone reading the manifesto might recognize something in it that would give clues to the terrorist's identity. The FBI offered a $1 million reward for evidence leading to an arrest. After considerable internal debate and the urging of the federal authorities, the manifesto text was published in the *New York Times* and the *Washington Post* on September 19, 1995.

Not long after that, a man contacted Susan Swanson, an investigator in my Chicago office. He said he had read the Unabomber's manifesto and found it very troubling. David Kaczynski told Swanson he was disturbed by similarities between the Unabomber's text and letters his estranged brother had sent to his family and to newspapers. Encouraged by his wife to pursue his concerns, David called Swanson looking for a quiet investigation into whether the manifesto's author might be his brother.

I was in our Washington office when Susan called to tell me about the case. We decided to have a conference call with David Kaczynski to learn more about his suspicions and explore what we might do to help him.

David Kaczynski was forty-five years old and working as the director of a shelter for runaway teens. He sounded cautious, hesitant, and probably scared about the possibility that his older brother could be the Unabomber. It seemed to me that he had decided to possibly expose his brother either to ease his conscience or satisfy his wife. Maybe it was both. Undoubtedly, he hoped that a discreet private investigation would show that his fears were not justified. But I think that deep down he had an instinct that his suspicion was well founded.

David told us that he had searched though old family papers and found some of his brother's letters containing ideas, vocabulary, and syntax that reminded him of language in the manifesto that he'd read in the newspaper. He told us that his brother, Theodore (Ted) Kaczynski, was a brilliant mathematician who had entered Harvard College at age sixteen. After graduating, he got a Ph.D. from the University of Michigan and was an assistant professor at UC Berkeley for two years in his mid-twenties. After a brief time living at home with his family, he had a falling-out with David and for years since had been living alone in a remote cabin in Montana. David had not heard from his brother for some time, and hadn't seen him for ten years.

Curiously, I realized that Theodore Kaczynski and I had been at Harvard during the same time, though I didn't know him. He had lived at Eliot House, one of the picturesque residences on the Charles River that was much sought after by upper-class students. Eliot's house master was a distinguished professor named Finley. Finley was very particular about the students he allowed into Eliot House, and hand-picked each one. I imagined he would have been aghast at the thought that a future terrorist was among Eliot House's residents.

Susan and I decided to contact an expert profiler named Clint Van Zandt. We asked him to compare Ted's typed letters to the Manifesto, looking for similarities in ideas, tone, syntax, and vocabulary. When I had consulted with FBI profilers in other cases, I was always impressed by how much they could discern.

Van Zandt's first report, though not conclusive, found striking similarities in the writings. He said there was a better than fifty-fifty chance that the man who wrote the letters also authored the Unabomber's manifesto.

At the same time, we matched the postmarks on the letters David's brother sent with the locations of various bombings. A pretty devastating pattern emerged. Ted Kaczynski always seemed to be in the right place at the right time. What had begun with a younger brother's anxious curiosity was now leading to something bigger: solving the Unabomber mystery. A man the authorities had pursued for nearly two decades was now quite possibly within their reach.

I called David personally to convey the results of the investigation thus far. I told him that the evidence wasn't conclusive, but it was persuasive that his brother was likely the Unabomber. As I relayed what we'd found, David seemed startled, if not shocked. However much he had feared that his brother was a terrorist, hearing of evidence supporting his suspicions articulated by someone else must have been very disturbing.

"I'm recommending that you go to the FBI with this information," I told him.

David had followed his instincts this far, but that didn't necessarily mean he'd go further. I knew that he and Ted weren't close, but it must have been daunting for David to recognize that the older brother he'd loved and grown up with was a terrorist. David might well have told us, *Thanks, but I don't want to pursue this any further.*

To my great relief, he didn't. He said, "I think you're right." Technically, David Kaczynski was a client. While he wasn't a paying client, he had put enough trust in me and our firm to have us check out the evidence that only he held. The relationship we have with our clients is one of trust, and we don't reveal what we find unless the client instructs us to do so. But the Unabomber matter was unique. Confronted with compelling evidence of the bomber's identity, I would have gone to the FBI if David hadn't. I had that moral obligation whether David liked it or not.

After the manifesto had been published, law enforcement authorities were besieged with tips from thousands of people who thought they had relevant information about the Unabomber's identity. How could David's evidence rise to the top of that pile? If the FBI was to become persuaded that Ted Kaczynski was a prime suspect, how could David feel confident that they would handle it appropriately? Just three years before, federal authorities had botched their encounter with Randy Weaver at Ruby Ridge. David wanted to be sure that if authorities approached Ted at his cabin in Montana, he would be treated carefully and not endangered. From that point, David Kaczynski worked with the FBI and a D.C. attorney named Anthony Bisceglie to locate and arrest his brother.

On April 3, 1996, Ted Kaczynski was apprehended in his wilderness cabin in Montana and placed under arrest. Tried in federal court in 1996 on charges of illegally transporting, mailing, and using bombs, he was convicted and sentenced to life in prison. David became director of a Buddhist monastery in Woodstock, New York, and a crusader against the death penalty. For years, he received no replies to letters he sent to his brother in prison.

Whenever I discuss the Unabomber case, I usually dwell on a single thought: What if David Kaczynski had done nothing? He could have ignored the tugs on his conscience. He could have dismissed his wife's prodding. Even after he had reason to believe that his brother was the Unabomber, he could have refused to cooperate with the FBI. He did the right thing, but as I've learned over the years, that was not by any means inevitable.

An investigator's job is to find facts that lead to the truth. But sometimes the truth isn't what people want to hear. I've seen many times over my career the great lengths that people will go to in order to avoid the truth, ignore it, or wish it away.

In early 1987, I received a phone call from a senior executive at Drexel Burnham Lambert, a major Wall Street investment banking firm. Drexel was very aggressive and successfully involved in mergers and acquisitions and hostile takeovers that dominated the business press in the 1980s. Its most notorious partner at the time was Michael Milken, who created the market for high-yielding "junk bonds." (In 1989, Milken pleaded guilty to securities fraud and served two years in prison.) The executive who called me wanted IGI to provide due diligence—a quick background check—on the owner of a California business for whom Drexel was preparing to raise money from investors. In this case, our target was a brash twenty-year-old carpet cleaner.

I thought I had misheard the age when the executive said it over the phone.

"No, he's a wunderkind," he said. He had started a business with the peculiar name ZZZZ Best in his family's garage. The company was billed as "the General Motors of carpet cleaners." Yes, that's what I was told. The kid's name was Barry Minkow.

One of Drexel's deal committees was about to go on the road to raise millions of dollars for a bond offering they were underwriting for ZZZZ Best's expansion. They wanted IGI to undertake a simple investigation. They were already confident that Minkow's business was sound and its prospects unlimited, but they needed an outsider's report to show investors they had done their homework. They just needed to make sure there weren't any major red flags. And they were in a hurry. "We'll be taking off soon," my client told me, "so let's get this done quickly." The implication, it should have been obvious enough, was that we would find nothing negative. Then they could get on with making ZZZZ Best an even bigger empire.

The oddly named company was trading on Wall Street at something like eighteen dollars a share and was valued at more than $200 million. Minkow was being hailed as a great American success story, a brilliant young entrepreneur who had started the company when he was sixteen and now boasted over a thousand employees. He was celebrated from Hollywood and Los Angeles, his hometown, across the country to Wall Street. When he entered negotiations to buy KeyServ, the Sears company's nationwide authorized carpet cleaner, Drexel offered to finance the $25 million acquisition through private placement of junk bonds. The folks at Drexel Burnham, all seasoned investors, believed in this deal, the kid behind it, and the hefty fees that would reward them for making it happen.

I called Barry Minkow in California, introduced myself, and told him I needed some answers to a few questions for a background check.

He was young—and that's how he sounded. "Sure," he replied. "No problem."

I asked him a few of my basic questions: Who are your chief officers? What are their backgrounds? Where did you receive your initial financing? How would you describe the company?

For a wunderkind, he wasn't very impressive. "I'll have to get back to you on that," he responded to most of my inquiries.

Minkow didn't seem overly concerned that he was being investigated. After all, his business had passed previous examinations by Big Eight accounting firms and prominent law firms when it went public and when its stock was sold in the 1986 IPO. He had become a multimillionaire when he was just a teenager. I'm sure he felt he was leading a charmed life. His vagueness, however, did give me a little concern. For a supposed whiz kid with a businessman's genius, he should have had an encyclopedic knowledge of his operations. The fact that he couldn't recall the name of his original financial backers was extremely suspicious.

After that phone call, I went to my usual sources for helpful information—former employees of his company—to ask about their experiences and what they might know about the company's financial background. We also dug into SEC, IRS, and other business records, from which we compiled a list of the company's officers and chief financiers.

It didn't take long to learn from court records that one of the original financial backers of the company had applied for a legal name change. His original name was problematic, since he had been convicted on charges involving organized crime. Knowing that a prestigious company like Drexel wouldn't want to be involved in a company that had begun with dirty money, I halted the investigation.

I called up the head of the Drexel team and told him the unfortunate news.

He paused. I figured he was disappointed, and that there was no way Drexel would want to ask people to invest in a company started up with dirty money.

"Well, did Barry do anything wrong?" he asked.

"I stopped the investigation," I replied. "I didn't go any further. I knew you guys wouldn't want to be involved with this."

Another pause. "Well, if Barry hasn't done anything wrong personally, I don't see a problem with funding him now."

"So you want me to keep looking at him?" I asked.

"Yes," he said. "Go ahead."

I went back on the case. We then discovered that the Los Angeles District Attorney's Office was conducting its own investigation of ZZZZ Best, specifically whether the company was a front for money laundering. I called up the Drexel Burnham team again with more bad news.

There was another pause. "Do you have any proof of that?"

I said the feds seemed to be finding evidence. I told them that we'd also learned that the *Los Angeles Times* was about to publish an article on the investigation and allegations against Minkow that should give the investors pause at least.

The Drexel team blew off my concerns. "Allegations aren't proof" was their attitude. It was now pretty clear that they were going to go ahead with their plans no matter what we learned. Which made me wonder why they were wasting my time.

I was afraid that Drexel was going to get into real trouble based on a couple of hucksters in California, and I was concerned for the firm. I made an appointment to see Fred Joseph, the head of the firm. I told him what I'd uncovered and of my concern that the deal team was more interested in the commissions they'd make from financing ZZZZ Best than they cared about the investors or Drexel's reputation.

But even Fred Joseph brushed off my information. "We have a compliance team here that looks at these kinds of problems," he said. He acted as if I were wasting *his* time. Drexel continued working the KeyServ deal despite my warnings.

Eventually the questions about ZZZZ Best became so great that one of the nation's biggest accounting firms, Ernst & Whinney, was retained to check out the reality of Barry Minkow's operation. Before they had authorized the IPO the previous year, ZZZZ Best's lawyer, an attorney with Hughes Hubbard & Reed, and a partner in Ernst & Whinney were invited to view a completed $7 million restoration project in a building in California. The tour was on a Sunday. They were told the eighteen-story building had been flooded by a burst water pipe and fire sprinklers. New carpet had been laid, walls had been painted, and the interior was about to be finished. The lawyer and accountant were impressed. They signed off on the IPO, and ZZZZ Best sold $13 million in stock the next month.

As federal authorities later revealed, it was all a scam. The pristine building that had been used to showcase the restoration was actually newly constructed. Minkow had rented out several floors of the building for a day, leased equipment, and brought in a team of people to clean the carpets, pretending that this was a standard ZZZZ Best operation.

There was no restoration business whatsoever.

The house of cards collapsed in 1987. On May 22, the *Los Angeles Times* featured a story about ZZZZ Best credit card fraud. Minkow had falsely charged past clients' credit cards to keep his business afloat.

The news article, appearing just before the KeyServ deal was to close, caused the stock to plummet and banks threatened to call their loans. Drexel put off the KeyServ closing for further investigation. At about the same time, a reporter exposed the fraudulent restoration. Ernst & Whinney resigned as the company's accountant, but did not disclose evidence of fraud it had found until later. Drexel finally pulled out of the KeyServ deal a few days later, after Minkow issued a press release implying that Drexel had cleared his company. His company's directors began their own investigation into the allegations, and when Minkow couldn't produce specific information about any of the restoration work he had claimed, Minkow abruptly resigned on July 2, 1987. The company declared bankruptcy on July 7, and Minkow declared bankruptcy a month later.

In January 1988, Minkow was indicted by a federal grand jury on fifty-four counts of racketeering, embezzlement, securities fraud, money laundering, and other crimes. After being found guilty on most counts, he was sentenced to twenty-five years in prison, though he served for only seven. In June 1989, a ZZZZ Best vice president pleaded guilty to insider trading for short-selling the company's stock and laundering corporate funds through Las Vegas casinos in mid-1987, when he knew Minkow was about to resign and the company was soon to collapse.

In fact, Minkow's entire operation turned out to be a giant Ponzi scheme. Even the IPO was basically a ruse designed to raise money to pay earlier investors. The company cost its investors and lenders $100 million. To this day, Minkow's business is considered one of the biggest accounting frauds in history.

By 1990, Drexel Burnham itself collapsed. The ZZZZ Best scandal was just the tip of the iceberg for a company that regularly tried to ignore the truth or skirt the law. Many of the senior officers at the firm were indicted on charges of insider trading, stock manipulation, and tax laws violations, and some went to jail. Drexel's heedless operation was an early precursor to a problem that would plague Wall Street over the ensuing decades in an unregulated atmosphere that encouraged risky investments with other people's money without due diligence or even common sense. If the Minkow experience taught Wall Street any lessons, they were quickly forgotten.

After Minkow's release, he became a minister and started giving lectures around the country, warning people about frauds like his and how to detect them. His entertaining presentations to law enforcement officials described how Ponzi schemes evolve: rarely intentional at the outset, but developing as the perpetrators need more money from new investors to pay off the early ones. For years, Minkow's life story paralleled that of Frank Abagnale Jr., the check forger who was the subject of the film *Catch Me If You Can*. Abagnale eventually went to work for the FBI to help expose other frauds. Minkow too collaborated on a movie about his life, but it didn't have a similarly happy ending. In 2011 Minkow was caught in another fraud, making money from deliberately driving down the value of a home-builder stock. He went back to prison.

It's a given that Barry Minkow was responsible for ZZZZ Best's fraud, but that doesn't let off the hook the many who rushed to embrace him. They enabled Minkow. Lawyers, accountants, Wall Street firms, and investors loved the idea of this prodigy making them millions. Greed distracted them and made them blind. Like victims of Enron and other financial scandals later, as well as those who lost millions in the Internet bubble and careless mortgages more recently, they forgot the most sensible adage: If it sounds too good to be true, it probably isn't true.

Like the ZZZZ Best case, my later experience investigating United Way of America demonstrated how oversight boards, their accountants and attorneys, tend to avoid inconvenient facts. In this case, some of the most respected leaders in corporate America were encouraged to sweep under the rug evidence of serious executive misconduct through governance failure. They not only tried to ignore the truth, but in effect conspired to subvert it.

I was introduced to the United Way by Frank Mankiewicz, a legendary public relations consultant in Washington. Frank had been Bobby Kennedy's press secretary, manager of George McGovern's 1972 presidential campaign, and president of National Public Radio. He had heard about IGI from an acquaintance, Brook Shearer, who was a member of my staff. In December of 1991 he called to enlist my help on a case.

Frank had been retained by the United Way, the huge national umbrella charity, to handle a problem confronting its leadership that he said was sensitive and required discretion. He told me that reporters from the *Washington Post* and a local business magazine, *Regardie's*, were looking into allegations by two ex-employees about United Way's president, William Aramony. They had been calling United Way headquarters and various local affiliates, asking probing questions. Mankiewicz told me that two whistle-blowers, former United Way employees, claimed that Aramony had misappropriated the charity's funds, which were considerable, in part to fund his romantic affairs. There were also complaints about his luxurious travel style.

As head of United Way for decades, Bill Aramony was a Washington fixture and a hero in the world of philanthropy. He had organized various local charities into a well-respected charitable empire. He had created the United Way of America name and iconic logo and developed a program to encourage annual workplace contributions to United Way affiliates from millions of Americans. The fourteen hundred affiliates, which funded local nonprofits in their communities, paid just under 1 percent of the contributions they received in dues to UWA. In 1990, that amounted to almost $30 million for UWA. In return, the affiliates benefited from the umbrella organization through training, marketing materials, and other support.

Aramony styled the organization to appeal to corporate executives and encourage corporate philanthropy. He forged a relationship with the National Football League, which gave the United Way the equivalent of tens of millions of dollars in free advertising by having football stars promote the charity in ads.

The United Way board of governors was a who's who of corporate America. Aramony had personally recruited some of the most prominent business leaders. At the time, the chairman of the board was the CEO of IBM. The vice president was the head of J. C. Penney. There were several others, including the head of one of the nation's biggest accounting firms.

The board members, like most everyone in Washington and the not-for-profit world, admired Aramony. When they learned of the impending critical press, they wanted to be able to defend Aramony from the attacks. Mankiewicz told me he was hired basically to find a way to kill the negative stories. As an ace PR guy, Frank was an expert at "spinning" the press. But he was also unique in his industry in wanting to know the truth. He needed convincing evidence to support his position. He told us that Aramony himself had suggested an internal investigation to clarify the issues and respond to the press inquiries.

As to the source of the allegations, I told Frank IGI would conduct background investigations of the former employees to see if there were any issues with their credibility. We would then check out the allegations against Aramony to see if there was anything we could find to back them up. Frank said that I'd need to meet Aramony and win his approval. This was a rather strange condition—to get the okay of the subject I was investigating. In any event, I went alone to meet with Aramony to see if he'd allow me to investigate him.

We met in his well-appointed office at the United Way headquarters on Fairfax Street in the Washington suburb of Alexandria, Virginia. The building was quite nice, an all-glass structure with views of the Potomac River. Aramony was in his midsixties. He was a trim, well-dressed man with a ready smile. He was very welcoming. In our first interview, we talked in general terms about the allegations about him, but I did not question him in detail. He was troubled by what was being said about him. He told me he'd been harassed for two and a half years by people making wild allegations. He expressed particular contempt for the Washington business magazine *Regardie's*, which he said "is on my ass now."

When I asked him about some of the allegations, he expressed complete bafflement. I asked him if there was anything he wanted to disclose to us. Was there anything IGI might find in a background check that we should know in advance? Did he own any property? He answered no to all these questions. He said that expenses he incurred for work at United Way had been recorded scrupulously and I could ask anybody on his staff about that. Aramony indicated no concern about any aspect of our investigation. Instead, he offered his full cooperation. He seemed like a nice guy, open and honest. In truth, I wanted to like him because of all the great things that the United Way accomplished. But in investigations, you have to avoid making assumptions based on appearances. They can be deceiving.

IGI was hired on December 17, 1991, with a contract signed by the general counsel. The next day, we drew up a memo outlining five areas for investigation: possible financial improprieties at United Way; Aramony's associates; his lifestyle and personal finances to support it; issues of corporate governance; and United Way's for-profit spin-offs and allied organizations. We listed steps we would take, including examining Aramony's corporate credit card records, his salary and other compensation, and his property and other assets. We would review internal financial reports and audits by UWA's accountant, Arthur Anderson, and interview UWA's financial staff. To investigate allegations involving Aramony's so-called cronies, we would do background checks and ask other staff about them. Aramony's connections to the spin-offs raised many issues, including nepotism and financial irregularities, that we would explore through documents and interviews. We were also asked to look into allegations about Aramony's girlfriends, gambling, and frequent first-class travel—rumors that were particularly troubling to the affiliates who heard about them. We learned that, sometime before, UWA officials had asked Aramony about two anonymous letters they'd received. One accused Aramony of using UWA funds to pay off a woman, and of improprieties with one of the spin-offs. The other was about one of Aramony's cronies and his contracts with UWA. There had also been a sexual harassment complaint against Aramony. We would have to find out more about these.

Our initial job was to collect background information about the whistle-blowers, looking through the standard databases. The results, described in a status report we wrote for United Way dated December 17, were unremarkable. Over the last two weeks of December and into January, IGI investigators interviewed dozens of United Way staff members and former employees to learn about how the organization operated and who was responsible for what. We asked about personal relationships among the staff and how key staffers interacted professionally with Aramony.

Curiously, IGI also was asked to arrange for sweeps of United Way offices and Aramony-related premises to search for listening devices. Clients sometimes ask for such sweeps, especially if they suspect corporate espionage. Did they think that Aramony, or United Way, was a victim of illegal snooping? If so, for what purpose? I wondered who they thought would have installed eavesdropping devices and what information they feared these bugs might reveal. We subcontracted the job to experienced former intelligence personnel, who scoured rooms for aberrational feedback on various devices. They unscrewed phones and looked into receivers. They examined fax machines for devices that could intercept facsimile transmissions, a favored way to steal confidential information through the interception of incoming and outgoing documents before e-mail superseded them.

United Way staff gave us a massive number of documents related to Aramony. Looking for irregularities, we examined telephone logs and bills, records relating to travel, Aramony's corporate American Express credit card records, checking accounts, appointment calendars, and select personnel records. We reviewed Aramony's consulting contracts, as well as material related to various United Way spin-off organizations. By the time we met with Aramony again, over ten hours on two separate occasions, IGI investigators had absorbed a lot of information and had a lot of questions.

Considering how openly he welcomed IGI's search, I don't think Bill Aramony really understood what an investigator does. It didn't take long to discover that Aramony had lied to me. A standard check of public records revealed that Aramony, who told me he didn't own any property, was in fact named on a deed for a condo in Coral Gables, Florida.

I called him on the telephone and confronted him with this discrepancy.

"Oh, I forgot about that," he said casually. "No big deal."

I guessed it was possible that the omission was an oversight, but Aramony's offhand tone rang an alarm bell. I told Frank Mankiewicz that we had to take a hard look at this guy. So with the grudging approval of the board, we opened up a more thorough investigation into Aramony's activities and spending practices.

Aramony was drawing a pretty substantial salary, which, including benefits, was north of $450,000 a year. There was nothing criminal or even unethical about that, but critics thought that level of remuneration was unseemly for the president of a charity that depended largely on donors of modest means. What was more surprising, given the ostensible purpose of the organization, was an extensive paper trail of memos demonstrating that Aramony was using the charity's funds to support his lavish lifestyle.

He behaved like a lot of people I've observed who have too much power in an organization—as if he were a potentate. We found memos asking staff members to repair his car, fix his VCR, and tar his driveway. He used a graphic artist on UWA's staff to be his interior decorator and paint his house. On several occasions he flew to Europe on the supersonic Concorde, and usually flew first class otherwise—often with a secretarial aide. He appeared to surround himself with a staff of yes-men (and -women) who carried out his every whim.

Aramony bought personal gifts, clothes, and golf equipment, all at the United Way's expense. He maintained accounts at florists in the Washington area that were paid by the United Way. He contracted with a limousine service, increasing his office budget by $30,000 to pay for it as an "administrative cost."

One did not have to hang around the United Way offices long before hearing about a woman named Lori Villasor. Aramony, who was sixty-four in 1992, had apparently met Lori when she was a teenager, and his relationship with her was mentioned by a number of aides. We discovered by checking the United Way's payroll that she was receiving a monthly stipend. Aramony paid for braces on her teeth and took her on vacations to Europe and Egypt. He sent her flowers often. We found records of a number of trips that Aramony made to Villasor's home in Florida that were charged to United Way.

Another woman, Anita Terranova, also appeared to have a relationship with Aramony that was more than professional. She also lived in Florida, where Aramony was from, and was interviewed by phone. She was employed at UWA or by a spin-off, United Way International, for twenty years, and retired six months before our investigation began. She had furnished and used an "office" in an upscale condo/hotel in Coral Gables that was bought in 1988 with United Way funds. The deed for this property had Aramony's name on it—the same property I'd called him about. Terranova's United Way American Express card was used to charge almost $40,000 in mostly travel expenses in the two years before December 1991, including $1,722 for two months' car rental in Florida. After she retired, Terranova used the card for $7,870 in expenses, including for a trip to Las Vegas where our investigators determined Bill Aramony was at the same time.

An attentive financial officer at the United Way would have spotted these abuses easily and called Aramony on them. But Aramony seemed to have thought of that. He removed the existing chief financial officer and replaced him with a handpicked employee he knew from Florida, Thomas Merlo. We found Merlo's name attached to records of legal proceedings in Florida, where he had been involved in lawsuits related to his business failures. He had been under investigation by the federal government in a case of Medicare fraud, and his work as an accountant had been examined by grand juries. (When Merlo's history soon became controversial, Aramony was forced to fire him.)

One of the most intriguing aspects of Aramony's leadership of UWA that we discovered was the for-profit subsidiaries that he created. These spin-offs were ostensibly designed, and approved by the UWA board, to provide services and products to the affiliated charities at group discount costs. Bill Aramony's son, Bob, had worked for three spin-offs, and was the president of a fourth, Sales Service/America, when IGI interviewed him. Bill Aramony said Bob couldn't have worked for UWA because of antinepotism rules, but they didn't apply to the spin-offs. He said that his son was hired by spin-off boards that were independent of UWA, although Bill Aramony had recruited the members of those boards. We found that Partnership Umbrella, one of the spin-offs, had used funds provided by UWA to buy and furnish an apartment in New York City that Bill Aramony used on his frequent trips to the city.

As for the rest of the organization, the employees who were not in cahoots with Aramony seemed shocked by the new allegations surfacing about their boss. Many of them seemed embarrassed. The atmosphere at the United Way offices reminded me of the White House during Watergate. People were just waiting for the next shoe to drop.

After reviewing documents and conducting interviews almost daily for three weeks, Bob Mason, one of our three crack investigators on this case, interviewed Bill Aramony. Bob's notes indicated that Aramony was far less cordial and hospitable than when I met him earlier. "I'm getting fucked," he said at one point. Yet he seemed to have a ready answer for every question.

"I'm not a detail guy," he said when asked about his expenses. "A lot of this shit bores the hell out of me."

He saw himself as a martyr, claiming he rarely got his out-of-pocket expenses reimbursed. "I make enough money here," he said. "I don't have to steal it." He spoke with pride about his work, remarking that he "worked his ass off" for United Way, which undoubtedly was true. His secretary came under fire, then various assistants who'd "signed off" on his expenses. "I don't know what happens to a receipt after I let go of it," he protested.

He denied any charge of sexual harassment or misuse of funds, saying, "I never had a problem like this in forty years." He denied that he ever made business trips to facilitate personal travel. He said that the apartment he used in New York, owned by a spin-off, saved travel expenses for UWA, and that he went to New York City "all the time." He said that gambling was "one of the few things that give me pleasure," and that he stopped off in Las Vegas if he had a trip to the West Coast. He referred to his "team"—presumably Merlo, Terranova, and others he'd brought to UWA from Florida—as the "Miami Mafia." When Bob Mason asked him about the Coral Gables condo, Aramony said, "We kept it for six months," and was now selling it because Terranova could "work out of her house." He described Terranova's job for UWI as running the "intern development program." He said she left UWA because the board chairman, John Akers, was downsizing at IBM and wanted UWA to downsize as well—so Terranova took early retirement. Then she was "picked up" by the spin-off. He said that although Partnership Umbrella is independent of

UWA, "I can absolutely install someone there." He acknowledged that he was vulnerable to charges of nepotism and cronyism—"I don't dump people. I take care of them."

As for the relationship with Lori Villasor, he said he was legally separated from his wife. "I haven't slept with my wife for twenty-eight years," he said in his defense. He mentioned having had treatment for prostate cancer.

He told us that he had never spent a nickel of United Way money on women. Then he boasted of what a hero he was in supporting the young woman. "She comes from a poverty background," he said of Villasor at one point. "I don't want her to slip back into it."

One of IGI's first interviews was with Steve Paulachak, one of Aramony's cronies who held various senior positions at UWA and the spin-offs. When Bob Mason interviewed him on December 20, Paulachak told us that the Securities and Exchange Commission had been investigating Aramony for insider trading. He said Aramony had bought stock in a savings bank connected to the chairman of Mutual of America who was a member of the boards of two UWA spin-offs. Mutual of America handled United Way's pensions and Aramony was on MOA's board. Paulachak said Aramony had not told the UWA board about the SEC investigation.

During the sweep of Aramony's telephones, a listening device was actually discovered. The bug belonged to the SEC.

When asked about the SEC investigation, Aramony brushed it off. Then he added that it would take him "two seconds" to find another job if things got too intolerable for him at United Way. He had used charm and guile to rise above modest circumstances as a young man and had built an organization that was the envy of its peers. He believed he could talk his way out of anything.

He was in fact a marvelous performer. Even as evidence of his malfeasance mounted, and even as he knew that we knew what he'd been up to, he never broke a sweat. Maybe he thought the board and the United Way structure was so skewed in his favor that he could get away with anything. He was almost right about that.

I realized that the board members were most concerned about the potential for bad press, even more than they were about financial issues in the executive office. Understandably, they were afraid that rumors about improper activities at UWA headquarters would deter donors. At the same time, they were so confident about Aramony that they couldn't seem to imagine that he could have possibly done anything wrong.

The board had designated a fourteen-member executive committee to oversee the investigation. The committee's chairman was Dr. LaSalle Leffall Jr., a prominent African-American doctor at Howard University's medical school who had a reputation for ethics and propriety. His personal integrity lent credibility to the committee's inquiry. On January 10 and 24, 1992, I spoke with Leffall and Kathryn Baerwald, who had become general counsel on January 1, to report on the status of the investigation.

At the end of January, while our investigation still was under way, I was informed that United Way staffers were preparing a report on Aramony's activities for the executive committee. This was news to me. They wanted to quote IGI saying that we had found "no problems" with Mr. Aramony's conduct. We made it clear that we could not agree to anything of the kind, that such a statement was untrue.

Later that evening, I received a telephone call from an Aramony aide named Gail Manza, who told me she was assisting on a draft report. I told Manza that the quote they wanted to attribute to IGI was a total misrepresentation of our findings to date.

An hour or so later, one of Aramony's cronies called us again. This time they had changed IGI's so-called quote and read it to us over the phone. The words were different, but they left the same impression:

that we were exonerating Bill Aramony. I ripped into them. They were preparing a report for which we had no notice, no input, and then had the gall to suggest, by quoting us, that we had approved it. I told them that if they kept in an erroneous quote from IGI, I'd denounce it and the report publicly. They finally agreed to remove the quote but indicated that they planned to send an exculpatory report to the board's executive committee anyway. Furious, I went to Frank Mankiewicz's house to inform him and try to figure out what in the hell was going on. Frank was as baffled as I was.

IGI prepared two memos for Leffall to share with his committee. One was an interim executive summary of the results of the investigation so far, and the other contained three pages of recommendations for new procedures the organization should adopt to prevent future abuses. The summary said IGI had found "no examples of misappropriation by Mr. Aramony of corporate assets," but identified several areas in which Aramony received inappropriate direct and indirect benefits. It highlighted Aramony's use of UWA credit cards for personal expenses that had not been reimbursed; personal services provided to Aramony by at least one UWA employee; benefits that Aramony, his son, and close associates received from their affiliations with spin-offs; the SEC investigation of Aramony for insider trading; Aramony's relationship with Thomas Merlo, his background, and questions about his hiring as CFO; Aramony's flagrant use of limousines; and the use of UWA funds by Partnership Umbrella to purchase and decorate the New York condo. The summary also detailed the complex relationship between UWA and United Way International, which operated with UWA funds and employed several of Aramony's friends.

Sometime in January, the executive committee brought in lawyer Berl Bernhard from the well-regarded Washington law firm Verner, Liipfert, Bernhard, McPherson and Hand. UWA's former general counsel, Lisle Carter, had been a partner at the firm. Verner Liipfert was formally retained on February 4 with a mandate to review our investigation's findings in light of nonprofit and tax law. They were to report to the board on April 2. The firm had done legal work for United Way before—even for Aramony personally, we later learned. I knew Bernhard from Watergate. In 1972, Bernhard had been the campaign manager for Senator Muskie's presidential bid. I had called him to testify to the Watergate Committee about the Nixon campaign's "dirty tricks." Now, hoping to clear Aramony, Bernhard pledged to cooperate fully with our investigation. To this day, Verner Liipfert takes credit for the UWA investigation, but, in fact, Bernhard and his associate, James F. Hibey, were often obstructionist.

I was invited to a prep session for Aramony on Sunday, February 2, at his home in Alexandria, Virginia. The chief executive was to be interviewed by a reporter from the *Washington Post* two days later. My role, I was told, was to provide factual information to help Aramony challenge the various accusations against him—a request I found bizarre, since IGI had discovered credibility in most of the allegations. I was disappointed that Dr. Leffall was not at the meeting. I was told that he had been called to the hospital for surgery. But when my secretary phoned his office the next day, she was told that Leffall rarely worked on Sundays and they didn't know that he had.

Berl Bernhard was at the meeting. For a lawyer who had railed so vigorously at Nixon's abuses of power, Bernhard seemed curiously uninterested in the problems we had found. At one point he complained that the session was getting "bogged down with facts."

Regarding our report, which was to be presented to the executive committee the next day, Bernhard insisted that I delete any references to the SEC investigation. I not only refused but said that I intended to recommend that the United Way establish a commonsense rule: that no United Way employee be allowed to trade in any stock of any of the companies represented on the board of governors to ensure that the charity would be free of even the appearance of insider trading.

The executive committee was to convene by phone conference on February 3 to discuss the findings of our investigation. I was asked to prepare an executive summary of our findings. When I asked the time of the call, I was told I wasn't to participate in it. The lawyers would brief the committee on the status of the investigation and answer all questions. We prepared an executive summary and gave it to the attorneys. They took what I submitted and then retyped it, removing reference to the SEC investigation and rewording it in the most favorable light for Aramony.

I was furious. Even thinking about it now, decades later, makes my blood pressure rise. I knew that I couldn't trust Aramony's cronies or the lawyers to deliver full and accurate information to the people who needed it. So I took that task upon myself.

On February 3, Bernhard informed the executive committee, meeting by phone, of the investigation's results. I don't know what was said. But Leffall reported publicly that the committee took a "resounding vote of confidence" in Aramony.

The *Washington Post* story about Bill Aramony and United Way of America finally appeared on the front page on Sunday, February 16. It was the first of nine articles the *Post* published during the next six weeks. By the time the series was concluded, local affiliates were clamoring for Aramony's dismissal. Five local United Ways in major metropolitan areas that had contributed a total of $2 million to UWA the year before announced they would withhold their dues.

On February 27, UWA headquarters held an hour-long teleconference with ninety-three locations to discuss the situation with local affiliates across the country. IGI's notes of the teleconference indicate that Leffall began by describing IGI and our investigation, saying the "external investigation is over." He claimed it found no "misappropriation," no "fraud or malfeasance," and no "impropriety" by Bill Aramony—just "procedural omissions." Nonetheless, Leffall said he had accepted Bill Aramony's letter of resignation with appreciation for his years of service.

The next day, the *Post* reported that Aramony had announced his retirement on the teleconference the day before, apologizing for "a lack of sensitivity to perceptions." He said he was "stepping aside to protect the United Way movement" but would remain in charge until a successor was found. For anyone who might be concerned about his well-being, Aramony told the audience that he would receive full pension benefits.

Around that time, IGI investigators searched Aramony's office looking for documents that had been eluding us. Among other significant documents, we found a bill from Verner Liipfert for representing Aramony in the SEC insider trading matter. This confirmed my suspicions that Berl Bernhard might have a significant conflict of interest that was not disclosed to the United Way board. The discovery for me was stunning.

I went to see United Way's board chairman, John Akers, at IBM headquarters in Armonk, New York, where he was CEO. Akers was basically a good guy, and an enormously busy man. The problems at United Way concerned him, but they were hundreds of miles away, literally and figuratively. He trusted United Way leaders to manage that ship without his interference. But he had invited me to contact him if I had a problem or had some information that I thought he needed to know.

When I told him about Bernhard's demand that IGI's report not mention the SEC investigation, and of the Verner Liipfert bill we had found, Akers sighed. "Terry, you never have any good news for me," he said.

I told him that I was concerned the lawyers were trying to white-wash the facts about Aramony's profligate use of UWA funds. After all, Aramony had said he was retiring, but he was still officially in charge. The board needed to recognize the facts. It troubled me that the executive committee's vote of confidence in Aramony, which Leffall still maintained, had been based on the claim that IGI's investigation had exonerated Aramony. "We have a real problem here."

Akers pledged to do something to counter any attempt by Verner Liipfert to cover for Aramony. What he ended up doing was bringing in another law firm to vet the reliability of Bernhard's April 2 report. That report is curiously prefaced with a letter from "Wilmer, Cutler and Pickering"—no individual lawyer named—that says "we have consulted extensively with the responsible lawyers [and] while we have not participated in the factual investigations, we have reviewed various memoranda prepared by Verner Liipfert lawyers and by Investigative Group, Inc. [and] we are satisfied with the methodology, objectivity and integrity of the investigation and concur generally in the findings and recommendations."

Verner Liipfert's fifty-nine page report, issued on April 2, 1992, relied entirely on IGI's factual findings.

In a letter to Akers, Aramony accused the board—the same group that had approved his management for years and defended him—of "convening a modern-day Salem witch trial." He continued to deny "any suggestion" of wrongdoing.

In 1994, after government investigations based largely on IGI's findings, Aramony and two of his cronies were indicted on seventy-one counts of fraud, conspiracy, tax evasion, and money laundering. They were accused of stealing $1 million from a United Way spin-off. The federal government's case described how the defendants used UWA money for personal gain, primarily to assist Aramony in his relationships with women. In April 1995, Aramony was convicted on twenty-five counts and subsequently sentenced to seven years in prison.

Aramony appealed the convictions and, in July 1996, the Court of Appeals affirmed the convictions on all but one count, which was dismissed because of a procedural error.

One ironic decision of the appellate court was that Aramony was not entitled to claim attorney-client privilege to dispute evidence against him. In his appeal, Aramony had asserted that his statements to IGI investigators were protected by his relationship with Lisle Carter, the general counsel, who had hired IGI. He claimed that he would not have made disclosures to IGI if he had known that what he said would be revealed outside UWA. He also claimed an attorney-client relationship with Verner Liipfert's lawyers, Berl Bernhard and James Hibey. To support this, he submitted an affidavit from his aide who said that when she asked the lawyers whom they would represent if Aramony and UWA "came to a parting of the ways," Bernhard and Hibey said they would represent Aramony.

Contradicting Aramony's assertion, Lisle Carter testified that his "sole and exclusive client was UWA." But he added that he had referred Aramony to outside counsel on two occasions for personal legal representation. Was one of those occasions the SEC investigation? Did Carter refer Aramony to his former partners at Verner Liipfert?

Bernhard's affidavit stated, "Aramony clearly understood that Verner Liipfert was being retained solely to represent UWA," and there was "no attorney-client relationship between Verner Liipfert and Aramony in this matter." Hibey's affidavit was similarly constrained: "At no time in my meetings or contacts with Aramony between late January, 1992 and early March, 1992 did I ever make a representation . . . to Aramony that Verner Liipfert or I represented him." The court denied Aramony's appeal, pointing out that he had not called Bernhard or Hibey to testify in his defense at the trial and had not asserted an attorney-client relationship sufficiently before his appeal.

The problems United Way suffered because of Bill Aramony's "lavish lifestyle" and self-serving administration did not end with his resignation, nor even with his conviction. For months, UWA had to borrow operating funds to offset the dues that affiliates withheld. And for years, UWA struggled with the issue of $4.4 million in retirement benefits that Aramony claimed. The existence of Aramony's huge retirement package was a shock to the affiliates and an embarrassment to the board. After lawsuits and countersuits, Aramony's pension claim was finally resolved in 2001, when a judge ruled that, given how much Aramony owed UWA for salary and "funds he received while he was stealing contributor money," he was entitled to only $7,781.

In many ways, Aramony's excesses were typical of for-profit corporate executives. The CEOs that Aramony hung with had lavish lifestyles that Aramony wanted to emulate. But he was head of a charity that should have required different standards. The lesson of the United Way scandal is for nonprofit board members, who too often neglect their fiduciary responsibilities. They aren't familiar with not-for-profit law and assume they can trust the charity's executives. So they approve inappropriate and even illegal retirement plans, compensation, spending, and spin-offs without careful consideration.

Aramony behaved like other wealthy men I've observed. They build monumental operations and then surround themselves with yesmen. In Aramony's view, he had worked hard to create the successful charity that UWA became. Bill Aramony believed he *was* United Way, so whatever he chose to do with its money had to be right and proper. His attitude was like Nixon's. As the disgraced president once said, "If the president does it, then it's not illegal."

To some extent, Aramony had cause to be angry with his board. Not only had he recruited many of them, but they had aided and abetted his behavior for years. They were nudged to action only because the press got wind of it. None of them was paying attention, not even the board member who headed an accounting firm. An objective audit should have revealed the misuse of UWA's funds. The board was made up of well-meaning people with busy jobs who were proud to think they were helping a prestigious organization. They failed to see that the board was being used by the CEO for his own purposes.

IGI's work in the United Way case exemplified what I'd wanted to do as an investigator—take on interesting and complex issues and assemble information to help remedy problems. What our investigators accomplished in a few weeks was stunning. Not only did our investigation provide the basis for Verner Liipfert's report, but it also provided a road map for federal prosecutors.

The United Way case demonstrates how hard it is for people in authority in a successful enterprise to recognize deception in their ranks. When people want to believe the lie, they will look the other way. I experienced another example of this in a case that *Vanity Fair* magazine called "the most sustained fraud in the history of modern journalism."

You might have heard of the *Shattered Glass* case—or the movie adaptation. For me, it started on a Saturday morning in May of 1998 with a 9 a.m. phone call to my home. Martin Peretz was on the line. He was the owner of the *New Republic*, a liberal magazine well respected in political circles. Among its contributors at one time or another were the civil rights leader W. E. B. Du Bois, economist John Maynard Keynes, Judge Learned Hand, and authors George Orwell and Virginia Woolf. Marty was a Harvard graduate, and I'd gotten to know him at various alumni events.

"Terry, I've got a problem with a reporter named Stephen Glass," Peretz said. He said he was worried that much of Glass's published work might have been fabricated. Glass had been fired the day before. Peretz wanted to know the extent of Glass's fraud as soon as possible. "Could you go down to the magazine's office and see what you can do?"

Like Barry Minkow, Stephen Glass, then twenty-five, was considered a wunderkind—a talented, appealing young man whom people wanted to like and believe. He had written articles not only for the *New Republic*, where he had risen to become an associate editor, but the *New York Times, Harper's,* and *Rolling Stone.* Glass had been accused of inventing facts in his journalism in the past, but had been given cover by the *New Republic*'s editor at the time, Michael Kelly. Glass's colleagues at the magazine liked him and wanted to give him the benefit of the doubt. Glass, who was studying law at Georgetown University, was said to be a stickler for fact-checking when he was editing other reporters' work.

Peretz told me to contact Charles Lane, the new editor who had replaced Michael Kelly a few months before. I told Peretz to secure and seal Glass's office and computer immediately, and to make sure that Glass had no access to the building. When I reached Lane that Saturday morning, he was eager to have my help.

What apparently had caught Lane's attention was a typically colorful article written by Glass called "Hack Heaven." It was about states' efforts to legislate against computer hackers. After examining the piece, editors from an online publication, *Forbes Digital Tool*, had contacted Lane on Thursday, claiming that the article was fictitious. For one thing, the article described how a California software company called "Jukt Micronics" was bending over backward to satisfy demands of a fifteen-year-old hacker in Bethesda, Maryland. They had done research online, and claimed that Jukt Micronics didn't exist.

Lane connected the *Forbes* editors with Glass on the phone, and listened as Glass defended his story and described his sources. The editors pointed out peculiar irregularities in the California company's website—a website which, Lane realized later, Glass had created. Beguiled by the young writer's earnestness, the editors suggested that he had been the victim of a hoax. Glass seemed to accept this, but Lane was not convinced.

On Friday morning, Lane asked Glass to take him to the hotel in Bethesda where Glass claimed he had met the software company executives and the hacker at a conference. Glass took Lane down the escalator to the adjacent office building where he said the conference had been held. Lane asked a security guard if he recalled such a conference. The guard said no, and added that the building had been closed on the Sunday that Glass said he had been there. Glass insisted that they had been in the building.

Driving back to the office, Glass broke down and cried to Lane about how much pressure he was under from his parents, law school, and the magazine. Lane became convinced that Glass was unreliable at best, and told him he was suspending him for two years, which Lane figured was tantamount to firing him.

When Lane returned to the office, he tried to contact "George Sims," who Glass said was the head of Jukt Micronics. A person claiming to be Sims called Lane from a phone number with the Palo Alto, California, area code and confirmed aspects of Glass's story. Later Friday evening, when discussing the situation with a colleague, Lane learned that Glass's brother was a student at Stanford University in Palo Alto.

Around 9:30 on Saturday morning, when I was talking with Peretz, Lane went to the magazine office and discovered that Glass was already there, working at his computer. Lane confronted him, saying, "Your brother is George Sims, right?" He then fired Glass and ordered him to leave the premises immediately without taking anything.

When I met Lane at his office that Saturday morning, I didn't fully realize all the reasons he had to be anxious. He was the new kid on the block at the *New Republic*. His predecessor, Kelly, who had fallen out with the magazine's owner, was missed by the magazine's staff. Lane was still struggling to gain command when he got the call from the *Forbes* editors. I don't know how much he knew of the history of Glass's other questionable articles, but he knew he was walking into a minefield.

I engaged a forensic technician to begin pulling documents and e-mails from Glass's computer that weekend. He managed to pull up more than five hundred data files from Glass's desktop computer and accompanying floppy disks, which were scattered around his desk, and about two hundred files that Glass had deleted.

Lane had given me a list of seven articles that he suspected of being fabricated. As we reviewed Glass's files, we expanded our examination to fifteen articles and accompanying notes. In the end, the *New Republic* had to apologize for twenty-seven, more than half the published articles Glass had written.

Glass's articles were famous for sources who had colorful, provocative, emotional, or embarrassing stories that shed light on the subjects of his articles. That was what made him such a draw. Few seemed to wonder if his sources were too good to be true. To cite one well-known example, Glass wrote about an entity called "The First Church of George Herbert Walker Christ," where parishioners, echoing the president (this was the first George Bush), swore off eating broccoli. It was weird and certainly would be intriguing if such a place existed. But did it really make sense? Would there actually be a church like that? Nobody had asked such things at the time. He also authored a parody of Federal Reserve chair Alan Greenspan, a portrait of President Clinton's detractors called the Commission to Restore the Presidency to Greatness, and "Monica Sells," ostensibly about garage sale items of the White House intern.

There are many ways to describe Stephen Glass, but sloppy isn't one of them. He took notes about sources for almost all of his articles, even those that were totally fabricated. He did it so that he'd be able to back up his stories if an editor or fact-checker ever asked to see his documentation. After we reviewed hundreds of pages of notes, it became easier to figure out which sources seemed legitimate and which were likely frauds. He had two styles for his notes. One style included full names, contact information, and long, coherent quotes. These were the ones that usually checked out. Other notes had partial names, sparse or nonexistent contact information, and garbled phrases, abbreviations, or half sentences that made little sense. Sometimes he wrote "Not for Attribution" next to a source as an excuse for not listing that person by name. Most of those people didn't appear to exist.

We went through all his files carefully, highlighting sources that appeared suspicious as well as ambiguous or anonymous quotes, and compared them with the finished articles. In some cases, we reversed directions by matching quotes attributed to sources in his articles to suspicious sources in his notes.

The more cumbersome task was to search through databases for the names of people in Glass's notes and articles to see whether they even existed. In one of his articles, for example, he referred to a woman named Rachel Hamford, whom Glass described as a San Diego housewife and a member of an online chat group called "Click for Christ." We found Rachel's name in Glass's notes. What purported to be quotes from a phone conversation with her was little more than a large block of unintelligible text—an obvious red flag. Glass seldom provided contact information—yet another of his trademarks. Finding no record of Hamford in online databases, we concluded that the data file was another of Glass's efforts to appease a fact-checker.

Glass had been doing this kind of thing for some time before he was caught. In a November 1996 article called "Deliverance," for example, Glass wrote about his frustrations ordering a Gateway desktop computer. His ordeal described a multitude of phone calls and colorful exchanges with various customer service representatives from Gateway, as well as with Federal Express when he allegedly attempted to track the shipment.

We found a letter on his computer dated September 24, 1996, that Glass wrote to someone at FedEx, claiming that a FedEx employee, Robert Maxwell, was fired after advising Glass never to ship a computer via FedEx. We then found a letter, dated a month later, to a FedEx employee appeals board in Memphis, Tennessee, concerning a FedEx employee named *Edward* Maxwell. According to Glass, this Maxwell had been terminated for "offending another employee after a scuttle concerning mailing a package after 7:30 p.m." In Glass's Rolodex file we found the name "Edward Maxwell (Robert)." We did not try to track down an actual FedEx employee named Maxwell because we concluded that Edward and Robert were creations of Glass's imagination. Glass had drafted these letters to FedEx to buttress his assertions in the article, just in case his editors ever asked for corroboration of his story.

There were no notes of any kind, not even incoherent ones, attesting to Glass's ten phone calls to Gateway or the alleged phone calls to FedEx. There was no record of a conversation Glass claimed to have had with a Gateway executive. We did, however, find earlier drafts of the article, which seemed to offer us a glimpse of Glass's penchant for embellishment in real time. In the first draft, Glass recounted his experiences with FedEx and a Robert Maxwell, but Glass did not mention any of the problems, frustrations, or anti-Semitism he allegedly encountered with Gateway employees, though those claims would find their way into the final published article. Neither did this early draft mention trouble with Gateway or the delay of his delivery. In a second draft of the piece, dated about ten days later, Gateway was suddenly a villain, and Glass added elements that eventually made their way into the published piece. We weren't able to ascertain whether Glass even had a Gateway computer.

As we reported our findings to Lane, he took the information calmly. I suspect that he was relieved, though saddened, that we confirmed what he already suspected or knew. We had retrieved from Glass's computer three files related to "Hack Heaven," including two that had been created the week that Lane started questioning Glass about the story.

On one of Glass's diskettes was a fifteen-hundred-word letter dated May 4, 1998, that was addressed to Lane and another colleague, Jonathan Cohn. Perhaps anticipating questions about his sources, the letter purported to provide "line-by-line" documentation of his article. The letter is interesting reading in hindsight, as illustration of the lengths Glass went to perpetuate his lies.

In one instance, Glass quoted a line from "Hack Heaven" describing what he said he'd been told about the hacker's effort to extort from the software company: "Across the table, executives from a California software firm, Jukt Micronics, are listening—and trying ever so slightly to oblige." Then he provided details to back up that scene. He wrote: "There were several executives there. Most of my actual processing of what went on was with George Sims, since he, among other things (for instance, he writes code also) deals with the press. He's in his mid-20s and helped start the company, I think. He told me I could call him at [650/906-7100]. He said company makes software that deals with genetics."

Quoting another line from the piece: "It's pretty amazing that a 15-year-old could get a big-time software firm to grovel like that," Glass wrote. "The word 'amazing' is my opinion. Calling the software company 'big-time' is an error. It wasn't in my original language, it was added in editing, I should have noticed it when I read through the piece again, I'm sorry that I did not." The letter went on and on like this.

We found another, shorter letter, also created on May 4, 1998. It appeared to be a letter Glass had written under the name of a Jukt Micronics executive. The executive supposedly was writing to complain about errors in Glass's article. We already knew that neither the company nor the executive existed. Looking through Glass's hard drive, our technician figured out that Glass was planning to insert this letter on a website he was creating under the name of Jukt Micronics, the imaginary software company.

My first thought about Stephen Glass as we uncovered his fabrications was that he was a lazy kid taking shortcuts. But the documents made it clear that he wasn't lazy. It took a lot of work to perpetrate his frauds—inventing complex stories with imaginary sources, creating fake websites, drafting fake letters, making up notes of fabricated meetings, even writing memos that documented errors. It was as much work as, or more than, it would have taken to do actual reporting in the first place.

One of Glass's articles offered one last twist in the case for me. As I was winding down my involvement, I paid a final visit to Glass's former office. There were various documents around, including a letter lying facedown on Glass's desk. Curious, I turned the letter over to read it.

The letter was written on the letterhead of *George* magazine, the publication of John F. Kennedy Jr., which folded after his death. The letter was addressed to Glass from one of the magazine's editors, stating that payment was being rendered for an article on Washington's "Power Players," which was to be published in the magazine's next issue. One of the so-called power players Glass had profiled was me. I guess it need not be said that Glass had never interviewed me and that many of the things he said about me were invented.

I brought the article to Charles Lane's attention. "I just read something else this kid made up," I said. "It's about me. But since it's really positive, let's not get rid of him after all." Lane laughed, though we both appreciated that nothing about this case was actually funny at all.

As I thought about it some time later, I wondered why Glass would have taken this risk. He had written an article that included a phony interview with a private investigator, a man whom he had reason to know uncovered secrets for a living. Even though he had no idea that I would be the one investigating him, it seemed pretty bold.

My guess is that, as Glass made up "facts" to embellish his articles and make them more interesting, he was emboldened by the success of his lies and the praise his writing received. In fact, we identified a chronological pattern in Glass's work. His early lies were little ones, no big deal, things that could be explained away. Over time, the frequency of the spurious material increased—from partially faked articles to complete inventions. *Vanity Fair* later recounted Glass's successful experiences in high school dramatics. The fraudulent stories of his articles came across as scenes in a clever play.

As with Barry Minkow, this was another case of smart people—the *New Republic* prided itself on catering to elites—getting fooled by a young guy who was too good to be true. In this event, part of the blindness resulted from arrogance. Editors at the *New Republic* expected their staff to be extraordinary, and they couldn't imagine that one of their own would be so dishonest. The editors liked getting good copy. Glass's colleagues liked hearing his stories and were attracted to his penchant for color and his enthusiasm. They wanted to believe.

CHAPTER 9

A SECOND PRESIDENTIAL SCANDAL

On November 14, 1995, the United States experienced a dramatic and unprecedented government-wide shutdown as a result of a spending dispute between the Clinton White House and the Republican-led United States Congress. All but the most essential government services—the postal service, armed forces, air traffic controllers—ran out of the funds needed to operate. This shutdown was yet another telling sign of the growing divide between the two major parties in Washington.

At the White House, many "nonessential" members of the staff were relieved of duty, as determined by the Office of Management and Budget, and sent home. Picking up the slack in some White House offices were interns, which, in 1995, included a young woman with dark hair and a penchant for dramatic gestures of her own.

In the spring of 1996, my office was contacted by a lawyer in California who was involved in a divorce case. He represented a prominent doctor who was seeking information about his ex-wife and her economic situation. The client was well known in California, but his name meant nothing to me. It was a rather run-of-the-mill case. We tracked down some information on the ex-wife, including the fact that she was living with their daughter in an apartment at the Watergate complex in Washington, D.C.

This was a simple exercise for a modest amount of time and expense. I promptly forgot about the case—and didn't remember it even when the client's last name came up prominently later, in a spectacular way. The Watergate apartment his ex-wife was living in was shared by their daughter, Monica, who, the world learned eighteen months later, was then involved in a difficult relationship of her own.

In early 1998, when I was in Moscow on a case, I received an unexpected phone call.

"Is this Terry?" asked a familiar voice.

"Yes."

"Terry, this is Bob Bennett."

Robert S. Bennett is a Washington superlawyer who is sought after by politicians, government officials, and corporate executives to help them deal with serious legal and public relations issues. He's who the major players call when they get into trouble. Bennett had represented former defense secretary Caspar Weinberger during the Reagan administration over a scandal involving selling arms to Iran in exchange for the release of American hostages. In general Bob usually represented Democratic clients, though his brother, Bill, who had been Reagan's secretary of education, was a well-known conservative author, pundit, and consultant.

I liked Bob. I knew him as a smart lawyer, and we'd worked together on a number of cases. I had no idea why he was calling now, but it must have been pretty important to track me down across nine time zones.

"Terry, have you ever heard the name Monica Lewinsky?"

On January 17, 1998, a fledgling website called the *Drudge Report* aired allegations about an affair President Clinton was said to have had with a then twenty-two-year-old former White House intern, Monica Lewinsky. This was followed a few days later by a front-page article in the *Washington Post*, "Clinton Accused of Urging Aide to Lie." The article said that Kenneth W. Starr, the independent counsel who had been appointed to investigate allegations of the Clintons' financial misconduct, was now expanding the inquiry to include charges that the president had encouraged Lewinsky to lie under oath. Mentioned as a witness to this was a woman who had worked with Lewinsky at the Pentagon. Her name was Linda Tripp.

Bob Bennett asked IGI to find out what we could about Lewinsky and Tripp through public information available on various electronic databases. He wanted to determine how credible they were and whether they had been influenced by Clinton haters. According to the *Post*, Ms. Lewinsky had given an affidavit in a lawsuit that Paula Jones brought against Bill Clinton for sexual harassment when he was governor of Arkansas. In her deposition, Lewinsky denied having had an affair with the president.

I knew the Jones case pretty well. IGI had been hired by Clinton's defense lawyers to look into Mrs. Jones's background. We searched public documents, especially those that might relate to her economic situation and sources of income. We conducted a database search for her name, finding various news articles about her and her associations. I learned that she had in fact received support from a group of conservative individuals as she pursued her legal case against the president. I knew this information would be used by the president's lawyers to question her credibility. That's when I first became involved in the fiasco that would draw the president, and the entire country, into the second impeachment scandal in which I was involved. Unlike the Nixon case, where the president resigned before impeachment, this time the president would be impeached.

My role in the Clinton situation was minor. But the media's hyped-up determination to find scandal and identify conspirators targeted me. I was portrayed as the leader of President Clinton's secret police. During these events and since, I have been called "the head of Clinton's KGB," one of "Hillary's private investigators," and part of Mrs. Clinton's "banana republic auxiliary police." The *Baltimore Sun* labeled me Bill Clinton's "private eye." *Newsweek* magazine had a double-page spread showing me in the center with links to all sorts of people.

The fact is that I don't know the Clintons at all. The closest I ever came to the president was across a crowded room at a private party early in his administration, and I shook hands with Hillary Clinton at another social event. Contrary to assumptions made by the media, readers may be surprised by how benign, ethical, and appropriate was the inquiry IGI conducted through analysis of publicly available documents.

When he was elected in 1992, Clinton was seen as a new kind of Democrat, not wedded to old party ideas. He was charming, appealing, and confident. But his openness and casual style rubbed many people, especially conservatives, the wrong way.

Clinton's detractors became obsessed. They suspected the Clintons were up to no good and were responsible for all sorts of crimes and mysterious coincidences. Like Nixon, Bill and Hillary became the poster children for duplicity, unethical conduct, and maybe even pure evil. While Nixon had imagined legions of enemies, Clinton had real enemies. The Clintons were accused of being behind drug running in Arkansas. George H. W. Bush questioned Clinton's patriotism, and Republicans were convinced there was a picture somewhere of Bill or Hillary burning an American flag. An official in the Bush Justice Department was caught rifling through Clinton's passport files, presumably to follow up on a rumor that Clinton once tried to renounce his U.S. citizenship.

In July 1993, Vincent Foster, a longtime Clinton associate who had come to Washington to be deputy White House counsel, was found dead of an apparently self-inflicted gunshot. Clinton antagonists suspected murder, and publicized their suspicions through magazine articles and even a movie, despite the fact that clear evidence from four separate investigations ruled the death a suicide. A torn-up suicide note found in Foster's briefcase had a cutting, and telling, last line. "I was not meant for the job or the spotlight of public life in Washington," he apparently wrote. "Here ruining people is considered sport."

The Clinton White House tried to ignore these allegations, but in January 1994, Attorney General Janet Reno appointed a special prosecutor, Robert Fiske. Fiske was a skilled trial lawyer who had been U.S. Attorney for the Southern District of New York. He had experience dealing with organized crime, financial misconduct, and a host of other activities. If the Clintons had been involved in anything illegal, Fiske would probably find it. Reno charged Fiske with investigating Vince Foster's death and the Whitewater controversy.

Whitewater was another of the supposed scandals that clung to the Clintons. It involved a complicated land purchase in Arkansas that had come under investigation before the president was inaugurated.

Fiske's interim report was released on June 30. Having interviewed more than one hundred witnesses, Fiske said he found no evidence that Vince Foster was murdered. He also cleared the Clintons of wrongdoing in meeting with regulators from the Treasury Department over the Whitewater investigation. But the Clinton's critics were not satisfied.

On the same day as the report's release, the Independent Counsel Reauthorization Act replaced the position of special prosecutor with a new position of independent counsel to be appointed by a three-judge panel instead of by the attorney general. Attorney General Reno recommended that Fiske continue his investigation with the new title, but she was overruled. Ten Republicans in the House and a conservative activist wrote to the three judges on the panel, all Republican appointees, charging that Fiske had a conflict of interest because he had worked with Democratic lawyers on past cases. They clearly wanted someone who would be more aggressive against the Clintons, and Judge Kenneth Starr was selected.

Judge Starr had been solicitor general of the United States under President George H. W. Bush, and then appointed to a federal appellate court. Because of his ties to the Republican Party, Starr was easy to portray as someone with a political agenda. Starr hired a team of lawyers with varying degrees of investigative experience. He also hired Sam Dash, the Ervin Committee's chief counsel, as a special advisor. Undoubtedly Starr saw an advantage in bringing in someone with Watergate credentials, but it was to little avail. From the outset Starr was seen as a right-wing partisan.

In 1996, IGI had been retained to investigate sources of contributions made on President Clinton's behalf. The Democratic National Committee asked me to conduct an investigation of thousands of dollars of contributions to the DNC that might have come from foreign sources, which was a violation of federal law. I was also retained by the Clinton legal defense fund, which had been set up to pay for the Clintons' defense costs in responding to investigations and lawsuits against them. Some of the contributions to the fund appeared suspect.

About $450,000 in defense fund contributions had been rounded up by a longtime Clinton associate, Charlie Trie, a Little Rock restaurateur who delivered the donations in two envelopes filled with checks and money orders. The defense fund immediately suspected about $70,000 of the contributions and returned them to Trie. They hired me to look into the rest. I could see why they were concerned; red flags were obvious. For example, the money orders had different names on them, but the word "presidential" was misspelled on all of them—in the exact same way and in the same handwriting. We started tracking down the alleged donors one by one. We found that many of the large contributions were actually from people with annual incomes of only $20,000 or $30,000. When I presented my findings to the defense fund trustees, they agreed with my recommendation to return all the Trie contributions.

The president initially was reluctant. I learned to my surprise that Clinton didn't want to return any of the money, and maintained that position until the two chairmen of the fund, Father Hesburgh of Notre Dame University and my former boss Nicholas Katzenbach, threatened to resign and make their objections public. In the end, the supposed donors whom we could locate received checks from the fund. I supposed a number of them might have been baffled receiving thousands of dollars in refunds that they'd never actually contributed themselves. Charlie Trie received whatever was left over.

In 1996, the year of Clinton's reelection, the Republican-controlled Congress decided to hold hearings on Clinton's foreign money contributions and their links to China and the Far East. A controversial Republican congressman, Dan Burton of Indiana, led the House investigation. Burton was known for his attacks on Clinton. He had asserted on the House floor that Vince Foster was murdered, and even described how he had reenacted the alleged crime in the back of his house, shooting a pistol at a pumpkin that was supposed to be Foster's head.

Having learned of my work on the DNC and defense fund contributions, Burton's committee issued a subpoena asking me broadly for any materials related to investigations IGI had done on behalf of political clients. I phoned a member of the committee and told him that, as a matter of fact, I'd had more Republican clients than Democrats. If I were to comply with the subpoena, I'd have to turn over all the information I'd collected on behalf of Republican clients, information that might be leaked to the media. I didn't hear another word from Burton on the matter after that.

Putting someone that partisan and prone to caricature in charge of a serious investigation was political malpractice by the GOP. With some justification, the media labeled the hearings a "travesty" and a "cartoon" and did not seem to take any of it very seriously. Thus there was little impetus for the Clintons or the Democrats to cooperate with Burton—and so they didn't.

A Senate committee also held hearings in July 1997 on illegal contributions to Democrats. The committee was chaired by Fred Thompson, who had been elected to the Senate from Tennessee in 1994. If Thompson intended to recapture the bipartisan spirit of the Watergate inquiry, he was thwarted by his Democratic co-chairman, John Glenn Jr. of Ohio, who had no interest in cooperating with the Republicans. Thompson and Glenn feuded in public on various occasions. (Later, some claimed that Glenn had done the Clintons' bidding in exchange for permission to make one last historic flight into outer space at the age of seventy-seven.)

The hearing also did not attract much media attention or scrutiny. Reporters did not follow the case with the zeal they did every twist and turn of Watergate. Little was said of the fact that as many as ninety-four people either refused to be questioned, pleaded the Fifth Amendment against self-incrimination, or left the country altogether.

Thompson also made a mistake, announcing at the start of the hearings that there was evidence that the Chinese government had used campaign contributions to interfere with the 1996 election. It was as if Sam Ervin had announced at the beginning of the Watergate investigation that he intended to prove Nixon committed impeachable offenses. An investigator should never make such a prejudgment. Trie had left the country and was unavailable to testify. In a highly partisan atmosphere, Thompson was never able to prove his allegation. (After

Trie returned to the United States in 1998, he was convicted of violating campaign finance laws and sentenced.)

Because of IGI's investigation of campaign finances, I was asked to testify. Senator Thompson acknowledged our past acquaintance with affection, noting in his deep Tennessee drawl that he and I were "young snappers" on the Watergate Committee back in the day. But soon the hearing went completely off the rails.

The same week as my appearance, *Newsweek* published an item linking me to an investigation of Republican senator Don Nickles of Oklahoma, who was on the Thompson committee. A Native American tribe in Oklahoma had approached me with their suspicion that Senator Nickles was involved in efforts to deprive them of revenues from oil wells on reservation land. I was not hired and did no investigation, but Nickles decided to turn the hearing into an attack on me. When I finally got a word in edgewise, I told the irate senator that I had never initiated an investigation for the tribe, but he went on and on, chastising me and asserting that members of the Senate ought to be above scrutiny by private investigators.

At one point I turned to Fred to ask him to refocus the committee on why I was called to testify in the first place. He shrugged, which I took as a signal that there wasn't much he could do about the ravings of his colleague.

What any of this had to do with Charlie Trie or Clinton was beyond me. It seemed obvious to me that neither Thompson nor anyone else had much control over the proceedings. I was amazed that the Clinton White House managed to get away with receiving hundreds of thousands of dollars in illegal foreign money—including from a guy in Little Rock who knew Clinton when he was governor. A clear attempt by foreign interests to influence our political process was greeted with a shrug. It was a brutal indictment of both parties. Partisan rancor in Washington was such that neither side was even interested in finding the truth.

Clinton's reputation as a womanizer got him into trouble from the very beginning. During his 1992 election campaign, a model/ actress named Gennifer Flowers claimed to have had a twelve-year relationship with Clinton. In 1994, another woman, Paula Jones, filed a sexual harassment suit against the president. She accused Clinton, who was then governor of Arkansas, of demanding oral sex in a Little Rock hotel room. The Jones lawsuit was stalled in the courts until May 1997, when the Supreme Court determined that a civil suit could go forward against a sitting president. Monica Lewinsky had been deposed by Paula Jones's lawyers, and had signed a sworn affidavit denying a sexual relationship with the president. As a father and husband, I found the allegations disturbing, particularly those involving a young intern.

On January 26, 1998, President Clinton addressed the allegations of an affair with Lewinsky before cameras at the White House. "I want to say one thing to the American people. I want you to listen to me. I'm going to say this again: I did not have sexual relations with that woman, Miss Lewinsky. I never told anybody to lie, not a single time; never. These allegations are false. And I need to go back to work for the American people."

When I saw that statement on television, I wanted to believe that the allegations were nonsense. It was hard to imagine that the president, already under attack for womanizing, would be so stupid as to have had a sexual relationship with an intern. But at the time, I was assembling information on Lewinsky and Linda Tripp for the Clinton lawyers. We pursued the same lines of inquiry for Tripp as we had for Lewinsky, examining various court records and her links to Republicans. Linda Tripp had worked for the Clinton White House as a holdover from the Bush administration. She had been transferred to the Pentagon public relations office, where Lewinsky also worked after she left the White House in 1996. I found there were definite issues relating to Tripp's credibility, including her connection to Lucianne Goldberg, a woman who tipped off reporter Mike Isikoff to the Lewinsky-Clinton affair. We were asked to investigate Goldberg's background as well.

In addition to knowledge about Lewinsky's relationship with the president, Tripp had also claimed to have witnessed another event involving a Clinton accuser. She said she saw Kathleen Willey leaving the Oval Office with her makeup and clothing in disarray—the result of an alleged Clinton advance. It seemed a little too convenient that Tripp had been in the right place at the right time to know of two instances of impropriety. Tripp had been employed in the Bush White House prior to working for the Clinton administration, which didn't necessarily impugn her capacity for honesty, but it was worth looking into.

As for Lewinsky, we conducted a standard database search on her, finding her Social Security number, residences, date of birth, and driving records. We searched various states in which she had resided for civil and criminal records and any bankruptcy proceedings—finding none. We tracked down the names of her friends and associates and compiled a list of news stories in which she or her friends were quoted. We tracked links between donors to conservative political organizations and various publications that trumpeted allegations against the president. We were asked to investigate the background of a retired Secret Service agent, Lewis Fox, who had told the *Washington Post* that he had seen Clinton and Monica alone together, contrary to what Clinton was then claiming. Lewinsky did show signs of naïveté and a capacity for exaggeration. That initially was the stance the White House took against her, and a storyline advanced for reporters.

We also constructed a chronology of Lewinsky's recent activities that might relate to her credibility, much of which was compiled from published reports. We included, for example:

1991: Graduates from Beverly Hills Prep. Attends Santa Monica Community College.

SUMMER 1992: Begins affair with married professor Andy Bleiler while student at Santa Monica College.

SPRING 1993: Moves to Portland to attend Lewis & Clark College. So do Bleilers, though there are contradictory reports regarding sequence.

JUNE 1995: Graduates Lewis & Clark; moves to WDC and joins White House as unpaid intern. Reportedly tells Bleiler, "I'm going to the White House to get my presidential knee-pads."

What I didn't know then was that Starr had detailed evidence of Clinton's relationship with Lewinsky. Linda Tripp had taped hours of phone conversations with Lewinsky during which the former intern described her encounters with the president, gifts he had given her, and the blue dress stained from one of their dalliances, which she had saved and never washed. Tripp gave the tapes to Paula Jones's lawyers, and to the independent counsel's office in mid-January.

For the next several months, rumors and salacious speculation headlined news reports, while Lewinsky refused to testify to the grand jury. Many Clinton loyalists steadfastly refused to believe their president would have been so reckless. But on July 28, after she was granted immunity against prosecution for her previous perjury in denying an affair under oath, Lewinsky testified to the grand jury about her affair with Clinton and turned over the semen-stained blue dress. In grand jury testimony that was taped on August 17, the president admitted to "an improper physical relationship" with Lewinsky.

When the famous blue dress emerged, the one allegedly stained by the president, it became clear that something inappropriate had indeed happened between the two. Based on the Tripp tapes and the blue dress, Ken Starr concluded that the president had committed perjury.

Had Robert Fiske still been the independent counsel and come across this information, I think he would have sent a private message to the president to stop fooling around with interns. Then he would have handed him a subpoena asking for his campaign contribution records and demanding his prompt and complete compliance. In other words, an effective prosecutor would have used the president's vulnerability about the tangential Lewinsky affair to pursue the more serious, and potentially fruitful, investigation that I believe the questions about campaign finance deserved.

That's not what Ken Starr did. Maybe he felt pressured to finally get the goods on Clinton and thought he had all he needed for that. For whatever reason, Starr turned the tawdry Lewinsky business into a national obsession, totally eclipsing any other aspect of his investigation.

As Judge Starr's tactics and preoccupations came under increased scrutiny, he became increasingly defensive, almost paranoid. When news reports offered unflattering descriptions of some of his deputies, he went ballistic. He became convinced that some sort of cabal was digging up dirt on his office and that I was the guy in charge of it. A Republican lawyer who likes to make headlines, Joseph diGenova, went on *Meet the Press* and claimed that I was investigating him and his wife. I had no idea who the diGenovas were, and no idea what he was talking about. White House press secretary Mike McCurry called the assertions "blatant lies." But, of course, people like diGenova and his supporters, blinded by their hatred of the Clintons and mass paranoia, would never believe that.

On February 23, 1998, I was at home in Washington when our doorbell rang. Before long, Margaret came to find me.

"There are two FBI agents here to see you," she said. I was as baffled as she was.

"Must be traffic tickets," I joked.

I went to the door. Neither of the men looked like FBI guys I've known—who were always clean-cut, professional, tough guys. These were scruffy looking, neither wearing a jacket or tie.

"Mr. Lenzner," one of them said, "this is for you."

I was handed a subpoena instructing me to appear before the Starr grand jury the next day, and to produce any and all documents "referring or relating to the Office of Independent Counsel Kenneth W. Starr," and "any contact, directly or indirectly, with a member of the media which related or referred" to Starr and his team. This was completely wild—Ken Starr was asking me for information, not about the Clintons or their activities but about Ken Starr himself and his staff.

As I studied the subpoena, I was struck by the signature at the bottom. It was that of a Starr deputy named Robert Bittman. His name rang a bell. Bob's father, Bill Bittman, was a criminal defense lawyer who'd represented E. Howard Hunt during Watergate. When Tony Ulasewicz delivered hush money to Hunt and other plumbers, Bill Bittman was one of the couriers. Ulasewicz had testified that he went to Bittman's office building near the White House, entered a phone booth in the lobby, and taped under the seat envelopes of cash for the Watergate conspirators. He then called up Bittman's office, left the phone booth, and watched until Bittman himself came down and retrieved the hush money. During the Watergate hearings, my public interrogation of Bill Bittman about this infuriated and embarrassed him.

I didn't want to be as paranoid as Starr was, but in the back of my mind I couldn't help but wonder if Bill Bittman's son, Bob, was trying for a little payback here.

I read in the newspaper that a White House aide, former journalist Sidney Blumenthal, had also been subpoenaed to testify about his possible involvement in the stories about Starr's deputies. When reporters asked Starr about the subpoenas, Starr said he was responding to an "avalanche of lies" about him and his team and he was using the grand jury to get to the source. He released a statement to the press. "This office has received repeated press inquiries indicating that misinformation is being spread about personnel involved in this investigation," the statement said. "We are using traditional and appropriate techniques to find out who is responsible and whether their actions are intended to intimidate prosecutors and investigators, impede the work of the grand jury, or otherwise obstruct justice." Apparently, Starr thought Blumenthal was doing this from the White House.

The whole thing was bizarre, and I was hardly the only one who thought Ken Starr was widely off track. The always colorful James Carville immediately went after Starr, labeling him a "thin-skinned fool." "This man is out of control," he said. Rahm Emanuel, another Clinton advisor, called Starr's inquiry an "abuse of power." It was painfully obvious to me that Starr had violated a rule of investigations: never make it personal. And another, more important rule: never decide the results of an investigation before you gather the facts. He was obsessed with the idea the nefarious Clintons and their all-powerful KGB network were snooping through his garbage and his underwear drawer. Back at the White House, they must have been laughing at their good fortune. How in the world had a case about Bill Clinton become focused on Ken Starr?

When word of my subpoena leaked, I became the subject of a slew of news stories investigating me. Most of them were silly and irrelevant. Some described details of my mundane personal life, which was hardly newsworthy, including my marriage, my kids, the price of my home, my relationship with my dad, and my "fanatical" diet. Articles discussing my professional life were usually loaded with error, false accusations, and innuendo. William Safire dusted off the columns he'd written about me during the Watergate hearings, calling me a "bully" and a "gleeful" savage. None of the articles had anything to do with the Starr investigation or campaign finances. In this atmosphere, the fact that I had investigated illegal contributions to the DNC and Clinton's legal defense fund were totally ignored. Though I personally had serious misgivings about the president and his behavior, I was now considered part of the Clinton tribe, by Clinton fans as well as by his opponents.

While my unwelcomed notoriety did attract some new clients to IGI, I did not appreciate the attention. I had always prided myself on the discreet way my firm operated. And I was distressed by articles that mischaracterized IGI as partisan. My involvement with the Clinton matter all but wiped out any work for Republican clients. To them, I was now an untouchable.

Some assumed falsely that I knew the Clintons well and was taking orders from them. There was an allegation that IGI's contract to train police in Haiti was "proof" of a payoff to assure my allegiance. This too was a total misconception. We were, in fact, hired for that job because of Ray Kelly, my deputy at the time. Kelly was the former New York City police commissioner and a former marine. The marines were desperate to have his expertise. Besides, if the Clintons were really going to buy my complicity, I'd like to think I'd be smart enough to ask for more than that.

Credulous partisans believe only what they want to believe, and they can cite "evidence" to support their beliefs. Whole books about the Clinton-Starr fiasco have been published with absurd claims—even about me. Kathleen Willey—whose maybe intimate encounter with Bill Clinton gave her fifteen minutes of fame—wrote in a 2007 book about my "long, intertwined history with the Clintons, especially Hillary." She wrote that I'd served with Hillary Clinton on the board of the Legal Services Corporation. (I was never on that board; the corporation was created after my time at OEO.) She claimed that I worked with Hillary on the Watergate Committee. (Mrs. Clinton never worked on the Ervin Committee; she was a young lawyer on the Rodino Committee in the House and I never met her then.) I had no connection to Hillary Clinton at all.

The stories and rumors kept gathering momentum. At one point I ran into a friend who had been a member of the news media. When she saw me, she whispered, "Terry, are you going to be okay?"

I was surprised. This woman had been in Washington for decades and saw the place at some of its roughest moments. Why would this be such a big deal?

"Of course," I said. "Why wouldn't I be?"

"Well, I've been hearing things," she said.

"Don't worry," I said. "I didn't do anything wrong."

Finding myself in a witness seat was a new experience for me. The grand jury room—some wag called it the Starr Chamber—was at the end of a hall on the fourth floor of a federal courthouse. A few other witnesses were seated on benches in the hall—waiting to be grilled as well.

The grand jurors were seated in chairs watching me come in. None of them asked a question, as is sometimes common. Starr's team was running this show.

It seemed that the Starr prosecutors had not done any of the open-minded background research that I always did before putting on a witness when I was a prosecutor. It was clear they thought they knew all about how the Clinton White House operated, were confident that I was part of that, and were not prepared for any inconvenient facts that contradicted their assumptions.

One of the prosecutors asked me when I had last reported to President Clinton. I responded, to apparent surprise, that I'd never met him. Another asked something to the effect of, "Mr. Lenzner, when Judge Starr was working on behalf of the cigarette industry, it says here that you were compiling negative information about him on behalf of your client. Could you comment on that?"

I looked at him incredulously. "As a matter of fact, I can comment," I said. "At the time Ken Starr was working for the cigarette companies, my firm was conducting an investigation of one of their whistle-blowers." My inquisitor looked shocked by my response. It hadn't occurred to him that IGI had the same corporate clients that Starr had.

I was shocked too—shocked that supposedly professional prosecutors would ask a question based on such ignorance of transparent facts. They should have known that IGI's client was Brown & Williamson, one of the biggest tobacco companies, and we would have had no reason to investigate the cigarette companies' lawyer. To the grand jurors, the Starr people must have looked as foolish and inept as I thought they were.

When it was Bob Bittman's turn, he was clearly annoyed with me. He asked me questions that had no real point—one being whether or not I knew what "the fraud exception rule" was. I had no idea, and said so. The question meant nothing to the grand jurors either.

During a break in my testimony, I went out and sat on one of the benches in the hall. A few minutes later a tall man with curly dark hair and glasses approached me.

"Terry Lenzner?"

"Yes."

"I'm Sid Blumenthal."

I said hello to him and we shook hands.

"Ken Starr believes we are in a conspiracy together," he said with a smile. He told me he was fighting a subpoena from Starr that asked for all of his contacts with reporters going back years.

I pointed back to the grand jury room. I said I just met with Starr's people. As Blumenthal recalled it later, I told him, "They're insane. Stupid and insane." Even if I had reason to damage Starr, why would I bother to go after him when he was doing such a good job of damaging himself?

When I returned to the grand jury room, one of the prosecutors fortuitously asked me when I had first met Sid Blumenthal. They believed that we were in cahoots.

In response to the question, I barely concealed a smile. Then I looked at my watch just to rub it in. "I just met him outside," I said. "About twelve minutes ago."

A few of the grand jurors laughed, but I don't think the prosecutors did. So much for their conspiracy.

A few months later, during the impeachment trial of President Clinton in the Senate, attorney David Kendall queried Starr about information that Starr had allocated funds for private investigators as part of his office's budget. What, Kendall queried with relish, were Starr's men snooping for? Were they digging up dirt on Clinton's former girlfriends?

Starr flipped out at the assertion. "We never hired *Terry Lenzner*," he snapped disdainfully. I had become his bogeyman.

The report of the independent counsel's investigation—the Starr Report—was submitted to Congress on September 9, 1998, and Starr posted it on the Internet two days later. It included intimate details of the Clinton-Lewinsky affair—almost soft porn. It went well outside the bounds of what a professional investigator would do, and was roundly criticized. On October 5, the House Judiciary Committee voted along party lines to recommend an impeachment inquiry and held hearings over four weeks. The hearings began in the lame duck session, after the Republicans lost a net of five seats in the November congressional elections. In contrast to the Watergate proceedings, the House of Representatives conducted no serious independent investigation of its own, and voted on December 19 to impeach the president for perjury and obstruction of justice. On February 12, 1999, after conducting a trial, the Senate voted against the impeachment charges and the president was acquitted.

The impeachment of a president of the United States is the most powerful responsibility given to the House of Representatives under the Constitution. The process should be handled soberly and dispassionately, without concern for party or personal interest. When the House's articles of impeachment are referred to the Senate for trial, conviction requires a two-thirds majority. Presidential impeachment has been attempted only three times in our history, and has never resulted in a conviction.

In 1974, President Nixon resigned, escaping the House's impeachment and trial by the Senate. Fifteen years later, President Clinton was impeached, tried, and acquitted. But these two impeachment events were vastly different.

One critical difference is the intentions and motivations that drove the Congresses toward impeachment. Sam Dash told Senator Ervin that his goal for the Watergate hearings was to "tell the story" of what happened through factual evidence obtained in public. In contrast, Starr's intention was to impeach the president; he had less regard for the evidence. As Starr said, "Whether the story reflects the facts is obviously a different matter."

The conservatives' determination to nail President Clinton fatally flawed Starr's investigation. Assuming the desired result of impeachment early in his investigation, Starr damaged his credibility and infected the inquiry with a terminal disease. The Watergate investigation in 1973 was the gold standard by comparison. Impeaching Richard Nixon, much less convicting him, had never been a goal of the Ervin Committee. We followed facts to discover what had happened. When the Ervin Committee first convened, none of us seriously considered that the Watergate scandal would implicate the president, or even his most senior aides. Every discovery, every revelation, was a shock. When the facts led to the Oval Office, we were as surprised, and sorry, as every other patriotic observer. Never did we recommend, support, or involve ourselves in Congress's decision to impeach Richard Nixon.

The quality and integrity of the leaders of the Watergate investigation in the Senate and in the House's impeachment inquiry were remarkable. Like Senator Ervin, Representative Peter Rodino was under the radar in national politics before he became chair of the House Judiciary Committee in 1973. When he organized the Nixon impeachment inquiry early in 1974, he said, "When this is done, the American public must be confident that this was a fair undertaking." Both chairmen recognized the need for transparency, high-mindedness, and bipartisanship. That's not to say that there weren't partisans on the committees, but all final votes of the Senate Committee were unanimous, as was the final vote of Rodino's Judiciary Committee to recommend impeachment to the full House.

The Rodino Committee appropriately did its own investigation of facts uncovered by the Senate committee hearings, with a staff of more than one hundred poring over documents for months. In contrast, the House of Representatives in the Clinton impeachment depended on the controversial Starr Report. When Sam Dash belatedly resigned as advisor to the independent counsel in December 1998, he admonished Starr: "You have no right or authority under the law, as independent counsel, to advocate for a particular position on the evidence before the Judiciary Committee." Dash's admonition helped to redeem his reputation, which had been badly tarnished by his work with Starr. But it had no impact on the House's decision to impeach President Clinton a week later. Dash's denunciation underscored my conviction that Judge Starr's appointment was the best thing that could have happened to the Clintons.

If Starr had been smart, he would have concentrated his investigation on Whitewater and campaign finance. It made sense to pursue some of the issues before Fred Thompson's committee—the lax fundraising rules, the suspect donations from the Chinese, the hundreds of thousands of dollars in illegal contributions. Having looked into some of those matters myself, I sensed there was more to find. A shrewd, seasoned litigator like Fiske—or an experienced investigator like me—would know where to look and how to go about it. Instead the Starr team went off on a completely different tangent.

Two other fundamental differences between the impeachment efforts were the nature of the offenses, and the role of the media. The Watergate issues—obstruction of justice, blatant misuse of presidential authority, and subversion of the democratic process—were huge, well documented, and obvious. There was little doubt that Richard Nixon's offenses met the standard of "high crimes and misdemeanors." Even the most defensive Republicans on the Judiciary Committee were persuaded to vote for impeachment when the president admitted, late in July 1974, to having halted the FBI's investigation of the break-in.

In contrast, Clinton's impeachers allowed the process to devolve to a focus on the president's intimate relationship. Their two charges—for perjury and obstruction of justice—stemmed from Clinton's attempts to conceal that relationship. The contrast between Nixon's crimes and Clinton's actions is stark. In Watergate, we would never have allowed our work to devolve into something so small and tawdry as a presidential dalliance with a young woman.

The role of the press and media were significant in both impeachments. In Watergate, live broadcasts of the Senate Committee's hearings brought the American people in on the investigation from the outset. Press and public could see for themselves what we were learning. They had the opportunity to judge a witness's credibility, to hear the discrepancies in various statements, to watch our investigation unfold and gather steam. In contrast, Starr acted mostly out of the public eye. As accounts of his investigation were leaked, Starr's covert operation allowed the White House and Clinton's supporters to characterize Starr successfully as a creepy monster looking for sexual secrets.

Television was fairly novel in 1973, but most Americans had access to it. The three commercial networks, plus the new Public Broadcasting System, carried staid, straightforward broadcasts of Watergate hearings, and the evening news shows reported similar accounts and commentary. We were all, in a manner of speaking, on the same page back then. Viewers weren't merely observers—they were participants.

The hearings became a national quiz show of consequential proportions. Every day, we received hundreds of letters critiquing the previous day's proceedings and offering suggestions for follow-up. Of course, the print press was enormously important in pursuing leaks and other leads for investigation. Woodward and Bernstein's early coverage of the break-in and trial of the Watergate burglars in the *Washington Post*—and that of other major papers that began soon thereafter—was essential. But the success and celebrity of investigative journalists in Watergate also had unintended consequences.

By the time of Clinton's presidency, reporters everywhere were looking for the big story—a *something*-gate scandal. The 24/7 news shows encouraged by the advent of cable television needed shockers to attract viewers. When Fox News began broadcasting in 1996, it offered competition to the supposedly liberal bias of other networks and provided an ideal outlet for Clinton's opponents. Print journalism was not immune to this new atmosphere. *Newsweek* reporter Michael Isikoff, for example, was relentless and creative in developing the Clinton-Lewinsky story for months before it became known. The bombshell revelations of that story were what redirected the independent counsel's inquiry away from the more serious, and perhaps more substantial, investigation of campaign financing.

In the Watergate investigation and subsequent consideration of impeachment, Democrats and Republicans were looking for the truth and willing to expose it. There was only one truth back then, one set of facts. To learn the truth, members of both parties had to acknowledge the same facts.

In the Clinton case, Republicans got rid of a first-rate litigator with a strong background in investigations in favor of people who were inexperienced, unprofessional, and seemed to have an ax to grind. Starr's bias and methods alienated Democrats who might have been otherwise inclined to cooperate, and discouraged their pursuit of the facts or even rational concerns about financial contributions or other misconduct. Both sides rushed to judgment—one side believing the president was guilty of every allegation and rumor, the other that he was an innocent victim of overreaching opponents. Neither of those extremes was likely to be true. If the facts didn't support one's assumptions, an alternate "truth" was out there to be embraced. By the time Clinton was impeached, "truth" had become relative. That impeachment inquiry was more theater than the pursuit of facts. The Clintons were criminals because Republicans decided they were, just as they decided I was in charge of the Clinton secret police because that's how they believed the Clintons operated. A sober, Watergate-style investigation was not possible in the highly charged, partisan political environment of 1998. It would be even less possible now, when partisan gridlock has rendered Congress impotent. This was the legacy of the Republican-Clinton battle. Neither side really cared about what was true. Each wanted to see what they could convince enough of the country to believe was true.

CHAPTER 10

REALITY FOR SALE

O n December 14, 2006, a man with a remarkable British title appeared before television cameras and announced the result of a three-year inquiry into allegations of a conspiracy that caused the 1997 death of Diana, Princess of Wales, along with her boyfriend, Dodi Fayed, and their driver, Henri Paul. There was "not a shred of evidence" to support a royal conspiracy in the deaths, declared John Arthur Stevens, more formally known as Baron Stevens of Kirkwhelpington KStJ QPM DL FRSA. Lord Stevens, formerly the head of the Metropolitan Police Service in England, said he had personally examined a long stream of documents from the British Secret Service and interviewed countless witnesses to reach his conclusion.

By some estimates, the various inquiries into Diana's death had cost the British taxpayers more than £20 million. Lord Stevens's report was more than eight hundred pages long. It examined all aspects of the police investigations into the crash and all the rumors and allegations that had circulated in the nine years since—that Diana was pregnant, that she was planning to marry Dodi at the time of her death, that

Prince Philip or Prince Charles, or both of them together, had plotted her demise, that British, French, and American intelligence services knew of the plan and either were complicit or did nothing to stop it.

If the goal of the inquiry was to lay to rest all the conspiracy theories about Diana's death and doubts about the prior investigations, it didn't completely succeed. As with the Warren Commission report on the assassination of John F. Kennedy, conspiracy theorists found any number of reasons to dispute the conclusions. A poll by the BBC, conducted after Stevens's report was posted on the Internet, found that 43 percent of Britons were satisfied that Diana's death was an accident. Nearly a third of Britons were not.

The inquiry would likely not have happened had it not been for the insistence of Dodi's father, the Egyptian billionaire Mohamed al-Fayed. He had not been satisfied with the investigations immediately following the crash, and spent years amassing information that he claimed pointed to a conspiracy and cover-up. Even after the Stevens report was issued, Mr. Fayed's attorney told reporters, "This was not a Saturday night traffic accident caused by speed and alcohol." He said he was "convinced" that the British Secret Service was involved and the French intelligence agency was either "complicit" or "knew what was going on."

"The most important thing is it is murder," Mr. Fayed said. In an interview with Fox News, Fayed said that Diana had told him she was threatened by the royal family and that they meant to do her harm. "All of this is documented," he said. He cited investigations and reports that supported his assertions. He didn't mention that one of the first investigators he'd hired was me.

Fayed's zeal to prove that the British royal family had murdered Diana and his son led many commentators to suggest he was motivated by revenge because he thought the royal family had treated him with disrespect. Others thought he had gone off the deep end, such as when he attacked a skeptical reporter as being a British spy. The situation was more complicated than that. On the one hand the Fayed case for me represented a troubling trend in the world of investigations—what I called "reality for sale"—the idea that a lot of money can buy a desired investigative result no matter the facts. It was also at its heart a very human story, perhaps a genuine response to trauma, guilt, and grief, which made it a complex and interesting case.

On August 31, 1997, I was on vacation in Nantucket when news of the crash broke. The first reports were that Diana had received serious but not fatal injuries. Then, at one in the morning, eastern standard time, CNN broke into its regular programming with a bulletin: "Britain's Princess Diana has been killed in a car crash in Paris." Her companion, Dodi Fayed, was described as "the man she had seemed to finally have found some happiness with." His father, Mohamed al-Fayed, was said to be immediately en route to Paris after receiving the terrible news. So was Prince Charles, to accompany his ex-wife's body back to England.

Watching on television, Margaret and I pieced together what everyone else also seemed to learn instantly—Diana, then thirty-six, was in a black Mercedes evading photographers along with her paramour, Dodi Fayed. The car's driver, head of security at the Ritz Paris hotel, which was owned by Dodi's father, was said to have been drunk. National grief and hysteria soon swept across England. Members of the royal family, who tried to mourn in private, came under enormous criticism for not caring enough. But nothing I heard about the death of Diana tingled my investigative senses, only my sympathy for her two young sons who lost their mother. As the death and funeral consumed the media, it really wasn't part of my life.

The next fall, I received a phone call from Mohamed al-Fayed. I knew Fayed was a wealthy man who owned the Harrods department store in London. I also remembered that his son was killed with Diana, but otherwise knew little about him.

I went to meet Mr. Fayed at a hotel. The clerk at the front desk told me to wait for an escort. Before long, two large men, who I assumed were Fayed's bodyguards, approached me. I knew at once these guys were professionals. As they escorted me to the elevators and upstairs to Mr. Fayed's room, we chatted about their training and I confirmed they had served in British Special Forces.

I've encountered all sorts of security entourages. Some wealthy people just like to have a show of protective muscle; others like it to be invisible; and some, like Howard Hughes, are really paranoid. Fayed's team had erected an impressive wall of security around him at the hotel. He had rented out an entire floor for his visit, which was now off-limits to any other guest for the duration of his stay. Cameras installed near the ceiling and sound detectors on the floor alerted security personnel if anyone was heading to Fayed's suite. A number of people were standing around trying to look busy.

After I was shown into the living room of Mr. Fayed's suite, he emerged from his bedroom, wearing a white bathrobe.

Mr. Fayed was nearly seventy years old. He was balding with gray hair, a healthy-looking bronze complexion, and a broad smile. He was a self-made man who rose from relative poverty in his native Egypt to become owner of one of the premier department stores in the world, along with other ventures, including the Ritz hotel in Paris, where his son, Dodi, and Diana spent the last night of their lives. Within a few moments of talking with him, I could see how that had happened. He was very charming and friendly, but also appeared shrewd as he sized me up.

"Terry, welcome," he said, as we seated ourselves. He spoke with an accent, but was very understandable. An assistant offered me a glass of iced tea. This is approximately how our conversation transpired:

"Now, Terry, listen," Fayed said. "I'm going to tell you a story that I want you to look into. And I know at the end of this story you are going to say, 'Mr. Fayed, you are absolutely right.'"

"Well, Mr. Fayed," I replied with a smile, "I'm sure you understand that the worst thing a professional investigator can do is to decide the conclusion of an investigation before it starts."

"Yes, yes, I understand," he said brightly. "But I have no doubt you'll be convinced."

He talked about his son's death in Paris. Having young adult children of my own, I felt tremendous sympathy for him. Dodi was said to have been his favorite. Then he leaned forward. "There was a plot between the British government and the royal family to prevent my son from marrying Princess Diana." Such a marriage, he noted, would have made Fayed a step-relative of the British royal family. "They couldn't afford to have this happen," he said.

Fayed said that he had a list of people from whom he had received information that he believed would prove his theory beyond any doubt. As outlandish as he thought the theory might have sounded to me, Fayed related it with what appeared to be total sincerity and conviction.

One of the names he mentioned stuck in my head because it sounded like a character in a James Bond novel: Oswald LeWinter. Mr. Fayed's theory seemed to depend on LeWinter's information. He had apparently told Mr. Fayed about a missing car that was involved in the Paris accident. The car, Fayed said, was a white Fiat, which he believed the British Secret Service used to conduct surveillance on Dodi and Diana. He claimed the Fiat intentionally collided with the Mercedes, forcing the car into the wall of the tunnel, and then sped off to the British embassy in Paris, where it was dismantled and its pieces thrown into the Seine.

Fayed said that some people on his list could give me more information about the Fiat. He also claimed that the United States government, and perhaps its intelligence services, were in cahoots with the British. The FBI, he said, was dragging its feet on following up on the leads he'd provided them.

Fayed and I talked for nearly an hour. He was not a foolish man.

He did not strike me as unstable. He had plenty of compelling arguments that he presented intelligently and logically. There wasn't a shred of uncertainty in his voice, not a hint of doubt. He was convinced that the royal family was perfectly capable of orchestrating convenient deaths. Dodi and Diana were an extreme problem to them, Fayed reasoned, and the royals took extreme measures to solve it.

Though he had told me what he hoped I would confirm, I wasn't sure what he expected to be the outcome of my investigation. As bright and successful as he was, he surely could not be entertaining a fantasy that Queen Elizabeth II and Prince Philip would be frog-marched out of Buckingham Palace and placed under arrest for murder. I figured his goal was to cause them as much pain as he believed they had caused him. If he could get the royals to undergo humiliating depositions and answer personal and embarrassing questions, then that was all the better.

"Will you help me, Terry?" Fayed asked.

I told him that I would take the case. For one thing, it was an interesting one. Though he implied that he expected me to agree with his theory, I would pursue the facts to my own conclusion. There was obviously a lot to investigate, and I was intrigued. He was a paying client who wanted some answers to questions about an event that affected him deeply.

Though I was highly skeptical of his theory, I also knew not to ignore a client's instincts.

As our meeting ended, Fayed handed me the list of names he'd mentioned. He asked me to verify their stories.

"I will do my best, Mr. Fayed," I replied.

Back in my Washington office, I conferred with a few people on my staff. None of us contemplated that we might solve the crime of the century. But there was a possibility that something suspicious did cause the crash. Perhaps one of the paparazzi was involved. Or perhaps the unknown driver of the mysterious white Fiat had important information.

One of my first tasks was to refresh my recollection on the Paris accident, and to gather relevant information from newspapers, magazines, and the Internet. I remembered some of it vaguely: the crash that occurred just after midnight; the reports of a paparazzi chase; news that Dodi and the driver, Henri Paul, had died instantly; a bodyguard named Trevor Rees-Jones, the sole survivor of the crash, who claimed to have no memory of the event. My investigators and I would have to look into all of this with fresh eyes to see what inferences we could draw and what evidence we might gather to corroborate or disprove Mr. Fayed's theory.

There were a number of conspiracy theories floating around, some crazier than others. One suggested that Diana had been killed in the wrecking yard where the Mercedes was taken after the crash. Another theory claimed that the Mercedes was driven up a ramp into the back of a truck in an effort to evade the paparazzi. Once inside the truck, the theory went, Dodi and the princess were murdered and their driver killed and injected with alcohol. Still another theory had the couple killed in the hotel while their alleged body doubles entered the doomed Mercedes.

Fayed's problems with the British aristocracy seemed to have started in 1985, when he bought Harrods, the enormous, iconic London department store. Almost at once, he found himself embroiled in a bitter dispute with the British government, which claimed that Fayed had misrepresented himself in negotiations to secure control of the business. It also resisted Fayed's efforts to obtain British citizenship. Considering that he lived in England, had sired four British-born sons, owned Britain's most luxurious department store, and had paid millions in taxes, it was easy to imagine that, to Fayed, the Crown's resistance was a personal attack. I could only imagine how Mr. Fayed got on with British lawyers, who from my experience were the epitome of the proverbial old boys' network, and undoubtedly sniffed at this immigrant outsider. I could appreciate the scope of the grievance that Fayed was nursing. I imagine that he had savored Dodi's relationship with the most famous and adored woman in England, whose son would one day be king. It was a perfect way to stick it to the people who seemed so hostile to him.

As for the investigation itself, our priorities were to ascertain the credibility of Oswald LeWinter and others on Mr. Fayed's list; to examine the role played, if any, by the British intelligence services in connection with the crash; to look into Mr. Fayed's allegations that the FBI had dragged its feet in investigating the information Fayed had given them; and to find out more about the mysterious white Fiat.

This obviously was going to be a complex and expensive undertaking. It would require sending investigators across the United States and Europe to interview witnesses. We would have to talk with intelligence contacts at embassies and with representatives of international media outlets. Because of the high-profile nature of the investigation, it was also important that we act with utmost discretion. For one, we did not want to cause any embarrassment to Mr. Fayed or bring him unnecessary publicity. For another, we did not want to invite false leads or scare off potential witnesses. IGI asked for an "evergreen" retainer with an initial payment of $50,000 and the expectation that the client will replenish the account to cover future expenses.

Over the course of several weeks, IGI staff conducted a thorough background check of Oswald LeWinter and his associates. This involved an electronic search of relevant public records to find any civil or criminal matters involving LeWinter, and identify his associates who might have information about his role in this matter. We searched international media for LeWinter's name and any corporate entities with which he was associated. We contacted our European affiliates to conduct an extensive French- and German-language database search for Oswald LeWinter's name. Every associate we identified was a possible interview subject.

We were told that LeWinter, who was then in jail, was connected to the international intelligence community. One of LeWinter's acquaintances told us that LeWinter inhabited "the murky world of rogue intelligence operations." He was, by most accounts, a convincing storyteller—one article labeled him "the most formidable confidence man in the world." He was one of those guys who absorbed conspiracy theories and spit them back out with pitch-perfect logic. In the past he had been accused of trying to leak "classified information" about other crimes, such as an effort to link the son of British prime minister Margaret Thatcher to an arms-for-drugs scandal. We heard he had obtained a New York City police badge to conduct a fraud, and had apparently found his way into teaching at several American universities with phony credentials. He was, at best, a problematic witness to stand against the British government.

There was also a woman named Linda who was said to have been living in LeWinter's home and helping him write a book. When we ran her name through the records and press databases, we found connections to various Hollywood celebrities, including the actor Steven Seagal. In his films, Mr. Seagal tended to play grim, tight-lipped men of action. That apparently was not all that different from his real-life persona. A graduate of a California police academy, Mr. Seagal was said to hang out with conspiracy theorists in what were called "rogue security circles." He was acquainted with the type of people who might be involved in a scheme to shake down Mohamed al-Fayed. Since he was linked to a woman living with LeWinter, I thought it might be worth trying to arrange an interview with Seagal. I contacted Fayed's office to make sure he was comfortable with my pursuit of this lead. Fayed told us to move forward.

We'd heard that Seagal had a reputation for being difficult. I tracked down the number for his office and got on the phone with his assistant, who repeatedly insisted that Mr. Seagal would not be available to talk, presumably ever.

The assistant sounded terrified of getting on the wrong side of his boss, but I insisted. "He is really going to want to talk to me," I told him. I left the impression that I had vital information to share with Seagal and that the assistant might get in trouble if he didn't put me through.

Once Seagal got on the line, I introduced myself and told him why I was calling. "My guy told you I don't talk to people," he replied.

Since I knew he was sympathetic to the concept of seeking justice— at least in his movies—I explained that I was trying to get information on the accident that had killed Mr. Fayed's son.

"No, no," he replied. "I really can't talk to you."

I kept him on the line by chatting about how much I liked his films. Finally, he agreed to answer some questions. He said he didn't know anything about the situation, he didn't know any of the names I'd mentioned, and he downplayed his association with Linda. Then, for the next forty-five minutes, he talked about his black belt in judo until I couldn't wait to get off the phone.

Other LeWinter associates were more forthcoming. One told us that LeWinter went to work almost from the moment he learned of the deaths of Dodi and Diana. When Mr. Fayed publicly offered $20 million for any information on the car crash, according to a LeWinter associate, "dollar signs flickered" in LeWinter's head. Another told us that LeWinter was at his home computer "day and night" in the days following the crash. The witness said he observed Mr. LeWinter typing a document that appeared to have a CIA emblem on the top left corner. He was working so long and so feverishly at his desk, the witness recalled, that LeWinter's feet began to swell.

LeWinter had told Fayed that he had sources who were "key

members of the investigating team" looking into the crash—suggesting intelligence service operatives. He said he had a file of documents that would shed light on a conspiracy. One of those documents reportedly "proved" that Princess Diana was pregnant, presumably with Dodi's child.

LeWinter had tried to sell these "blockbuster" documents to various media outlets, including *Star* magazine. According to a witness, when a reporter for *Star* first encountered LeWinter's file, the eyes practically "popped out" of the reporter's head. LeWinter was quoted as saying *Star*'s offer was "too cheap," so he next turned to Sky News, owned by Rupert Murdoch, and met with network officials by phone. When that didn't pan out, LeWinter decided to approach Fayed.

The evidence we collected supported the conclusion that Oswald LeWinter was not a credible source. The most surprising discovery, however, was that Mr. Fayed knew much of this already. Earlier in 1998, LeWinter had been arrested in Austria for attempting to extort money from Fayed by offering him fraudulent documents. Fayed had played a key role in the arrest, and was praised by authorities for his assistance. "The Harrods boss has seemingly foiled a scam and caught a fugitive," the *Independent* in London reported. Why, I wondered, had Mr. Fayed not told me this? And why was he paying good money to follow up on the assertions of a man he already knew to be a fraud? I never had the opportunity to ask Fayed this, though in retrospect I wish I had.

As to the second aspect of our investigation—Mr. Fayed's frustrations with the FBI—I queried our bureau contacts, including some I'd known for decades. Eventually we interviewed agents directly involved in the case. They did not attempt to hide their annoyance with Fayed or his allegations. Contrary to ignoring the case, the agents told us they were being pressured by higher-ups to "get results" on the investigation and to follow up on any leads provided by the Fayed family. But the agents saw the case as a waste of time, an imagined conspiracy that had little evidence behind it. If anything, the agents said, pursuing it was diverting the bureau's resources and attention from more important investigations. The conspiracy-minded would argue that this was exactly what you'd expect the agents to say. But I found their statements credible.

As for the white Fiat, one of my investigators spoke to a contact in the French government. He learned that there had indeed been another car involved in the crash. This was the first evidence that any aspect of Mr. Fayed's theory was true. French police sources said that traces of paint and glass found on the damaged Mercedes indicated a collision with a white car. According to news reports, experts who analyzed the paint marks believed that the Fiat had struck the Mercedes with insufficient force to drive it into a wall. A search for the white Fiat and its driver was under way.

I never came across any evidence tying the car to the British government or any intelligence services. Still, the disappearance of the Fiat did pose some legitimate unanswered questions, which buttressed the suspicions of conspiracy theorists. Who had been driving the car? Why did they speed off? Why hadn't the driver come forward? There were a multitude of possibilities other than that the car was driven by a British spy intent on killing the princess.

After several weeks, I reviewed with my investigators what we'd learned about the case. The primary witness Fayed cited was an accused con artist. His associates backed up claims that he was trying to get money from Fayed with false information. In fact, Mr. Fayed himself made this charge to the authorities. There was no evidence the FBI was slow-rolling the case. The missing Fiat was interesting but not proof of a conspiracy, nor that the royal family had anything to do with the crash.

The theoretical motivations behind the plot that Fayed claimed seemed weak. Maybe it boosted Mr. Fayed's ego to think he was so distasteful and threatening to the royal family, but it didn't seem to make much sense to me. Ironically, the only conspiracy we actually discovered was the one Mr. Fayed had himself exposed. There were plenty of red herrings and avenues to explore. But I felt it was unethical to waste more of my client's money on a wild-goose chase.

I called Fayed to report on our conclusions. "I'm sorry to inform you, sir, that we can find no evidence to corroborate your theory of what happened in this case." I told him that his sources appeared to have been perpetrating an elaborate hoax, that there was no tangible evidence linking the British government, MI6, or any other intelligence service to the crash that killed his son. I also told him what our intelligence contacts had told us—it was just impossible in this day and age for a conspiracy this vast to have succeeded and been kept so secret.

Mr. Fayed's response was short. "Thank you," he said when I was finished. "You're fired." That was it, and he hung up the phone. He did not pay all he owed for IGI's work, but his lawyer paid the balance some time later.

I didn't give much more thought to this case again until it was all brought back to the fore with Mr. Fayed's dogged insistence on an official British inquiry. I had to wonder why he had gone to so much trouble, expense, and time to try to convince the world of something that was so implausible.

What makes a case like this complex and challenging are the personalities and emotions involved. Undoubtedly Mr. Fayed was fueled in part by his resentment of the royal family. Did he intend to pay them back for his perceived mistreatment the same way that Princess Diana did: by using the media to embarrass them? If anything, Mohamed al-Fayed was proving that the royal family was right to be wary of him all along.

During the British inquest into Diana and Dodi's death, Mr. Fayed finally had his day in court. He made the most of it. His accusations and theories were far more conspiratorial than anything I remembered from our conversations. British reporters called his appearance before the inquest "a spectacle." He labeled the royal family "terrorists" and "thugs" and called them "a Dracula family." He said that Prince Philip, who was born in Greece, was a German-born "racist" and a "Nazi" and the mastermind of this fiendish plot. Charles wanted Diana dead, Fayed asserted, so he could marry Camilla Parker Bowles, whom Fayed called the "crocodile wife." The list of conspirators was broadened to include Diana's sister, emergency services personnel in France, and British prime minister Tony Blair.

The brilliance of conspiracy theorizing is that doubters can discount everything they don't want to believe and seize every coincidence or corroborating claim, no matter how off the wall, as proof that a conspiracy exists. During the inquiry, letters from Diana emerged, including one in which the princess speculated that the royal family—she named her former husband, Charles, in particular—wanted her dead. In a letter written a few years before her death, the princess handwrote the following: "My husband is planning an accident in my car—brake failure and serious injury, in order to make the path clear for him to marry." Six days before her death, a friend claimed that Diana had warned her that the royals—this time Prince Philip—planned to murder her.

Having gone through some of the evidence, I simply don't believe that the royal family could possibly have been involved. The consensus of the intelligence people we spoke to in embassies in Paris and London was the same. If such a plot had existed, there just were too many incentives and ways for someone involved in it for the plot to have been kept secret. If the British government and the royal family truly had conspired, someone by now would have spoken out. Just as John Dean and "Deep Throat," the mysterious informant for Woodward and Bernstein, had during Watergate.

Though the details of Mr. Fayed's accusations have varied over the years, from the very beginning he held fast to one assertion: that the accident could not have been caused by a driver going too fast and having had too much to drink. Fayed, in fact, repeatedly insisted that Henri Paul was not drunk, and that the blood sample showing his high alcohol level had been tampered with. Over time he went even further, disputing that Henri Paul had been driving the car at all.

I realized why it was so important to Mr. Fayed to dispute the evidence about the driver: Henri Paul was his employee. He had worked for the family for more than a decade. If his conspiracy was not true, then the man he had handpicked to protect his son and the princess was the one who had killed them both. I imagine that parents who lose a child must go over in their minds again and again what they might have done to prevent the tragedy. I came to the conclusion that Mr. Fayed was chasing his conspiracy theory to absolve himself of a terrible guilt he could never deny or forget.

After firing me, Fayed hired new investigators—investigators who found the evidence he was demanding. In short, he bought a different reality, one that he could live with. I don't know if Fayed believed every aspect of the conspiracy he alleged. What I do know is that he wanted to believe it. He is a smart businessman. I doubt he would throw away millions of dollars simply out of spite. So he found people who would make it true. He spent a small fortune to buy his own reality. Mohamed al-Fayed was my first encounter with this phenomenon but not my last.

In the fall of 2005, I received a call from a lawyer in Los Angeles. "Terry, I've got a client who's got a problem and needs you to come out to California and meet with him immediately," he said. He mentioned the name of a well-known movie director, one I knew only vaguely.

He told me that the case had something to do with a possible security threat to the director's family. I asked Jack Barrett, a very smart and careful investigator who worked in my D.C. office, to fly out to California with me. I chose Jack because he had been a FBI agent and police officer and had exceptional investigative skills.

The director put us up for the night at a little inn along the Pacific Ocean, not far from his estate. His compound, as I encountered it, was heavily secured. A couple of guys who looked like they'd served in the marines or special forces were walking with guard dogs along the perimeter, which was enclosed by a seven-foot-high fence. Whatever I was being called in to discuss I figured had to be serious.

The director met me inside his oceanfront house. His security director sat beside him. From the time our meeting began, the director was directing, running the conversation and very commanding. He did not suffer from modesty. He boasted of his elaborate security measures. While we spoke—we met for hours—security men in combat boots would occasionally walk through the house with guard dogs.

The director said that he had funded an operation that conducted maritime exploration. He said he'd been involved with Russians for the past decade in these types of adventures.

A relative who had been managing this operation had hired a Russian woman as a stewardess and the two had some sort of personal relationship. The director believed the woman had been looking for a rich American to seduce. At some point, the relative and this woman were in a Moscow hotel room when a group of Russians burst into the room and took the relative into custody, charging him with assault and rape. They demanded money to make the problem "go away," and the director had paid the ransom.

The director told us that he had been receiving mysterious communications ever since. He had received calls from people with Russian accents, threatening harm if he didn't pay them off. He had concluded that these callers were connected with the Russian Mafia. What particularly spooked him, he said, was something that occurred a few weeks earlier. He said he was working late in the evening in his office near the house and heard a knock on the double glass doors. He said he looked out the window, saw no one, and ordered his security people to do a sweep of the area. No one was found, and nothing was amiss, but he assumed the knock was a threat.

When he returned to the residence, he said he received a call on his unlisted phone line. The voice asked for him by name. The director did not identify himself and instead told the caller he'd take a message. The caller then hung up. The director said he believed the voice on the phone was that of an Israeli with a Russian accent. How he came to this conclusion was unclear. Like other take-charge clients, he had lots of conclusions, each delivered with great assurance.

After we agreed to take a break for the day, he invited us to tour the compound with his guards. The house itself was austere, with little to indicate that the director spent a lot of time there. There was a small building on the estate that had been turned into a surveillance shack with cameras watching the grounds twenty-four hours a day.

Later that evening, the relative arrived. He was a likable guy who seemed to be living in the director's shadow. He told a harrowing story about his ordeal, which clearly had shaken him. The Russians he described were big, thuggish brutes who were connected to law enforcement somehow. In Russia, he said, there was a class of people who were able to drive around the city recklessly without any fear of being stopped by the police. These apparently were the same type.

The relative then told us about his arrest. He said he was with a woman named Irina in a hotel room. Shortly after she left, plainclothesmen identifying themselves as Russian police came to his room and told him he was under arrest. They put him into a car and took him to a local police station, where he was placed in a cell. He said the officer told him that his trouble could go away for fifty thousand rubles. The Russians said something to indicate that they knew he was related to the director, who they knew had a lot of money and could cover this demand. Eventually the relative was able to phone his country's embassy—he was not an American citizen—which was able to secure his release. He was never charged with a crime, and he said he left Moscow the next day.

As we listened to this story, the director interrupted constantly. Sometimes he insisted on making his own points. At other moments, he denigrated his relative with comments like "This guy did a really stupid thing," or "He never should have gotten involved with this girl." It was clear that in the family dynamic the director was the big shot.

The director's security people had traced some of the threatening calls and the director gave us a list of phone numbers he wanted us to check out. Then he indulged in more theories about what was happening, and insisted that the Russian Mafia was after him.

I asked the relative more questions about Irina. At least, he *thought* her name was Irina. I realized that nothing about this was necessarily true. He said that Irina told him she was a trained sniper who had targeted President George W. Bush. Irina had mentioned that the Bush daughters were coming to Moscow and she was studying their likely routes while in the city. The relative said he was stunned by this. Which, of course, begged the question: If this was true, why didn't the family report any of this to the Secret Service? The relative also said that he and Irina went to a war museum, where Irina discussed shoulder-held weapons in detail—with the kind of specifics he believed only a sniper would know. He also claimed he had been told by mutual friends that Irina was a KGB agent, and said that Irina had once given him something to drink. It didn't taste right and he threw it away. In short, he knew he was with a woman who was either dangerous or deranged or both. I told the director that I would ask our Russian contacts to see what they could find out about the people and incidents in the relative's story.

The key item on our agenda upon returning to Washington was to find out whether any of the people that we'd been told of in California were actually connected to the Russian Mafia. From my work on the Copperfield case, I knew some Russian mob figures, and they were right to be wary of them.

In Europe there is a network of former intelligence officials who offer their services for hire. Since the Cold War ended, these have included former agents from the CIA and KGB, who often work together on various investigations. I used these same people a few years earlier to help the magician David Copperfield reclaim the trucks carrying his equipment that had disappeared while he was on a Russian tour.

One of my chief contacts for work in Eastern Europe was formerly with the FBI, where he had trained foreign law enforcement officials who came to the U.S. from Russia and elsewhere. When they returned to their home countries, my contact stayed in touch with them. They were a valuable source of information and assistance.

We gave him the names the director had given us. The word came back from Russia that they were petty crooks, shakedown artists who took advantage of foreigners in the country. Not one of the names was a significant figure in the Russian mob. I was pretty confident that the director and his family were not in mortal danger from any of these characters.

After our results came back I telephoned the director and delivered this news to him personally. "We've checked out the people whose names you provided," I told him. "They are known to be petty crooks who take advantage of foreigners in Russia. We don't believe they pose a significant threat to you or your family."

I thought that at the very least he'd be relieved to learn that the Russian Mafia was not sending hit men to kill them. Instead, he dismissed me brusquely.

"I've hired another group of investigators," he announced. "They are less expensive, and they are coming to a different conclusion."

I called the attorney who had gotten me involved in this case and told him what had happened. He confirmed that the director had hired some former FBI agents to look into the same claims that he'd hired me to look into. These investigators did indeed come up with different conclusions, implicating Russian Mafia figures just as the director had wanted.

I asked to see their report. When I received it, I saw that it did not come close to the scope of work my office had undertaken, nor did it have most of the information we'd uncovered from our contacts in Russia. But it did tell the director that he had cause to believe his life was at risk. This, I realized, was what he wanted: substantiation for his own theories, "proof" that he was in the middle of massive international intrigue.

What I've learned about this director's movies is that they usually involve huge, threatening crises that the heroes solve with complex and violent action. It occurred to me that the director was so caught up in inventing these scenarios that he saw himself as the star in his own drama—a man of action hunted down by the Russian mob. I was, in effect, a writer he hired to develop this scenario for him. When I didn't do the job, he hired some other writers who were more accommodating.

A few years later, I had another client who wanted proof of his scenario. This case involved a popular singer and an attractive blond woman who made a career through her associations with rock stars. She claimed to have become romantically involved with the singer and to have borne his child.

The singer's lawyer told me that his client was extremely upset over photographs published in a tabloid, which claimed to show the singer's alleged mistress and their love child at the Dallas airport, where they were to be picked up by the singer's private plane.

The lawyer wanted me to send a team of investigators to Texas to interview the various players. They wanted to learn who took the photographs, how the tabloid got them, and if anyone in the reclusive singer's organization was involved. The matter was considered so urgent—the singer was said to be on the verge of hysterics—that his lawyer called repeatedly that day to see if anyone was yet on their way to Dallas.

I couldn't figure out why this was such a big deal. A celebrity as popular as this singer was had undoubtedly been hounded by paparazzi and been the subject of tabloid gossip many times before. What was so upsetting about a photo of a baby in one tabloid? And why was it so important to find out how the photographs had been taken? But I was used to how narcissistic and demanding celebrities can be. So I sent a couple of my investigators to Dallas. We assembled a timeline of events involving the singer and his alleged mistress—a woman I'll call Lucy—and the names of some of their associates. What I found only made things more confusing.

It appeared that shortly after the child's birth, according to a website, the married singer publicly acknowledged that Lucy was not only his manager but his mistress too. The website also announced the birth of their child. A few days later, the singer's publicists contradicted the announcements and denied the singer's paternity. They said the earlier acknowledgment had been a hoax, and claimed that the singer did not know Lucy at all. Days later, that statement was recanted also. The publicist admitted that the singer did in fact know Lucy, that she did work for him, but that the baby was not his. The singer threatened to sue any tabloid claiming he was the father. Months after that, he was seen and photographed with Lucy and the baby at various hotels in California. I didn't know what was going on, but it was clearly not a good PR strategy.

All this appeared, at first anyway, to be a curious sidebar. At issue for IGI were the two photographs taken at an airport. One showed Lucy standing alone outside an airport terminal. The other picture, allegedly taken at the same time, showed the child being held by a nanny. The singer's lawyer wanted us to verify his conviction that Lucy or someone who knew about her itinerary was responsible for the photographs and their publication.

When the tabloid's photographs were examined by experts, it was obvious that they could not have been taken by a cell phone camera, nor at close range. They had been shot from a distance with a tele-photo lens, from an elevated location. But the lawyer insisted that we interview those who might be involved anyway. We put together a list of potential suspects and went to interview them one by one to assess their credibility.

Suspect #1: The nanny. My investigators sat down with the nanny shown holding the baby in the photograph, a woman I'll call Joy. Joy had been employed for six months, and said she was one of three nan-nies who provided twenty-four-hour care for the baby. She said she did not see anyone taking a photo or acting suspiciously at the airport terminal.

Joy said that after the photos were published, she had remarked to Lucy that the photo of her appeared to be "posed," which Lucy promptly denied. Joy also noted that the entourage had been driven to the airport by a man who was not their customary driver, which led us to look into him.

Suspect #2: The driver. There actually were two drivers that day, who were previously unknown to the women. The first, described as a white man in his forties, drove the limousine carrying the passengers. A second driver followed them in a van carrying their luggage. The drivers denied knowledge of the photographs. Both had been hired by the man I'll call Fred who handled the singer's personal security.

Suspect #3: Fred. Fred was the first person that Lucy suspected when the investigators interviewed her. She indicated that she and Fred did not get along well and she had persuaded the singer to relieve him of his duties for a time. She said Fred was standing near her when one of the photos was taken—the one of her alone outside the termi-nal. His cell phone made a sound she described as "zzzzzt," and he told her he had accidentally taken a photo of his left foot.

Suspect #4: The mistress. Lucy herself also denied any responsibil-ity for the photos. In the first place, she said, the photo of her was unflattering—she said she was recovering from cancer treatments. She also said that, for security reasons, she didn't ever want a photo of her baby to be made public. "All it takes is one crazy," she said.

After these preliminary interviews, I proposed to the lawyer a list of actions that we might take to get to the bottom of the matter. I sug-gested, for example, checking Fred's background for litigation or a history of press leaks or similar instances involving his other famous clients. I also asked to interview Fred himself to get his side of the story. I suggested interviewing the other nannies to see if any of them had a motive or opportunity to have these photos taken. But the law-yer didn't want us to go that way.

Instead, I was urged to keep the focus on Lucy. It seemed obvious to me that she was the singer's mistress and her baby could well be his. In fact some of the singer's security people reported that their boss would often sneak into her hotel room on road trips. The lawyer told me that the singer, or perhaps his wife, believed that Lucy had ar-ranged for the photos in order to force the singer to divorce his wife and marry her.

The lawyer directed me to a composer friend of the singer, named Mike, who supposedly knew all of the characters in this case. Mike was very critical of Lucy. He disputed, for example, her claim that she was suffering from cancer and getting radiation treatment. He claimed this was her cover story for plastic surgeries and that her drivers saw her heading to appointments "dressed to kill." If she was really suffer-ing from cancer, he maintained, then why did she work so hard on her appearance? That was probably the kind of question only a man might ask. It was Mike's opinion that Lucy and her friends were after the singer's money and "milking the cow dry." Mike said Lucy was not an attentive mother, that her nannies "quit a lot," and that Joy, who he said hated Lucy, was going to quit as well.

Mike asserted that Lucy was responsible for the tabloid photos. After they were published, he said he overheard Lucy as she spoke to a friend.

"Couldn't they have used a better picture of me?" she reportedly asked.

"Yes, I know," the friend replied.

This was hardly damaging evidence. Mike also spoke about a massage the singer received at a hotel from an "over-friendly" masseuse. Mike said he later saw a picture of the masseuse in the house of one of Lucy's friends. This led him to surmise that "they had something going." This, again, proved little—but it was becoming obvious that I was supposed to draw the conclusion that Lucy was the villain in this story.

None of this was adding up, so I pressed the singer's lawyers for more information. Finally, one of them came clean. He said the singer wanted to end his association with Lucy. He would provide for the child, but otherwise he wanted both of them out of his life. Asking IGI to track down the source of the photographs was a ruse. Nobody in the singer's entourage really cared that they were likely taken by a paparazzo. They wanted to blame the mistress as an excuse to push Lucy out of his life, and they wanted us to provide evidence of her complicity. I refused. That's not where the investigation was leading. Maybe another investigator would come to the conclusion they wanted, but I wouldn't, and I told them so.

A few days later, I received a voice mail from the singer's counsel objecting to IGI's bill. He said his client was not going to pay it because we hadn't concluded with the result he wanted. After I calmed down and considered what a jerk the singer was, I called the lawyer and told him I was drafting a legal complaint that would spell out the work we had done. A check for payment arrived in a FedEx envelope a few days later.

About a year later, Lucy died. She had been suffering from cancer, just as she said. The child died shortly after that, of an undisclosed illness. Tabloids reported the singer's devastation. The singer "loved" the woman, his friends told the newspapers. Lucy's death and that of their child was said to have left the musician heartbroken. During the publicity of his grief, the singer received sympathetic wishes and support from countless fans. If only they knew the truth.

Like tabloids, some newspapers also take advantage of readers' credulity in publishing stories to appeal to their readers without verifying the "facts" they assert. Even well-respected papers sometimes report the reality they think their readers believe rather than more complex truth.

In 2005, I was contacted by a representative of Petróleos de Venezuela, the state-owned oil company controlled by the government of Hugo Chávez. It was managed by Asdrubal Chávez, the president's cousin and a longtime employee of the company.

In April 2005, *El Nuevo Herald*, a Spanish-language affiliate of the *Miami Herald*, published a series of articles accusing the oil company, and by extension the Chávez administration, of official corruption. Namely, the articles claimed the company was funneling millions of dollars in money and contracts to a bunch of Chávez cronies. The articles contained references to specific agreements and documents and the names of people who were to receive payments under these agreements.

The oil company insisted the allegations were not true. It asked IGI to investigate and identify the articles' sources. I flew down to Venezuela and met with the Chávez cousin. He was a friendly guy who claimed I could look at any documents I wanted. "Hugo wants to get to the bottom of this," he said. I didn't know why Chávez was so concerned about this particular series of articles and their allegations. The Chávez leadership had been accused of far worse. On the other hand, the news articles made charges he believed were false.

My investigators made several trips to Venezuela and interviewed eleven of the sixteen individuals mentioned in the news articles. They all admitted that they would have liked contracts from the Venezuela government and the revenue from them. But they all denied they had ever received a contract. More significantly to me, each of the people named in the articles whom we interviewed said they had never been contacted by the Miami reporter about the assertions.

One claimed he had contacted the paper to correct inaccuracies but never received a response. Another said he'd considered a libel suit but, daunted by the cost, let the matter drop. Another told us that the articles had put his family in danger by suggesting that he had a lot of money; he was afraid of being kidnapped by antigovernment guerillas.

The *Miami Herald* had published numerous articles attacking the Chávez regime, which appealed to its wide readership of Cuban-Americans who were fiercely anti-Castro and anti-Chávez. The publisher, Alberto Ibargüen, had close ties to Chávez opponents. Both the *Miami Herald* and *El Nuevo Herald* had published news reports apparently intended to undermine the Chávez government. We discovered that the documents used for the articles about the oil contracts were prepared by someone with close ties to the Chávez opposition—raising serious questions about their legitimacy. Regardless of what one thought of Hugo Chávez, it appeared that at least in this case, his government had been wronged.

The *Miami Herald* is respected as a reputable and reliable newspaper. I found the paper's own rules for its reporting, including its commitment to being "fair, accurate and objective," and went to see the *Herald*'s general counsel at his office in Miami.

"Your reporters never tried to contact any of these individuals," I told him. "That can't be the *Herald*'s policy."

Like any careful attorney, he did not acknowledge that my assertion was correct, but said he would look into the matter. He had little sympathy for my inquiry or for the Chávez government.

Twenty-three people were named in the *Herald's* articles and I presented the general counsel documentation from twenty of them that the allegations were not true. "Twenty?" he asked. "Why didn't you talk to all twenty-three?"

Taken aback by his casual and off-the-point response, I banged my fist on his desk. "That's an outrageous thing to complain about," I told him. "Your guys didn't talk to *any* of them."

The general counsel smiled slightly. He may have shrugged. As far as I know the paper never changed or corrected its story.

To most Americans, at least, Hugo Chávez was not a sympathetic victim. Because he was a "bad guy," I was left to assume that the *Herald* reasoned it was okay to lie about him and invent facts. That's not the role of the media, at least not as I knew it. It's an example of why public faith in the veracity of media accounts today has reached a historic low.

CHAPTER 11

THE POLITICS OF TRUTH

IGI has had a number of political clients. At one time, we had a small division for this called Campaign Facts. I thought we could be nonpartisan and work with politicians of every stripe to seek truth. I'd always resisted labels for myself, and was amused by how readily some people assumed I was a knee-jerk liberal when others thought me a die-hard, law-enforcing conservative. Eventually, I realized that most wanted to peg IGI on the left side of the spectrum.

In 1994, two years into Clinton's first term, I was involved in a political campaign that later had consequences more far-reaching than I expected. That spring, I received a call from my old friend Jim Flug, whose office I used during my first days on the Watergate Committee. He was now a lawyer in private practice and was helping Senator Ted Kennedy in his race for reelection, which was turning out to be the fight of Teddy's political life.

A number of embarrassing incidents and scandals were finally catching up with the legendary senator, even in his home state of

Massachusetts. It was the twenty-fifth anniversary of the incident at Chappaquiddick, and there was a trial in Florida regarding his recent involvement in a late-night escapade with his twenty-something nephew William Kennedy Smith that led to the young man being charged with rape. Instead of maintaining his usual margin ahead of the challenger, Teddy was struggling to maintain his Senate seat. His opponent was a wealthy Republican, Willard Mitt Romney, the son of a former Michigan governor and a successful Boston businessman with a family as clean-cut and photogenic as he was.

To strengthen the campaign, Kennedy had hired his longtime political consultant Bob Shrum, a smart strategist who has worked for nearly every Democrat anyone has ever heard of. He and Flug were very worried about the race. They asked if I could identify some issues that could be used against Romney. As we discussed terms and strategy, I sensed that some on the Kennedy team were unhappy that IGI expected to be paid for my services and wasn't offering them gratis for "the cause." They had also made the assumption that I was on their "side" of the Washington brawls.

The first campaign hurdle I had to overcome was dealing with its titular head, the senator's nephew Michael Kennedy. Bobby's son suffered from an overblown sense of his authority. Every time I offered an idea for the investigation, he'd reject it summarily. Before long I was reporting directly to Shrum and finally got to work.

Since Romney was campaigning on his record as a successful businessman and job creator, I told Shrum we ought to fully examine Romney's company, Bain Capital, and its relationships. "The question you ought to ask," I suggested, "is how did Romney become a successful businessman in the first place?" I knew from past experience that there might be skeletons in his closet. In some instances, some of the most prominent businessmen in America—including household names in the country today—have started their careers with a little help from organized crime. I had no reason to expect to find that with Mitt Romney, but I was curious about what we would find.

After examining hundreds of pages of documents, articles, and filings, we put together a chart of Bain Capital's corporate structure to determine what Romney's role was at the company (he was one of twelve partners at the time), who his associates were, who else worked there. We examined financial documents that were in the public record—SEC filings, annual reports, communications with shareholders and investors—and looked at various transactions, such as if Bain Capital had made any payments to foreign officials.

Bain Capital had a reputation for extreme secrecy. It was called the "KGB of management consultants" and did not even issue business cards for its first seven years. Employees were required to fill out elaborate confidentiality agreements and refer to clients by code names. Among the companies that at one point or another had been under the Bain umbrella were interesting little coincidences. One company was Vetco Gray, which had taken over the Hughes Tool Company. One of Bain's foreign investors bought Bebe Rebozo's Key Biscayne bank and kept Bebe on as president.

Using confidential sources in Panama, El Salvador, the United States, and Switzerland, we identified six Bain Capital investors who were tied to the powerful oligarchies in El Salvador and Panama. Some of them were accused of funding Panamanian dictator Manuel Noriega. The Salvadoran millionaires were said to have directed and financed right-wing death squads that were trying to destabilize El Salvador's moderate government and terrorize its supporters with kidnappings, violence, and even murder.

For me the issue with the most potential for Kennedy's campaign was the pattern of behavior we identified from an examination of Bain's business practices. In many instances Bain would take over a company, invest in it, cut back on employee healthcare and pension benefits, lay off workers, and sell off the less profitable assets. This happened with a company called SCM, in Marion, Indiana. Bain Capital borrowed money to buy the company, loaded it with debt, slashed wages and benefits, and ultimately closed the plant. This kind of ruthless practice for a man who was touting his business success struck me as an issue worth highlighting for the Kennedy campaign.

I accumulated hundreds of pages of materials and gave the package to Shrum, who was thrilled with our findings. He started using Romney's record of layoffs in the campaign. He brought a group of workers from Marion, Indiana, to Massachusetts to videotape them for campaign commercials.

In one Kennedy ad endorsement, a laid-off worker declared, "I would like to say to Mitt Romney, if you think you'd make such a good senator, come out here to Marion, Indiana, and see what your company has done to people." Another said, "He's cut our wages to put money back into his pockets." Romney faced what the *New York Times* described as "a series of devastating advertisements that challenged Mr. Romney's proclamations about his record as a venture capitalist in creating jobs in recession-battered Massachusetts." Shortly thereafter, the *Boston Globe* published its own investigation of Bain Capital layoffs at a company in the state. Largely as a result of the Kennedy ads in October, by early November Romney was trailing the senator by fifteen points. On election day, Kennedy was reelected by a margin of 58 to 41 percent.

I was one of the first outside investigators hired by a major political campaign to conduct opposition research. I know this is because my hiring became a news story in itself. Payments to my firm were disclosed on the campaign's financial reports. In order to keep my involvement below the radar, those payments were supposed to go through a law firm. But the filing became public and the press picked it up. So did the Romney campaign. One of Romney's top guys, Charles Manning, called a press conference to respond to the "revelation" that Senator Kennedy had stooped to hiring a "sleazy" "international spy firm."

Mitt Romney understood the value of the service we performed. In fact, he hired IGI in 2002 to investigate his Democratic opponent when he was running for governor. I was greatly complimented when his campaign retained us, though I wasn't totally surprised. During my work with Bain, I came to know one of its senior managers, an impressive guy with whom I got along well. I found Romney to be impressive in many ways too. The Romney team also hired us in 2006 when he was planning to run for president. He wanted IGI to find out everything it could in his background so he could be prepared for attacks. It was ironic, of course, that one of the primary attacks used against him—by his Republican primary opponents and later by the Obama campaign in 2012—was the issue I identified in 1994.

Maybe it was his business background, but Romney understood better than most politicians the importance of conducting due diligence investigations. He obviously wasn't happy about the election result against Kennedy, but he appreciated that my firm was doing in the political sector what we'd done for years in the business world. We performed background checks, tested credibility, and armed people with information that they could share with the public. I thought of it as a public service and still do.

I was once hired to work on a case involving a candidate for governor of California. He was an extremely wealthy person, and I was asked by an advisor to conduct due diligence on the candidate's own background. Without much effort I discovered that he had misrepresented his intentions to buy a Catholic Church property. He had promised the Church that the property would be used for low-income housing, so he got it at a discount. Instead he flipped it for a huge profit.

When I presented this information directly to the candidate, he lied. "I don't remember any of this," he said in a tone that I found difficult to believe.

Then he summoned his wife. "Wasn't this a case where my signature was forged?" he asked her.

She didn't seem to have any idea what he was talking about, and she wasn't about to play along. "No," she replied, "it wasn't."

"You have to learn to toughen up," he told her. In other words, she was supposed to have lied.

"So what is the answer?" I asked the candidate. "What should I do?"

He thought for a moment. "Eh, no one is going to find that," he said.

This was typical of many a politician's attitude, one that gained even more prominence after the Clinton impeachment scandal. The rules don't apply to everyone—all that matters is the spin.

In 2001, when President George W. Bush came into office, a representative from a consortium of prominent women's groups called me. The consortium was looking to hire an investigator to examine Bush's potential Supreme Court nominees.

Bush had been in office for only a few days. "Won't there be plenty of time for this later?" I asked. She responded that her organization wanted to get an early start and needed research on potential candidates to begin as soon as possible. After I met with them, the group decided to hire IGI and asked to meet with the person whom I would assign to manage the case.

I told them they were in luck. I was going to assign one of our top people, a woman who was a terrific lawyer and investigator. The next day I got a call from the group. They said they'd met with our investigator and were dissatisfied.

"You didn't tell us she works from home," the woman said. I confirmed that, yes, she had young children, lived in the suburbs, and often telecommuted from home. I also said I was sure that her work would be satisfactory in every respect. I figured a woman's organization of all places would appreciate IGI's flexible work policy.

That wasn't going to satisfy this group. They wanted her to be available downtown at a moment's notice. I was baffled. For one thing, why would an investigator doing background research be needed at a moment's notice? For another, they had no reason to think that she wouldn't be able to accommodate them. So I told them it was her or no one. They chose to go elsewhere. A few months later, the group came back to us. I was still upset with the original decision, so I turned them down. Here was a group that advocated for the rights of women and yet they discriminated against a woman because she worked from home.

I encountered one presidential candidate when it was too late to affect his campaign. In July 2004, four months before the November elections, Massachusetts senator John F. Kerry was poised to become the next president of the United States. In the Gallup poll, he was five points ahead of President George W. Bush, whose administration's invasion of Iraq and the continuing war there, along with a wobbly economy, put his reelection in doubt.

A month later, a group no one had ever heard of, Swift Boat Veterans for Truth, began airing devastating campaign ads against the Democratic candidate. One showed a young John Kerry giving testimony to the Senate Committee on Foreign Relations in April 1971. Kerry had left Vietnam in 1969 with three purple hearts, a silver star, and a bronze star after captaining a swift boat on the Mekong River. By 1970, he had become involved in the antiwar movement as a leader of Vietnam Veterans Against the War. He believed that returning veterans who were disillusioned with the war could give credibility to the antiwar movement by speaking out. He organized a veterans' rally on the National Mall, and the Senate Committee invited him to testify at the same time. Just three weeks before the veterans converged on Washington, Lieutenant William Calley had been convicted of the massacre at My Lai, the atrocity that had brought national and congressional attention to the magnitude of war crimes. In his televised Senate testimony, Kerry argued against Nixon's war policies and the policy makers who "have attempted to disown us and the sacrifices we made for this country." Wearing his military fatigues with the ribbons from his medals, he famously asked the senators, "How do you ask a man to be the last man to die in Vietnam? How do you ask a man to be the last man to die for a mistake?" On CBS's *60 Minutes*, Morley Safer portrayed Kerry as "an eloquent man of turmoil with a Kennedy-esque future."

But the most eloquent and memorable line in Kerry's speech is not what the Swift Boat Veterans for Truth highlighted. Their ad spliced quotes from that testimony and displayed them on-screen: *"They had personally raped, cut off ears, cut off heads . . . randomly shot at civilians . . . razed villages in a fashion reminiscent of Genghis Khan . . ."* The videotaped image of Kerry's delivery shows him as an imposingly tall, earnest, and insistent young man with a patrician Boston accent that some found off-putting.

Interspersed with Kerry's statements in the ad were comments from Vietnam veterans who accused Kerry of undermining the troops and betraying his country. "John Kerry gave the enemy for free what I and many of my comrades in North Vietnam prison camps took torture to avoid saying," one veteran said on-screen. Another said, "He betrayed us in the past. How can we be loyal to him now?"

It was rough stuff, and it reawakened the country's mixed feelings about the Vietnam war. It played perfectly into the Republican Party's subliminal message about Kerry and the Democrats opposing the war then under way in Iraq—that he was unpatriotic, maybe un-American. Observing Kerry's 1971 demeanor, some voters perceived him as arrogant and discounted his policy experience and lifetime of public service. It was almost irrelevant that what Kerry had said thirty-three years earlier was true about the actions of some American soldiers in Vietnam. The Bush campaign repeatedly denied any connection to the ads, and by the fall, Bush was ahead in the polls and headed for a narrow election victory in November.

I was surprised in late 2004 when my secretary told me that Senator Kerry was on the line. He asked if I could come to a meeting at his house that evening.

At the appointed time, I went to Kerry's residence in Georgetown. The senator was in his home office with two of his aides, and soon had two other advisors participating by conference call from Boston.

Kerry waved hello to me. He appeared to be in a thoughtful mood, which was understandable for someone who, but for sixty-five thousand votes in Ohio, would have then been planning his first term in the White House. I had no idea why he wanted to see me, but he soon got to the point.

"Terry," he said, "I want you to prove that the things I said about Vietnam in 1971 were factual."

Isn't it a little late for that? I thought. Many Democrats had been appalled by the attack ads, and disappointed that Kerry had made little effort to rebut them. He seemed to believe that his record of service in Vietnam spoke for itself, and that history had proved the rightness of his antiwar activities.

"What do you want to do with that information?" I asked Kerry. What I really meant was, *What do you want to do with it* now?

"I want to use it to rebut the swift boat stuff," he said. He seemed genuinely baffled that so many voters believed the allegations in those ads—that Kerry was not only unpatriotic, but had lied about his military record, and lied about the actions of American soldiers.

I was sympathetic to Kerry's frustration and what must have been his considerable regret over not having challenged the attacks before the election. But I didn't see the point of getting into all this now—with the election over, and the considerable expense that such an investigation would entail.

What bothered me most about his request was that it might have made a world of difference had he considered this early in his campaign, when animosity from some veterans to his 1971 Senate testimony was not unknown. Many observers surmised that some of those veterans were behind the attack ads.

So many candidates neglect due diligence before the lies and dirty tricks begin. If candidates aren't prepared to defend and explain their own records before their opponent takes a whack, they risk allowing voters to be misled and distracted from the real issues.

Four years later, when the Obama campaign was up and running, they could have avoided or at least been better prepared for vexing challenges that came as complete surprises. They should never have been blindsided by Reverend Jeremiah Wright, the pastor of Obama's Chicago church, who railed against America as the "U.S.-KKK-A.," and almost destroyed Obama's candidacy in April 2008. No doubt, it's hard to imagine how viciously the opposition will seize on and distort even simple facts—like Barack Obama's birthplace—but good due diligence can help campaigns to anticipate potential problems in the candidate's history and the issues opponents might seize on. Maybe it's overconfidence or maybe it's carelessness, but it's a mistake to underestimate the opposition.

As for Kerry's assignment, I expressed some misgivings, but he seemed eager to correct the record. We talked about his military service and about who might have been behind the Swift Boat Veterans' ads. He then spent considerable time on the phone with his aides in Boston, debating aloud about whether or not he wanted to pursue this.

As Kerry continued his back and forth, it occurred to me that if he really wanted to go this route, he did have a pretty good case. Only one of the ad's Swift Boat Veterans had served directly with Kerry in Vietnam, and then only briefly. Every other one of Kerry's "band of brothers" vouched for him, stood by him, and supported his presidential campaign. The Swift Boat Veterans for Truth ads were funded by millions from major donors to the Republican Party, including people with close ties to the Bush White House and its campaign guru, Karl Rove. But even if I proved that everything the Swift Boat Veterans said were lies, or at the very least half-truths, what possible difference could it make now?

Finally the senator turned to one of his aides. "Can you coordinate with Terry?" he asked. Then he turned to me. "Can you write something up and give us a sense of how you'd do this?"

In the next few days, I wrote up a proposal and sent it over to the senator's office. But I never heard another word about it. I assume, and appreciate, that Kerry decided to go forward instead with concentration on his leadership role in the Senate.

Had I been given the assignment to look into the Swift Boat Veterans and Kerry's antiwar history, I might have found out more about this that would have intrigued me. For example, John F. Kerry—like another senator from Massachusetts, John F. Kennedy, with the same initials—was anathema to the Nixon White House. The Nixon tapes recorded conversations the president had with his aides in 1971 that show they thought Kerry was a real threat, and they mounted a dirty tricks effort to discredit him.

Only a handful of people really know what it feels like to lose the presidency. But it's a pretty safe bet that it feels lousy. Especially if you think you lost because some guys were lying about you and questioning your integrity.

One of the chief instigators of the attack was a man named Jerome Corsi, whose other claim to fame was accusing the United States government of a massive cover-up of what he claimed was advance knowledge of the 9/11 attacks. Corsi later wrote a book accusing Barack Obama of lying about his U.S. citizenship, which he described as part of the greatest fraud in the history of the American presidency.

One prominent and intentionally nonpartisan fact-checking group described the Corsi book on Obama as "a mishmash of unsupported conjecture, half-truths, logical fallacies and outright falsehoods." So did dozens of editorials across the country, any number of Republicans, and the state of Hawaii, which produced Barack Obama's birth certificate. It didn't matter much. The Corsi book on Obama, like the smears against Kerry, was convincing to many. The allegations live on to this day, just like those claiming George W. Bush was a secret alcoholic in the White House who snorted cocaine, and Bill Clinton murdered Vince Foster.

Forty years after Senator Ervin's committee hearings, our country has forgotten the lessons of Watergate. Howard Hughes's secret contributions intended to influence White House policies were shocking in the 1970s. Big money is now more prevalent in politics than ever before, especially since the Supreme Court's 2010 *Citizens United* decision that money is effectively speech, protected by the First Amendment. Donors across the political spectrum fund all sort of activities whose origins are hidden from voters.

There are no legal standards of conduct for political campaigns, no legal consequences for false assertions, and few press outlets or institutions voters can trust for an honest examination of facts. During the Republican primary in 2012, Mitt Romney spent a considerable fortune on an effort to characterize his Republican primary opponents— conservatives like Newt Gingrich and Rick Santorum—as corrupt liberals. Billionaire Sheldon Adelson almost single-handedly kept Gingrich's campaign alive, even paying for an attack ad on Bain Capital that was filled with loose reporting and outright falsehoods. No one was penalized for this.

Money funnels into campaigns from big-money donors on both

sides of the political spectrum without transparency, much of it to fund all sorts of devious activities designed to mislead the electorate.

Manipulation of political campaigns through dirty tricks and smears has become common since Donald Segretti became notorious for such activity on behalf of Richard Nixon. There's little question that the collapse of Senator Muskie's campaign in 1968 led to McGovern's nomination and finally to Nixon's election. When John McCain led George W. Bush in the 2000 presidential primaries, voters in South Carolina received phone calls claiming that McCain had an illegitimate black child. It's hard to imagine that such a claim could have been sufficiently credible or potent thirteen years ago to take down a prime candidate, but McCain's loss in South Carolina diminished his candidacy. The Bush campaign denied a role in the false attack and to this day no culprit has been uncovered. McCain's loss to Bush in that South Carolina race may have changed history.

There have been mudslinging and crazy rumors about America's leaders since the founding of our republic. That isn't new. What *is* new is that so many people don't seem to care about facts anymore, or understand even that there is factual truth. As in the Clinton-Starr era, the truth is what you can get enough people to believe; or, as with Aramony and Stephen Glass, it's whatever the folks in charge wish it were.

It's impossible to imagine that a congressional investigation as serious, open-ended, and bipartisan as Watergate could happen in today's political and media climate. Half the country would just reject the facts we uncovered and be seduced by media to believe instead another version of truth. The Republicans would have been backed by super PACs waging war on Sam Ervin, and Democratic donors would have funded Nixon's opponents to demand impeachment. Cable news shows on one side would air and discuss any rumor about Richard Nixon—the more outlandish, the better—and its viewers would believe it. Another program would defend Nixon, question the motivations of Ervin and Rodino, and tell its viewers exactly what they want to hear.

The tribal mentality that grew after Watergate and Vietnam and strengthened through the Clinton and Bush years has poisoned our political system. If you watched MSNBC and Fox News channel's election coverage, you'd think you were watching two different elections in two different countries. The media on the left and the right draws opposite conclusions from the same events. How can voters discern truth when even basic facts are in dispute?

In the final days before the 2012 election, a number of bloggers, columnists, and an entire news network stubbornly rejected polls that predicted an Obama victory. They trumpeted instead a few "unskewed" polls predicting a Romney win. These partisans dismissed as part of the "liberal media bias" any journalist, analyst, statistician, or election official who tried to defend and explain the mainstream media polls. Romney supporters were so determined to deny Obama a second term that they really believed the nonsense. After the election, Karl Rove and other right-wing pundits struggled to explain how convinced they had become of their own dreams.

This book describes situations I was engaged in over the past fifty years. While the nature of these cases and my work varied widely, they all required good instincts, sound judgment, and "good old-fashioned shoe leather"—gathering reliable information, chasing down leads, and triangulating facts and testimony.

In establishing rapport with clients and witnesses, good investigators know how to assess a person's credibility. They rely on intuition and what they have learned through experience. They are skeptical, and question the motives and intentions of clients and witnesses. They ask the right questions to corroborate or dispel the accuracy of information. They develop solid leads and are persistent in following them. Most important, they are objective. They never decide the results of an investigation before gathering the facts. These practices reflect the professional and ethical standards that all investigators should observe.

The proliferation of media and manifold increase in access to information through the Internet that has happened since I began my career is truly stunning. Those developments should facilitate the job of any investigator—whether a professional or not—but that's not always the case. So much information is unreliable that it often takes a seasoned and sophisticated investigator to discern true facts and assemble a coherent narrative. Simply assembling downloaded information may be a quick, easy, and profitable way to produce a result for a client, but that should be only a beginning.

To understand the truth of any case, it's valuable if all the facts can be established for common agreement. In contested situations where all facts aren't apparent or agreed to, advocates "spin" the useful facts they have in order to persuade. In Watergate, the pursuit and acceptance of straightforward facts is what led to that event's sound conclusion. The senators, representatives, and the public who were the "clients" all embraced the facts the investigation revealed. But that situation is rare.

It's increasingly difficult to establish the reliable factual information that is essential to drive sound personal, corporate, government, and political decisions. Internet websites are filled with errors, distortions, and outright falsehoods. And media outlets profit from oversimplification, rumor, and diatribes. If people won't accept even the most obvious facts—like the president's birthplace—it's hard to imagine how they can be effective in a civil society.

ACKNOWLEDGMENTS

I imagined writing a book about my professional experiences for years, but that always seemed to be a project for later. When I realized some time ago that "later" was "now or never," I didn't fathom how challenging an enterprise writing a book would be. That *The Investigator* is now in print is due to the assistance of several invaluable people. What finally got this project under way are my associations with Gail Ross; David Rosenthal and Sarah Hochman of Blue Rider Press; Matt Latimer; and Anne Walker Browning. Gail led me through the maze of the publishing world and its processes with fortitude and acumen. David's enthusiasm for my proposal inspired me with confidence to believe that my story was worth telling. Matt Latimer was patient, diligent, and tireless in prompting me to dig deep into my memory and files, and arranging my stories into a coherent narrative. Anne was an amazing researcher, organizing my files and verifying facts with persistence and efficiency. Sarah Hochman, as the book's editor, has been unfailingly encouraging, appropriately questioning, and insistent when insistence was needed.

My wife, Margaret, who journeyed with me and knows my stories well, helped enormously to reorganize drafts and safeguard my literary voice. This book would not have been written without her. Our children, Emily, Jonathan, and William Lenzner, have encouraged me affectionately with perception and understanding. They are my legacy and I hope they will learn from this book.

My brothers, Bob and Allan, have been unfailingly supportive of this and all my endeavors. As a business reporter, Bob's excellent analyses of economic trends and exotic financial transactions are always timely and insightful, as is the advice he has given me. He always looked out for his younger brothers, and Allan and I depended on him to provide early warnings of challenges at home and at school. Allan was my partner in deciphering and navigating the rocky shores of childhood. To this day, his unique observations, sense of humor, and personal loyalty sustain me.

My colleagues and friends at Investigative Group International have tolerated the extra burdens that this project has placed on me and on them with grace and good humor. Rina Aaron, Jack Barrett, Ann Cochran, Jenni Crocker, Magda Cupo, George Fields, Adam Harsha, Jennifer Hoar, Rich Hynes, Dustin Kahlson, Ann Keating, Jonathan Lenzner, Bob Mason, Regina Mellon, Michele Strickland, and Tom Wendel all deserve my heartfelt thanks.

I am grateful to several friends who read drafts of various chapters— Jill Brett, Eleanor Dunn, John Eastman, Debra Knopman, Cokie Roberts, Deborah Spencer, and Sarah Spencer—and offered wise advice and encouragement.

Another group I want to acknowledge are those individuals whose guidance influenced the broad scope of experiences in my career. I would not have these stories to tell without them.

Lloyd K. Garrison, a senior partner in the law firm where I worked one summer during law school, was the first. I'll never know why he pointed me toward the Civil Rights Division, but I am eternally grateful that he did.

John Doar was the best first boss a lawyer could have, and has been my mentor and friend since. Working under him in the Deep South and with him at the New York City Board of Education were privileges that I cherish. He deserves more credit than current history accords him in civil rights, and as counsel to the House impeachment inquiry in 1974.

Robert Morgenthau has been appropriately celebrated for the intelligence and integrity with which he led the U.S. Attorney's Office in the Southern District of New York and the Manhattan District Attorney's office later. Working under him as an assistant U.S. attorney was another privilege that I had no reason to anticipate.

The lawyers and staff of the Legal Services Program deserve more than simple acknowledgment for their energetic commitment to improving the lives of America's least fortunate through equal access to justice. They inspired me, and supported me with their loyalty.

Father Philip Berrigan and Sister Elizabeth McAlister, along with their cadre of Catholic antiwar activists, exposed me to a level of commitment to a cause that was profoundly enlightening. Working with Ramsey Clark to defend them, I learned how criminal defense can be effective, creative, and worthwhile.

Edward Bennett Williams, Washington's premier lawyer at the time, befriended me after I was fired by the Nixon administration and promoted me to others in the D.C. bar. He went out of his way to recommend me to the Watergate Committee. This was a fortuitous relationship that made a world of difference for me.

Sam Dash, Senator Sam Ervin, and Senator Lowell Weicker defended me against the attacks of the Nixon White House and encouraged me to pursue the facts of my "dirty tricks" and Hughes-Rebozo investigations.

David Mugar and the state of Alaska deserve credit for putting their faith in me to investigate and pursue their claims. Working on those challenging cases introduced me to new areas of practice, and formed the basis for my investigative firm. Best of all, I continue to enjoy a rewarding friendship with David.

The history of IGI involves a number of great leaders whose exceptional work ethic and creativity have helped to generate solutions for our clients' complex and challenging matters. Prime among those leaders were New York City police commissioner Ray Kelly, who helped to bring IGI into twenty-first-century international operations, and Larry Potts, the former deputy director of the FBI, whose calm demeanor I still try to emulate. Tom Wendel, IGI's current president, brings extraordinary forensic analysis to complex issues and develops sound strategies for solving clients' problems.

IGI has been blessed to have among its clients major law firms, corporations, and nonprofits who seek our assistance. I appreciate the challenging and interesting problems that they present and the opportunity to contribute to their solutions in a collegial atmosphere of mutual respect.

This isn't meant to be a history book. The stories in here are the fruits of my memory, such as it is. To verify facts and sequences, I've reviewed case sheets, congressional hearing records, and news articles. I've been aided by the accounts in many books, four of which are Sam Dash's *Chief Counsel*, Taylor Branch's epic history and John Lewis's memoir of the civil rights movement, and Anthony Summers's *The Arrogance of Power*. These and many other excellent histories of the events that I participated in are far more comprehensive accounts than I have attempted here.

INDEX

author's meeting with, 316–19
British government against, 320–21
British inquest and, 326–27
conspiracy theories of, 318–19, 321, 324–27
FBI and, 318, 321, 324–25
Henri Paul and, 328
Oswald LeWinter and, 323–24
security for, 316–17
white Fiat and, 318, 320–21, 325
FBI. *See* Federal Bureau of Investigation
FCC. *See* Federal Communications Commission
Federal Alaska Pipeline Commission, 222
Federal Bureau of Investigation (FBI), 14, 42–43, 302–3
Berrigan case and, 81–82
Boyd Douglas and, 93
Mohamed al-Fayed and, 318, 321, 324–25
Operation MIBURN, 14, 17–21
Unabomber and, 256–57
Federal Communications Commission (FCC), 155, 210, 215, 216
RKO TV station and, 215–16, 232
Federal Energy Regulatory Commission, 222, 231–32
Fiske, Robert, 294–95, 302
Fleming, Peter, 134
Flowers, Gennifer, 299
Flug, Jim, 113
Edward Kennedy and, 341–42
FOIA. *See* Freedom of Information Act
Forbes Digital Tool, 282–83
Ford, Gerald R., 187
on Frank Olson, 189–90
Foreign Corrupt Practices Act, 214–15
Foster, Vincent, 294, 296
Fox News, 312, 315, 354
Frates, William, 164
Freedom of Information Act (FOIA), 201, 245
Freedom Summer, 10–11, 13. See also Civil rights movement; Mississippi; Selma, Alabama

Gallup, George, 138
Garment, Leonard, 133
Garrison, Lloyd K., 5, 12–13
Gateway computer company, 285–86
Gelernter, David, 252–53
General Tire and Rubber Company, 249
Bob Curtis and, 211, 212–15
bribery by, 214–15
corruption at, 213–15
David Mugar and, 210–15
Howard Swires and, 211, 212–15
secret bank account from, 214–15
Genovese family, 61–62, 150, 175
George magazine, 288
Gesell, Gerhard, 200–201
Getty, J. Paul, 164
Giancana, Sam, 174–76
Gingrich, Newt, 352
Glass, Stephen, 281–89

background on, 281–82
Charles Lane and, 282–84, 286, 288
"Deliverance" article by, 285–86
falsified notes of, 284–88
on FedEx, 282–86
firing of, 283
"Hack Heaven" article by, 282–83, 286–87
Jukt Micronics and, 282–83, 287
Martin Peretz on, 281–82
Glenn, John, Jr., 297
Goldberg, Lucianne, 300
Goldwater, Barry, 69
Goodman, Andrew
death of, 13–15, 17–18, 31–32
disappearance of, 10–11
and Freedom Summer, 9–10
group implicated in murder of, 31–32
Gottlieb, Dr. Sidney, 6
author's meeting with, 190–92
background of, 193–94
and CIA assassination programs, 194–95, 198–200
defense strategy for, 196–204
Edward Kennedy and, 201–4
handwriting analysis and, 191–92
immunity for, 196–97, 200
lawsuit for, 200–201
LSD experimentation and, 189–90, 195–96, 198
MK-ULTRA, 198, 201
patriotism of, 193, 196
60 Minutes and, 245
Greenspan, Alan, 284
Greenspun, Hank
author's meeting with, 149–56
Edmund Muskie and, 148–49
and Howard Hughes–Richard Nixon relationship, 147, 151–53, 158–61, 163
Operation Gemstone and, 147–53, 156–57, 163, 171–72, 183
on Richard Danner, 163
Gurney, Edward, 108

Haig, Alexander
Jimmy Carter and, 207
on Operation Gemstone, 177–78
partisanship over, 204–8
Watergate scandal and, 204–5
Haldeman, H. R., 100, 119, 122, 130, 144, 164
Hamer, Fanny Lou, 47
Hamilton, James, 105, 116
Hanrahan, John, 234
Harr, Jonathan, 240
Harris, Billy, 24–25, 31
Harris, Lou, 118
Harris, T. O., 50–51
Harrisburg Seven. *See* Berrigan case
Harvard College, 6
Harvard Law School, 4, 6–7, 11
Harvard University Board of Overseers, 79
Helms, Richard, 201

ABOUT THE AUTHOR

Terry Lenzner is the founder and chairman of Investigative Group International (IGI), and the former assistant chief counsel to the Senate Watergate Committee. Prior to establishing IGI, Lenzner also served as a Justice Department attorney with the Civil Rights Division, a federal prosecutor in the Southern District of New York, and in private practice.